DEAD: 57,661.

HERE ARE 33 WHO SURVIVED...

> *"We have tried to put into honest words the raw experience of what happened to us. We have reflected upon that experience, recalling, among other things, that we were once idealistic young people confronted by the awesomeness of fighting other human beings...*
>
> *"Please understand that we are not asking for a parade, a monument or pity. But we do ask you to remember in your own way the 57,661 Americans who died in the war. Perhaps all of them died in vain. But if we as individuals and as a nation learned something of human value for having been in Southeast Asia, their sacrifice, we maintain, was not futile..."*
>
> *from the preface by*
> *AL SANTOLI*

EVERYTHING WE HAD

"NO BOOK ABOUT VIETNAM, OR ABOUT AMERICA ITSELF, WILL EVER HAVE THE POWER FOR ME THAT THIS ONE DOES, with its haunting, remarkable, ghastly memories of what the young were required to endure. Any woman in this country who does not know much about war will learn everything from these voices." *Gloria Emerson*

(more)

EVERYTHING WE HAD

EVERYTHING WE HAD

EVERYTHING
WE HAD

An Oral History of the
Vietnam War by
Thirty-three American
Soldiers Who Fought It.

Al Santoli

BALLANTINE BOOKS • NEW YORK

Library of Congress Catalog Card Number: 80-5309

ISBN 0-345-30336-9

This edition published by arrangement with
Random House, Inc.

Manufactured in the United States of America

First Ballantine Books Edition: March 1982
Seventh Printing: October 1982

ACKNOWLEDGMENTS

There are millions of Vietnam era veterans whose voices aren't in this book, but many not heard here speak eloquently and powerfully elsewhere. The idea of this oral history of the Vietnam War originated with Rick Weidman and Robert Muller, veterans who founded and currently lead the Vietnam Veterans of America, Incorporated. Both men have done much to lobby in behalf of the Vietnam veteran and to keep the media fully aware of his concerns. I thank them.

I would also like to thank:

Grant Ujifusa, my editor at Random House, for understanding and believing in the project from the beginning. Ruth Hagy Brod, my literary agent, who passed away during the course of the project, and John Thaxton, who took her place, for their guidance and expertise. Gloria Emerson for her loyalty. My family, Deshung Rinpoche and Dr. Nima Labrang, William Packard, Larry Epstein, Frank McCarthy, Christine Wright, Maggie Schmidt, Kyla Williamson, Michael Sulsona, Mike Pahios, Alexander's Deli, Robbie Long, Carmella LaSpada and the Veterans' Ensemble Theatre Company for their friendship and support. The staff at Vietnam Veterans of America for their assistance. Jack Bloomfield and his typists, who transcribed many hours of interview tapes, and Joan Siegel, who made my travel arrangements. Reverend Roberta Palmer and Pir Vilayat Khan, who convinced me not to give up.

My hosts on the road: Linda Andrews in Killeen, Texas; Walter Rutherford and Rick Brown in Burlington, Vermont; Shelley Oemeler in Wilmington, Delaware; Dan Stack at DAV in Cleveland; Joan McCarthy and John Terzano in Washington, D.C.; Diane Rudolph in San Francisco; Mike MacAfee, Michael and Theresa Reese-Cowen and their daughter Hanna in San Diego; and Fred and Debbie Katz in New York City.

A special thanks to the veterans I interviewed whose experiences are very much a part of the manuscript but whose stories do not appear in the book: David Laine in Cleveland; Robert Borden in Milwaukee; Tim Kolly, Ian Sturton and Mary Bielefeld in Washington, D.C.; Marty Oemeler in Wilmington, Delaware; Brad Krichbaum in Burlington, Vermont; Chris Noel in Los Angeles; Joe Simonetti, Patrick Dillon and Brian McDonnel in New York.

*For the families of the men and women
who served in Vietnam*

At the beginning of an undertaking
the enthusiasm is always greatest.
And at that time both in the
Peloponnesus and in Athens there were
great numbers of young men who had
never been in a war and were
consequently far from unwilling to
join in this one.

   —Thucydides, *The Peloponnesian War*

"I have asked Commanding General William Westmoreland what more he needs to meet this mounting
aggression and he has told me. And we will meet his
needs . . . We do not want an expanding struggle with
consequences that no one can foresee, nor will we
bluster or bully or flaunt our power. But we will not
surrender and we will not retreat."

   —President Lyndon B. Johnson, July 28, 1965

Though it be broken—
Broken again—still it's there,
The moon on the water.

   —Chosu

"... see what we saw ... feel what we felt ..."

Douglas Anderson
Major Michael Andrews
Thomas Bailey
Mike Beamon
Jan Barry
Thomas Bird
James Bombard
Lee Childress
Brian Delate
Ralph Dennison
James Hebron
Scott Higgins
Samuel Janney
Stephen Klinkhammer
Kit Lavell
Bruce Lawlor
George Lawrence
Admiral William Lawrence
Luis Martinez
Herb Mock
Dennis Morgan
John Muir
Warren Nelson
Karl Phaler
Jonathan Polansky
Robert Rawls
Lieutenant Colonel Gary Riggs
David Ross
Al Santoli
Robert Santos
Donald Smith
Gayle Smith
Lynda Van Devanter

Preface

THIS is a book by thirty-three veterans of the Vietnam War. We have tried to put into honest words the raw experience of what happened to us. We have reflected upon that experience, recalling, among other things, that we were once idealistic young people confronted by the awesomeness of fighting other human beings. Now as parents and as citizens we feel an obligation, for the sake of our children if for no one else, to say what we could not or did not say in the past. It has taken most of us many years to come to terms with the violence that we practiced and encountered.

Please understand that we are not asking for a parade, a monument or pity. But we do ask you to remember in your own way the 57,661 Americans who died in the war. Perhaps all of them died in vain. But if we as individuals and as a nation learned something of human value for having been in Southeast Asia, their sacrifice, we maintain, was not futile. At least thirty-three of us feel that we are wiser people for not running away from our memories of combat and those who died in it.

Our book is called an oral history because the thirty-three tours of duty in Vietnam presented here will take the reader more or less chronologically from December of 1962, when John F. Kennedy was still alive, to the fall of Saigon in April of 1975, when Gerald Ford was President. Our personal accounts span almost the entire period of the nation's overt involvement in that distant place.

As a group of veterans, we profess no collective set of political beliefs. We do feel, however, that anyone who wants to test his or her or the nation's mettle in a presumed rite of passage—war—should show care and wisdom. It must always be remembered that the Vietnam War was a human ordeal and not an abstract heroic adventure as might be understood by Hollywood or a politician's speechwriter.

It is often said that it is impossible for the uninitiated to understand war. But in our book we hope you will see what we saw, do what we did, feel what we felt. Until the broader public fully comprehends the nameless soldier, once an image on your television screen, the nation's resolution of the experience called Vietnam will be less than adequate.

The American people have never heard in depth from the *soldiers themselves* the complicated psychic and physical realities of what they went through in Vietnam. To encompass those realities in a book, one veteran traveled around the country and spent countless hours, talking crying and laughing with other veterans and their families. I was that veteran, and we present our story.

Al Santoli
October 1980
New York City

Contents

IV BARREN HARVEST

V OPERATION NEW WIND

1

Gathering
Clouds

David Ross
Medic
1st Infantry Division
Dian
December 1965-July 1967

Welcome
to the War, Boys

A couple of us were just kind of hanging loose out in front of the main hospital building, which was a big corrugated-tin pre-fab. About forty new guys were lined up there to have their shot records checked before being sent to their units.

The guys were all new, their first couple of days in-country, and they were all wondering what it was going to be like. Joking, smoking cigarettes, playing grab-ass in the line—it was pretty loose. I mean, nobody was saying, "Straighten up. Stand in formation," none of that. People were just kind of leaning up against the building.

All of a sudden, four choppers came in and they didn't even touch down. They just dumped bags. One of the bags broke open and what came out was hardly recognizable as a human being. For those of us that were just sort of standing there looking in the direction of the new guys . . . it's not the kind of thing you laugh at. Irony or satire . . . things get beyond words. All the guys stopped laughing. Nobody was saying anything. And some people were shaking and some people were throwing up, and one guy got down and started to pray.

I said to myself, "Welcome to the war, boys."

3

Jan Barry
Radio Technician
U.S. Army 18th Aviation
    Company
Nha Trang
December 1962-October
    1963

The
Nine-to-Five War

I arrived at my unit in Nha Trang on Christmas Eve. I had spent something like four days in Saigon waiting to get a ride from a little replacement camp that looked like something out of a South Seas World War II movie, palm trees and tents and dust. I was told to get on this airplane, a tiny little thing. It had a crew chief, pilot and copilot. This plane flies very slowly and I think it took four hours to go two hundred miles. It just drones and drones and drones, going from Saigon to Nha Trang, across an immense expanse of changing terrain.

When we landed, it was almost dusk. As soon as the plane stopped, the pilot, the copilot and the crew chief jumped out and into a jeep. They drove off. I hadn't even gotten my bags out of the airplane and I'm left standing there alone in my class-A uniform. I hadn't the faintest idea where I was, no one around, it's getting dark. There's these strange lights out in the mountains. I don't have a weapon.

It was a base camp. But I didn't know whether I was on the edge of the perimeter, whether there was a perimeter. I couldn't see anything. I had no idea whether

4

they had left me in the middle of nowhere and the guerrillas were going to come and carry me away.

And while I'm standing and standing and standing there absorbing all of this, eventually a jeep comes by and this guy who's really drunk says, "Oh, sorry I didn't pick you up before." He takes me to the company area, where there's no one. He's the only person. He's the CQ [command of quarters], the driver. As far as I know, he was the guard for the whole air base. I never saw anybody else.

He says, "Everybody else is downtown drinking. I'll find you some civilian clothes." And he leaves his post. He gets me civilian clothes and says, "Let's take these bicycles," and we ride off post. We're riding down to the seacoast, where the wind is blowing, a very strong wind. I don't see any other Americans, just lots and lots of Vietnamese, strolling the streets, in and out of little tiny beach bars. He keeps taking me into places and disappearing. I'm left there. Clearly he or somebody has paid for my drink. So whenever I'd finish a drink I would just get up and leave. I couldn't speak a word of Vietnamese and nobody knew the crazy American. I never saw another American the entire time and I didn't know where the air base was. I spent half the night trying to figure out which of the side roads to the beach led back to the airfield.

I kept trying different roads until I finally hit upon one that seemed right and eventually rode this bicycle up to the main gate. The next morning when I woke up all these people were there. It was Christmas day, everybody drunk. And that was my introduction to the war.

I began to realize many months later that *we* were the war. If we wanted to go out and chase people around and shoot at them and get them to shoot back at us, we had a war going on. If we didn't do that, they left us alone. After a while it became clear that there was a pattern here. Our people, including Special Forces, used to stop at four-thirty and have a happy hour and get drunk. There was no war after four-thirty. On Saturday, no war. On Sundays, no war. On holidays, no war. That's right, a nine-to-five war.

At dawn aircraft would go out, the patrols would go

out. And if no one went, no one attacked the military units. But when we were pushing, they would hit anyplace, including a place like Nha Trang. I got blown out of bed one morning at three. We didn't know what had caused it, and just as some idiot turns on the lights, this old sergeant screams, "Mortars!" What a feeling—that some jerk has just turned on the lights where a whole bunch of us are sleeping while somebody's mortaring the camp.

It turned out not to be mortars but sappers who had come through the fence, blown up a couple of airplanes and slipped right back out again. But the worst part of it all is the Army couldn't trust us with weapons. The people who had been stationed there before me had shootouts, acting like Wild West characters. They would get drunk, take their weapons and have fast-draw contests. So all of our weapons were locked up at night in a connex, for which only the armorer had a key. And the night of this attack the armorer was downtown with his girlfriend. So everybody is running around saying, "Where is the armorer? Where is the key?" Nobody could find him or the key and there's all this tremendous shooting going on down along the flight berm.

We had a guard for our area. There were Vietnamese perimeter guards out there someplace. They were all shooting like crazy—probably at nothing, just to make sure that they weren't going to be blamed later. But we didn't know that. I mean, as far as we knew, Ho Chi Minh could've been leading all of the North Vietnamese Army straight across the airstrip.

Everybody's running around like crazy without a weapon, not having the faintest idea what to do next. I remember having this strange feeling: "Our guard is down there all by himself on the flight line. Somebody ought to go get him." So I got into a jeep and started driving with the lights out down to the airstrip. I didn't even think of the consequences. Fortunately, by the time I got down to the flight line all the firing had stopped.

I was nineteen and turned twenty when I was there. I joined the Army in May of 1962 and was in Vietnam in December, just as I finished radio school. That was my first assignment. I could've had orders, as everyone else in the class did, to Germany. Two of us had orders to Vietnam. Before I even joined the Army I ran into a guy who'd graduated from high school a year or two ahead of me. He had just gotten out of the Army from Alaska. He said, "Wow, the place to go is Vietnam. You get combat pay in addition to overseas pay. You can really clean up." In the Army there was an undercurrent that there was someplace in the world where you could get combat pay. But there was no real discussion in the newspapers, as I can recall.

Some people in the unit had no conception where they were in the world, they didn't care. It wasn't Tennessee. It wasn't the state they came from. So therefore they had no interest in learning anything. Other people were very interested and learned Vietnamese and became very close with a number of Vietnamese people. At some point you began to realize that the people around the military base were clearly cooperating with the guerrillas because they were able to infiltrate the inside of our bases and we hadn't the faintest idea where the guerrillas were.

When the Buddhist demonstrations began against the Diem government, it became very clear to most Americans there who probably hadn't been paying attention that we were supporting a police state which, against its own people who were peaceably having demonstrations, would turn loose tanks and machine guns and barbed wire all over the country. From May of '63 all through the summer we'd get caught up in them, just trying to walk around in civilian clothes to go to bars.

The first one I saw was in Nha Trang. Several of us were downtown along one of the main streets on a midday, and all of a sudden the street was full of people marching with banners. Looking at the crowd going by, I recognized several of them as bar girls, as people who worked at the base, KPs who worked in the mess hall. We hired women who came and made our beds, shined our boots, kept our little hootches spick-and-span. After a while you began to feel that we had transformed ourselves into the British imperial army in India, where we had all these servants.

I mean, all of us felt we were entitled to our servants. Twenty guys in a hootch would chip in and pay twenty dollars for a woman to come and do all the cleaning, make all the beds and shine all the boots. And for that woman, twenty dollars a month was a lot of money. We didn't make much in the Army—fifty or sixty dollars a month, that's what it was when I started. For us to be able to afford a servant just had mind-expanding or -exploding consequences.

Some people became very arrogant and ordered their servants around. Some people became rather involved in a compassionate way, finding out what the woman's family situation was, and tried to help out, even visiting the family and getting to know the kids and getting more involved on a personal level. Other people took an in-between position of just accepting the situation and enjoying the fact that they had somebody, who was going to take care of all their usual Army duties. We didn't have to do KP. We didn't have to do all the rigmarole of spit-shine. Somebody else was going to spit-shine for us. And under those kinds of circumstances, most people, not having any historical perspective, didn't think about this. I did because I specifically was interested in the military, wanting to make a career of it, and started associating this with the British army in India and the French colonial army in Indochina. You would hear little bits and pieces, like the base where we were had been a French base, with these big imposing brick buildings that clearly had been French army barracks.

We'd talk about it with the interpreter for our unit. He would talk about when the French army was there, most of them spoke German. We asked why they spoke German. He said because they came from the German army after World War II into the French Foreign Legion. So he could speak German, he could speak French, he could speak English. He spoke three dialects of Chinese and of course Vietnamese. This man was making a paltry salary as an interpreter for this American Army unit. A very cultured man who spends his days with PFCs and Spec. 4s, being ordered around by people who didn't even have high school educations.

There were two or three of us who got to know him very well. One friend was German. His father had been killed in the German army and then his mother married an American soldier and came to the U.S. My friend spoke German with him and we learned this past history of the French Foreign Legion.

In addition to that, I learned that the telephone lines that we used from Nha Trang to Saigon had been put in by the Japanese army. And then someone told us that in the bay at Nha Trang there's an old Japanese airplane that was shot down. We began to get a sense of this place and this history and these people seeing armies come and go. And we're just another one.

I can remember the encounters I had with Vietnamese students. They would stop me at the beach. If we had an afternoon or a weekend off and it was a nice day, we could walk a half mile to the beach, lay out the towel, and have this tropical bay with nice rolling waves that compared to the Riviera. The French had built villas all along the seafront. It was like being stationed in Atlantic City in the middle of a war.

On the main beach road, students would come along on their bicycles or come walking along the beach and try to have a conversation with you, try out their English. Sooner or later they would come around to that they had been reading about Lincoln, they had been reading about Jefferson, about the Declaration of Independence. They felt all this was great. Often they would start out by saying, "I'm a Christian and I'm a student"—very excited and wanting to talk. But at some point in the conversation it would come to "But your army, you know . . ." and sort of an unstated question: What does it have to do with the Declaration of Independence? Because they knew, and we were beginning to know, that the Saigon government was a police state where three people getting together on a sidewalk was illegal, the people were so closely watched by their own police.

Then these odd things would happen. This German friend of mine played very good tennis, so he found himself being invited to tennis clubs through the interpreter and playing tennis with the likes of the town's chief of police and other more highly ranked Vietnamese than a PFC would generally meet. One day he casually happened to say that he wanted to get rid of his Vietnamese girlfriend . . . She was imprisoned the next day.

And then the demonstrations broke out. The one at Nha Trang was not forcibly attacked; it was one of the early ones. By the time they were having demonstrations in Saigon, however, the army [ARVN] was out in full force. There was barbed wire and tanks everywhere.

Two or three of us had met through a teenaged girl a whole American family that lived in a villa in Saigon. The father was an adviser to Saigon University. They had a full house of servants. So we again had this great dichotomy of meeting people who were living a great luxurious life in the midst of a war. We went to visit this family during the demonstration period, and there were barbed-wire checkpoints everywhere on the block where they lived. It was completely ringed by barbed wire and ARVN guards. I went up to the barbed wire and said to the guard, "We want to visit the people in the house." He hauls off with his rifle and aims it right at me. I was going to take this guy on. Fortunately, the officer for that unit came running over. I'm sure he was having night-mares of this guy shooting an American. He cooled things down and let us through.

Well, this continued to happen. We would hear stories from officers that in Saigon, Mme. Nhu would tell American officers straight to their faces that her government did not like Americans but it liked having our money. They were very arrogant and very well knew that they had the Kennedy government in their pockets by just screaming "Communists!" They didn't have to tell us that they liked us. They didn't do anything except show utter contempt for Americans who were there. In addition, they had a rigged election in 1963 in which single candidates ran for seats in the assembly. Mme Nhu was a candidate. No opposition. The whole family of President Diem put themselves up as members.

With experience like that, many of us began to realize that something was really wrong and what our purpose there was—being a trip-wire protection of this police state. The Americans were waiting for something to happen so that they could bring in a larger force. I thought, "This is what happened in the Philippines to those soldiers who got caught on Bataan." We were there as bait. If the ten or twelve thousand of us got overrun, we were the excuse for an even bigger war.

The entire contingent of Americans in Vietnam was so thinly spread out that there probably weren't more than five hundred in any one place. Tan Son Nhut had the highest concentration. And it was becoming apparent that the ARVN might turn on us. That became a real worry in the summer of 1963. It became rather apparent from discussion going on that there was going to be a coup. I recall going to Saigon several times and hearing this undercurrent in bars where Vienamese officers would be.

I left Vietnam in mid-October 1963 and the coup happened two weeks later. One of the people who was still there said that the night before the coup took place they were told to get packed up, be ready to leave the country, be ready to blow up their equipment. At that point one of the options was to completely leave Vietnam.

I came back from Vietnam to go to a preparatory school for West Point. In November I was at school. We were having an assembly; everyone was in one room. One of the officers said, "There is a report that President Kennedy has been shot." Everybody was shocked. My feeling was, "The beginning of this month the President in Vietnam was shot, and now I come back here and our President is shot. Here comes what I left, following right behind me."

Almost no one in the Washington area knew we had anything like what was going on in Vietnam. Those of us who had been there wore our military patches on our right shoulders, which denoted that we had been in the war. Colonels would stop me and say, "What war have you been in, son? Where is that? We have people fighting over there?"

Karl Phaler
Communications Officer
U.S. Navy   Destroyer
    Richard S. Edwards
Tonkin Gulf
September 1964-Spring 1965

Patrolling
the Tonkin Gulf

WE were in the second Tonkin Gulf incident. The *Turner Joy* and the *Maddox* went into the Gulf in July 1964 and were fired on August 2 and 4. We relieved them on what used to be called the DeSoto patrol.

The DeSoto patrols were two destroyer patrols that would go above the 17th parallel—above the DMZ—theoretically staying in international waters in the Tonkin Gulf. The *Maddox* and the *Turner Joy* had been on DeSoto patrol when they got hit, which triggered the Tonkin Gulf resolution. We were involved in an incident, shortly afterwards, and all three of those attacks were used to justify bombing raids against the North.

We were in transit from San Diego to the Philippines in a convoy of eight tin cans [destroyers]. We were headed for Subic Bay. Midway in the Pacific we got word that the *Turner Joy* and *Maddox* had been hit. The carrier *Ranger* and my destroyer, the *Richard S. Edwards*, were detached in a group and made a high-speed transit to Subic Bay.

Turner Joy and *Maddox* were in Subic Bay next to us. They had .50-caliber damage on them. I talked to some of those people and they were very enthusiastic about it. That was the first blood that the Navy had drawn in a

12

while. They had little PT boat emblems painted on their gun turrets for the number of claimed kills. They were all gung ho. And of course, we were wound up tighter than a clock, too.

We sat offshore on the 17th parallel for about four or five days while the decision was being made whether or not to go again with the DeSoto patrol. The last ship sent in received hostile fire. And the decision was made *right up at top.*

At the time I was the communications officer. I was manning the radio net, what they called high-com net, which was a direct voice to the Seventh Fleet and then to COMNAV, SINCPAC in Hawaii and to Washington. I was on the radio net when we got the green light to go: *"Parkland, Parkland. This is American Eagle. Over."* American Eagle was the Man and that was Lyndon Johnson. Of course I didn't think it was him, but it certainly was one of his aides actually speaking on the net. *"Parkland, this is American Eagle. Green light for tomorrow."* It meant we were going into the Gulf. The President himself had authorized that mission.

At that time the Vietnamese government was in a revolving-door phase. It seemed there was a new government in Saigon every two or three weeks. We were preparing to invest ground forces. The DeSoto patrols into the North were being undertaken largely for showing the flag and also for some ECM [Electronic Counter Measures, radar surveillance] collection purposes. It was very difficult to figure out exactly what was going on. The nominal instructions were simply to patrol offshore. There were other kinds of information being fed to us in very secure channels—usually going only to the commanding officer—concerning coordination in liaison with the OPLAN 34 Alpha missions being run out of Saigon by MACV-SOG. They were infiltration missions into North Vietnam by people who had come south after the partition. MACV-SOG, Military Assistance Command Vietnam—Studies and Obeservation Group, was largely an Agency [CIA] operation.

Most of those operations, to my knowledge, were terminally fruitless. They were going back in to make reports on radar sites and emplacements and arms transportation and so on. The North Vietnamese snapped up these people as fast as they hit the beach, or else the boatmen surrendered to the other side, which is a very typical experience in Vietnam—whenever you give somebody an asset to take with them someplace, he hands it over immediately. Anyway, that was a form of warfare being directed against North Vietnam by the South at that time. And our involvement in it had to be very carefully distanced, officially. These PT boats were high-speed ocean-going crafts. We would have occasional radio contact with them. Once in a while we'd refuel them.

The North Vietnamese came to the rather ready conclusion that the destroyers in the Gulf and these PT boats that were attacking their territory had something to do with each other. And that, at least nominally, was the basis for their strikes against American destroyer patrols.

The only things that had ever happened were the *Turner Joy* and *Maddox* incidents, and then, while we were on patrol one night, we made radar contact with some small, very fast-moving craft. Ourself and another destroyer. (We had a Navy captain aboard who was acting as commodore of this two-destroyer detachment.) Contacts closed. We fired a couple of warning shots. They kept on closing. We were at ready condition. We went to general quarters and began evasive maneuvers and began firing.

A night naval surface engagement is one of the most beautiful things God ever revealed to a human being. As far as I know, I fought in the last one ever. The second Tonkin Gulf incident was the last time an American force was ever engaged by other naval surface forces in gun battle.

It was a moonlit night, hazy, and we were moving at flank speed, making tightly coordinated turns with guns going off in all directions. It was very difficult to tell what you could and could not see. Some of us thought we saw the ships. I spent the whole time in CIC [Combat Information Center] giving ranges and bearings for the gun-control equipment. There were definitely radar contacts.

I couldn't have told you whether it was spooks, ghosts or real boats out there. There was some damage to the superstructures of the ships, which could have been the enemy. It would have been ourselves. We don't know. We went back and forth through the area the next day. We did not come up with much in the way of wreckage or anything. I don't know whether anybody ever torched us off or whether they were just feigning at us to distract us. We didn't suffer any casualties. No systems were put out of order. We're not too certain whether we were shooting at the real thing or ghosts.

The Gulf is a very funny place. You get inversion layers there that will give you very solid radar contacts that will have courses and speeds that are very trackable. There are places in the world where weather conditions are such that you get phony returns on radarscopes, depending on the frequency of the radar band and the time of day. You will see very real and very live contacts on a scope that just aren't there. That may have happened to us. Or we may have been feinted at and got panicky and started shooting at phantoms. We don't know.

I think the ultimate denouement of that contact, the second Tonkin Gulf incident, was hushed up very beautifully. It only leaked into the press some months later when one of our kids wrote home to his mother and said, "By the way, Mom, I was in the war too." Initially we had been authorized combat pay for that month, then it was withdrawn. We never did understand why, having actually been fired upon, we were denied combat pay, whereas every wimp in the world simply had to get into the airspace to draw it.

The presidential campaign was that fall. I was sitting on the radio listening to Lyndon Johnson tell the people he was not going to send American boys to fight an Asian war. I looked over across the water and there was a whole bunch of American boys in battle dress getting ready to fight that Asian war.

2

Sand
Castles

Washing Ashore

I was laying in a swimming pool in Subic Bay one afternoon, and they came and got us out of there and said, "They're landing in Vietnam and we're on the way." There were only six of us beachmasters in Subic Bay and the only airplane they had was an old C-47. So they got that thing charged up about dark and we flew in and landed at Danang, Vietnam. It seemed just like any other peacetime Air Force base at that time. It was fairly open. They were flying cargo in and out, and that seemed to be about it.

There had been an Air Force base there for I don't know how many years. Danang, it seemed, was kind of an R & R port for the Viet Cong for some time. They knew if they caused any trouble there, the Air Force would cancel the shore leave for their men and the local economy would be hurt considerably. Many of the merchants in Danang were supporting the Viet Cong and they were getting money from the U.S. military and passing it on to the Viet Cong.

The beachmaster's job is to maintain salvage and communication on the beach during amphibious landings. I always kind of think of it as "Marines get there first, the

19

beachmaster shows them where to go." The Marines started landing early in the day, and it was three o'clock in the morning of the first day's activity before I actually got there. They had shifted the landing site to the sand ramp in downtown Danang. The boats came up the river, right up the center of town. There was a hotel on one side, a hotel and a motel, and a sand ramp in between them. We just walked the troops right up the ramp and sent them on their way to the air base. As a matter of fact, we spent three days and nights getting the Marines ashore. They went immediately to the air base and dug into their foxholes and did whatever Marines do when they're in that kind of situation.

In our case we never seemed to have any opposition. Later on, the beachmasters did take some casualties, but during the time I was there it seemed like it was a piece of cake, a real nice little excursion into a tropical climate that was fairly pleasant. You would get a little too much sand every now and then, but other than that it wasn't ncessarily bad. You worked some long hours, but it kept your weight down and you didn't have to worry about dieting.

Living
Off the Jungle

THE Marines' 9th Expeditionary Brigade landed in '65, the 1st Marine Division came along shortly behind them in '65 and I came along right after that. We were officially designated "the last Marine Corps Raider Company." We really weren't anything out of the ordinary, but we had that title and General Krulak took it seriously. Anytime the shit would hit the fan anywhere, he would call us in to help.

General Krulak's son commanded Golf Company, and Kobi Tan Tan was where Little Dicky Krulak walked into an ambush and really started getting chewed up bad. They called us for help. So we went charging over there by foot. We were wading through thigh-deep water, practically running through it. We got over there, formed on line and started into the area.

It was a relatively open village surrounded by rice paddies on three sides. Steep hills ran up behind it, heavily brushed. Little Dicky Krulak walked his platoon into this village that was right snug up against the hills and they just chewed him up. We got there, our full company on line. It was really impressive. You don't often get a

21

chance to see a classic book-type assault: two platoons in front and one platoon in reserve, double-arm interval [two arms' length between each man], rifle under your arm firing as you go. I was in the back because I was the company radio operator and I was carrying the company commander's radio. It was just so fascinating to watch all this stuff in person. And there's these little puffs of gray smoke going off all over the place. It never occurred to me—I said, "I wonder what all those little puffs of gray smoke . . . Oh, shit, those are mortar rounds." It was just like the movies, for chrisakes. Here were all these guys spread out going through mortar fire. I didn't hear the explosions. It's really funny because every time I've ever been in a real emergency situation—I mean, everything from Vietnam to a car wreck—my hearing gets shut off. I don't hear. I was concentrating on the radio so much I didn't hear the explosions. I just saw little puffs of smoke. I didn't see anybody go down because of them.

Little Dicky Krulak's boys were pinned down in the village. We were a little bit off to their side and coming in on kind of a sweep flank. We got there and broke into our three platoons. I was with company headquarters section, directly behind first platoon. We came up to this pathway with a line of trees alongside of it. Beyond was an old foundation for a house. There was a big pepper field with a line of bamboo running down its side, perpendicular to the trail. As we went across the pathway and out into the field, I noticed Heath, from the first platoon, was laying in the pepper field. He was quite obviously dead. I went down because when you carry a radio you're a very obvious target. I crawled up to him and grabbed him because I wanted to check his pulse, which was beside the point because the guy was turning green and he was dead, dead, dead. I started backing up and I ran into the XO. He said. "What's going on?" and I said, "Heath's dead and something's going on here." Everybody seemed to be laying down, but nobody was shooting at anything. I looked over and there was another guy from the first platoon that was dead. Reports started coming back from first platoon that they'd been hit real hard. We were coming up from behind and started backing up to the tree line, trying to get radio communications. Radio was the pits down in that valley, it was really a dead spot. We started using runners.

I backed up from around a tree to tell one of the runners which way to go, and the radio just . . . blew up on my back . . . just disintegrated. I jumped back around the tree and took some of the pegboard off and said, "Oh, shit." Just one round. It hit dead center through—I mean, the guy shot me right dead in the middle of the back. But for some reason it didn't come through. Battery stopped it.

The whole thing was the work of one sniper, who had dug himself a tunnel inside a rice-paddy dike. He had three shooting locations that covered the same killing zone, anybody who walked in there. He shot everybody in the chest. He did no wounding at all. He killed eight people that day. Two guys were wounded, if you count me, because my radio was a casualty, but I wasn't hurt. Scared shitless, but I wasn't hurt. And Sergeant Mac-somebody got hit in the arm because just as the guy fired he turned to see what was going on and it went through his bicep. If he had been standing still, he would've got hit right in the middle of the chest. Another guy was hurt, but we aren't sure if it was by friendly fire, maybe his own, because he was hit in the lower leg. This sniper was shooting only from shoulder to hips. So naturally he was killing everybody he hit. He was a real pro, as good as you're ever gonna see when it comes to snipers.

We finally located where the hell he was. We just put one rifle squad on line and assulted his position with our M-14s. We chewed up the whole length of the rice dike, blasted it, bulldozed it.

Peter Wa Ju went to look at the guy and, himself being Chinese, said, "This guy is Chinese." The sniper was blasted. He was eaten up. But he was still reasonably intact, enough for Peter to make a definitive statement. He was absolutely positive that this guy was Chinese. We also found a lot of white powder on him. We didn't know enough about dope, but it seemed like the guy was doped up—either that or he was awful good. It would have made it easier for us to accept if we believed he was doped up. But either way he was awful good.

We operated out of Phu Bai for several months and then we did Operation Yo-Yo. I don't remember what the real name of it was, but everybody referred to it as Yo-Yo because we were in and out of the Kobi Tan Tan Valley. We started down the road and we stopped; and we started down the road and we stopped; and we started down the road . . . This was in the area just immediately west of Khe Sanh. The VC had been operating here since at least '54 andmost of the people were sympathetic to them. We owned them in the daytime and the VC owned them at night. It was pretty well clear-cut. We really didn't contest it that much. We stayed the hell out of villages at night. We set up ambushes in the surrounding countryside and did a lot of security patrolling, just clearing the area so we could set up an air base, surrounding an Army radio-relay unit, which had been there since God was a pup. These guys just sat around in Bermuda shorts all day inside this big wire compound. It was a semi-spy situation and the CIA had been paying money to keep them healthy. They were there by themselves before we landed. Now they had a regiment of Marines around them. I guess they decided not to pay anymore.

During this time was our first experience with prisoners. We were on a company sweep and we got word from an aircraft that there was somebody with a weapon out in this field. We went out there, and there was a big sinkhole and water and drainage ditches leading into it. The pilot was trying to signal to us from the air where they were, and we couldn't find them. He was flying over us, radioing, "They're right down there, man." We set up a quick perimeter around the whole sinkhole area. Unfortunately, I was one of the guys who had an old K-bar knife, and the gunny sergeant saw it and said, "You, with the knife, come here." I was wading along into these holes, reaching down with the knife, feeling for them. I found a foot. The pilot had told us that one of the guys had an automatic weapon, because he had been fired upon, and I didn't know whether this guy had the automatic weapon or not, but I had a foot. So I very gently started poking him with the edge of the knife, working my way up the leg, up the body, because I wanted him to know I had the knife. I found his throat and I stuck the knife up under his chin and pulled him up. Him, me and the knife all came up together.

His eyes were as big as mine, because he was sixteen, seventeen years old. He was very scared, I was very scared. I looked up and there was a company of Marines in a circle all the way around me with about one hundred and fifty M-14s pointed at us. It was the world's largest Polish firing squad. If one guy would have fired, they would have wiped themselves out. Everybody would've opened fire and it would have been an absolute massacre.

I'm just standing there saying to the guy, "Jesus, guy, I don't know whether you can understand me, but don't move, don't make any sudden movements whatever you do or we're all gonna be in trouble."

We did find the automatic weapon. It was down in the ditch. A lot of people kind of wanted to brutalize the prisoner in relatively small ways. I don't mean in an atrocity sense, but we'd been getting a lot of heat, getting incoming fire, and people had been getting hurt and they really wanted somebody to take it out on. Here was somebody they could lay hands on. It took a lot of effort on the part of the NCOs and officers to keep this guy from getting banged around a lot. This taught me pretty much because a lot of times later on we would take prisoners. Most of the time it was VCS, Viet Cong suspect. We had very little evidence with which to judge these people, mostly because of the language difficulties. We hesitated to use ARVN interpreters because their methods of questioning people was to slap them upside the head with a revolver or shoot their foot off and say, "You VC?" The guy says no and BANG. "You VC?" Sooner or later, after losing enough pieces, the guy would say yes and then he'd be shot because now he's guilty, you know. We had a lot of trouble with that.

As a matter of fact, I severely injured one of our ARVN compatriots because of that. I butt-stroked him in the kidneys. I was trying to break his back. I had just had enough of it, you know. Here's this little guy and he's all trussed up, he's tied, no longer a combatant, he's now a prisoner. His status had changed, he was not a VC anymore, he was a prisoner, and this ARVN was getting

ready to kill him. And I just . . . didn't want that anymore.

Once when we were operating in the same area as the
Koreans, we went into a village and were looking around.
This Korean lieutenant who spoke excellent English, obviously well educated, a really nice guy, asked me,
"You've been into villages like this before. Do you see
anything that would make you suspicious?" I looked
around and said no. He says, "Well, what do we have
here? We have a little old lady and a little old man and
two very small children. According to them, the rest of
the family has been spirited away, either by the ARVN
or by the VC—they'd either been drafted into one army
or the other. So there's only four of them and they have
a pot of rice that's big enough to feed fifty people. And
rice, once it's cooked, will not keep. They gotta be feeding the VC." So they set the house on fire and the roof
started cooking off ammunition because all through the
thatch they had ammunition stored. They arrested the
four of them and sent them off to a relocation camp.

That was an example of the kind of cultural lesson
that I was beginning to learn. I had no idea—my experience with rice up until then had been either Minute Rice
or Uncle Ben's. It never occurred to me that even in your
refrigerator rice won't keep very long after it's cooked.
And they certainly didn't have refrigeration; they had a
pig in the kitchen, which the Koreans confiscated and ate
that evening. We did a lot of foraging off the land when
we operated in the field.

When we were in Kobi Tan Tan, most of the time we
got one C-ration a day. What else you wanted to eat you
foraged for. But it was an agricultural area with lots of
peppers and rice. A lot of times when we'd find a little
old lady who was all by herself, supposedly, with a big
vat of rice, we would just appropriate it. We'd just pull
off a banana leaf, line up, and everybody would walk
by and take a banana leaf full of rice from her. She never
said a word, she didn't care, she'd just dish it up and
we'd go on about our business eating rice.

This was an area heavily sprayed with the herbicide
Agent Orange. We were not only wading in it, we were
eating and drinking it, too. There were lots of particu-

larly hostile forest areas withered away where there were suspected ambush places. But the herbicide planes would also destroy whole crops, rice crops. So we were wading in it and drinking the water.

By the time we finished Kobi Tan Tan, after thirty days of eating C-rations, the only C-rations I could even look at was beanies and weenies. And Christ, we used to fight over who was gonna get the ham and lima beans. They were not called ham and lima beans, by the way; they were called ham and motherfuckers. They were ungodly, terrible. We had one guy who used to like them, and he used to collect all these peppers, rice and everything you could think of, and he poured it all into a helmet with his ham and lima beans and mixed this ungodly concoction of stuff and he'd eat that. But he was from West Virginia and we'd take that into account.

In June they sent us up to Dong Ha, which was a little Air Force radar station about five miles south of the DMZ. There was a Vietnamese infantry school there and they had one company of Marines on a rotating basis to protect the airport, which was a little dirt strip, and the radar station. Very quiet. We also had a squad of reconnaissance Marines with us.

We got a radio call from the reconnaissance saying they needed some assistance. So we mounted one platoon out on operation. Sergeant Hickock got out of the helicopter, grabbed the radio and said one word: "Help." Two divisions of North Vietnamese were coming across the border and we were sitting there watching them. There was a sort of a valley that they were coming through and a hill right in the middle of the valley. We took the hill. We just stayed there and died. And stopped them. They set the hill on fire and they had the high ground on either side of us. It was an impossible situation.

The DMZ didn't look like anything, didn't have a fence or anything. I expected to see a big white stripe down the side. Wasn't there. There was one little road. It was flat. A river that meandered through the middle of the DMZ and a bridge across Highway 1 at this point. We were about fifteen miles inland.

These two divisions of North Vietnamese came overland, parallel to and just west of Highway 1. They knew just

one company of Marines was there. There was nobody
to stop them. We weren't supposed to. There was no reason why we did. Why did we? We didn't have anyplace
to run. Nothing else to do. It was either stop them or die
there. In four days we went from almost full strength
down to ninety-one effective, all of whom were wounded
in one degree or another. We just came up, grabbed the
hill and started digging real fast. We set up machine guns,
whatever we had with us. Water was our biggest problem, ammunition was second. We didn't eat. We didn't
have time. We were fighting day and night and they tried
every trick in the book. They tried an artillery assault,
they tried to machine-gun us off, they even set the hill on
fire—looked like a forest fire. We let it burn over the
top of us because they were right behind it. We just got
in our holes and let it burn, then stepped back out and
started shooting again.

They put artillery up above us and were shooting
down right on top of us. Rockets, machine-gun fire, rifle
fire, everything you want. It was all point-blank.

Helicopters kept resupplying us. They would take a
quick, low pass at the top of the hill and zoom by there,
throwing out water and ammunition, grabbing as many
wounded as they could. The North Vietnamese were at
the bottom and either side of us. I have a little problem
here because there's three days that I don't have any
memory of . . . I lost my entire squad and I kind of went
berserk. At least I'm told I went berserk. I don't have
the foggiest idea what I was doing. I was told that I was
throwing rocks at people. I was really gung ho. I have no
memory of it. We did hand-to-hand fighting, we hit them
with rocks, but they didn't get behind us. I hit one guy
right between the running lights with a big old rock the
size of a softball. Knocked him right back down the hill.
Got two points for it, too. These were actually uniformed,
well-equipped regular army forces. They had helmets,
web gear, the whole thing.

We really didn't think about the future. I had no ex-
pectation of making it out of there. I don't think anybody
else did, either. We didn't discuss it. We really didn't have
a hell of a lot of time to sit around discussing things. I

had written us off. People were too tired to cry. It was physical exhaustion—you had no energy left for anything else. You would stay awake and keep firing, drink some water, make sure your ammunition and weapon were in good shape and eat when you could, stuff some food into you just to keep fueled up so you could keep going.

Sometimes they'd come on a dead run, hollering and screaming. Usually they came in a well-organized, well-controlled assault. We knew we were up against professionals; we knew we were up against some good ones. But as I say, there wasn't any way out for us. After the fourth day, the 4th Marines came in and overran our position, which pushed them back a little farther and gave us a little breathing space. The battle went on for over a month.

Coming back out, we were just numb. Just exhausted. We didn't have any emotions left, we were just drained, it was just . . . knocked out of you. It was a major battle. Of course, once you left the area you had no more news of what was going on unless you knew somebody who was there and you talked to him. What happened after we left . . . I don't know. We couldn't read about it in the paper. The only paper we got was the *Stars and Stripes*. You ever hear any news in the *Stars and Stripes?* The only good thing in *Stars and Stripes* was the Sergeant Mike cartoon.

We did a fine job there. If it had happened in World War II, they still would be telling stories about it. But it happened in Vietnam, so nobody knows about it. They don't even tell recruits about it today. Marines don't talk about Vietnam. We lost. They never talk about losing. So it's just wiped out, all of that's off the slate, it doesn't count. It makes you a little bitter.

I still am deeply disturbed by the fact that so many people died. The young Marines that I served with thought at the time that they were doing what they were supposed to be doing. Nobody had educated them in the politics of the situation. We went into the Marine Corps with the same feeling our fathers and grandfathers had gone into the service. There wasn't anybody around to tell us that we hadn't done the right thing. And then to find out later that all those people had died in vain, or that the largest percentage of the American public be-

lieved that they died in vain, is very disturbing to me.
But like I say, there isn't one hell of a lot I can do about
it, so I just try to roll along with it.

Driving back down Highway 1 after the battle of Dong
Ha, we saw all the Buddhists had little wooden temples
out in the middle of the road. They were in rebellion and
we had to weave the trucks through them. It was about
110 degrees and we had to slow down to five miles an
hour.

The Vietnamese had a little internal squabble going
on at the time in an area south of Danang, a place called
Henderson Trail. There was a fortress there, an ARVN
encampment. All the army troops from the encampment
went up to Danang to join the Buddhists. The South Vietnam marines came in and kicked their ass.

The ARVNs had almost gone to war with some American Marines who were holding the bridge, south of Danang. These guys wanted to cross and the commanding
officer of the Marine company said uh-unh. And he had
two Phantom jets come in and fly about fifty feet above
the bridge, just to sort of punctuate his statement. The
ARVNs were going to Danang to fight against the South
Vietnamese marines. So in essence, if they had gotten
there, the battle might have turned the other way.

Throughout the war the Vietnamese army and the
Vietnamese marines and the Vietnamese forces in general
were given a great deal of lip service as far as coopera-
tion and things like that. But, for instance, the railroad
bridges across Danang were held by the U.S. Marines.
The airport was held by U.S. Marines. The key spots in
the city, the harbor, the bridges leading out of town,
were all held by us, not by Vietnamese. We let them
kill each other in town, we didn't care—we held the keys
to the city.

Before the ARVNs abandoned the encampment at
Henderson Trail, we had given them thirty-six thousand
Bouncing Betty mines. When they came back there were
thirty-six thousand 60-millimeter Bouncing Betty mines
missing. The VC just came right in and picked them up,
and we had to go out and find them one at a time. Meaning, BOOM.

After Dong Ha they had brought us back to troop strength. Within a period of about a month we received one hundred brand-new guys. And we're trying to teach these people, in a field-expedient method, how the hell to stay away from Bouncing Betty mines. It was carnage. We had a lot of guys get hurt.

They were trip mines. All you had to do was bury them and pull the pin. You could rig them up sixteen different ways. Step on them and they usually go off waist-high. It's a 60-millimeter mortar round, called a daisy cutter, with a super-fast fuse, designed to go off in a flat disc explosion. Bouncing Betty . . . It's supposed to cut you in half, groin level. It's a psychological thing. Everybody would hit them. They were up in trees, they were all over. The VC had a picnic, just like decorating a Christmas tree. Yeah. Goody time. It was the only time they ever had enough to spare because normally they had to carry that stuff down from the North one at a time. They put them everywhere, scattered them around like snowflakes. They were killing more water buffalo than anything else. Villagers were hitting them too. I didn't speak any Vietnamese, but I know how they felt about it—they were scared shitless. And that's the way I felt about it.

We had one guy who got a whole load of it in the cheeks of his behind. He was laying there and we were treating him. The corpsman had given him a shot of morphine and we were waiting on the helicopter. He was joking about his million-dollar wound, joking about how he'd be chasing the nurses by tomorrow afternoon. They put him on the helicopter and he went into shock and died on the way to the hospital ship.

I stayed with the company, but I became one of the office clerks in addition to being a radioman. They pulled me off patrol duty because they were afraid I would go off my nut again. By the way, I got no psychiatric care for that—because I came out of it on my own. The doctor said, "How do you feel?" I said, "Fine." And he said, "Okay, that's it." That's it?

That's like I was wounded three times and I don't have a Purple Heart. It's chicken to get a Purple Heart, nobody gets Purple Hearts. I got mostly shrapnel, pieces of my own radio. Twice I had a radio shot off of me and once I got hit with a rock. A concussion grenade went off and I got hit in the shin with a rock. You can't get a Purple Heart for getting hit with a rock unless your rank is major or above or you're anybody at regimental headquarters. But it was about this time that we discovered that three Purple Hearts gets you sent home. That's when everybody changed their minds about Purple Hearts . . .

By this time Danang base camp had been built and Dong Ha and Phu Bai were starting to be built up. Dong Ha got built up accidentally because of that charge over the DMZ, but Phu Bai . . . I went back to Phu Bai and I couldn't believe it. Just in a couple of months it had changed drastically into a huge international air base where before they had a dirt strip.

Danang was a circus. A friend of the first sergeant, his daughter's husband or fiancé, was at division headquarters and we stopped in to see him. He said, "Come on home with me and I'll give you a beer." He had a house he was sharing with two officers. It wasn't a hootch, it was a house. They had stereo gear, cooking utensils and a refrigerator full of beer. And twenty miles away we're up to our ass in mud. It just bungled my mind.

He had this big poster of Ann-Margaret taken when she was over there in a USO show. Very famous photograph. She was wearing a pair of Capri pants and a sweater that went right down to her mid-thighs. When she was up on stage the photographer was down below shooting up at her. She raised her arms in the middle of a song and it pulled her sweater up. You could see the very clear outline of her crotch through her trousers. It was an extremely famous photograph. Thousands of reprints were made. Scattered all over the world.

Thomas Bailey
Interrogation Officer
525th Military Intelligence
    Group
Saigon
January 1970-August 1971

The Prayer Wheel

WHEN I was in Cambodia we were trying to interrogate this Buddhist monk, Cambodian, who had seen a chopper go down. We were trying to figure out where the hell it went down. This was in the TOC bunker—where they were running fucking battles—so it's chaos city in there. We were sitting on the floor, myself, the interrogator who knew English, an American major who was fluent in French, a Cambodian colonel who knew French but no English, who was trying to get some money and guns for his troops, and then this monk, in a circle.

So I would ask a question and it would have to go through the whole chain to get to the monk and then come back again. I pinned down where the chopper was, got it oriented on the map and what time of day, what the weather was like, to figure out how far away it was. To try to get more information, I asked the monk, "after you saw it go down, what did you do?" So that went around the chain and when it came back, everyone laughed. The answer was "I offered up the appropriate prayer." We were all laughing, and the Cambodian, who was a kid—he was nineteen and had a shaved head—started rubbing my arm and smiling. He had never seen hairy arms before.

33

Thomas Bird
Rifleman
1st Cavalry Division
An Khe
August 1965-August 1966

Ia Drang

P RESIDENT Johnson deployed the Air Mobile Division,
as he called it, to Vietnam on a nationally televised
press conference on Juy 28, 1965. I was stationed in the
1st Cavalry at Fort Benning, Georgia. Air assault was a
new concept in warfare—fast deployment of troops, fast
evacuation, fast medevacs, fast resupply. Everything was
helicopter-oriented.

The reaction within the division was very mixed emotionally because what the division had been preparing for
the past two years was now going to happen. There were
a lot of career soldiers, many of them married, lots of families. They all lived around the Columbus, Georgia, area.
Everything was being uprooted so fast. I got myself a
quick pass to go home.

On August 15 I went over on the aircraft carrier,
the USS *Boxer*. After a very violent cruise we pulled up
to the coast of Vietnam. Over the PA system they said,
*"We are now off the coast of Vietnam. You can go up
on the flight deck and take a look."* We all had this feeling that we were going to see a war going on—artillery
exploding, jets strafing. I remember getting up on the
flight deck and seeing one of the most beautiful visions

34

I've ever seen in my life . . . a beautiful white beach with thick jungle background. The only thing missing was naked women running down the beach, waving and shouting, "Hello, hello, hello." I said, "Wait a minute, wait a minute, what's going on here? We must have the wrong place."

We came down off the *Boxer* on wet nets into these landing crafts. Everybody saw the movies going on in their heads, thinking we would be getting shot at. It was the movies, except it was real. We were carrying our duffel bags and saddle-up gear, but nobody'd been issued ammo. I thought, "What are we going to do when we hit the beach?" I came off the wet net very afraid. Everything I did seemed huge in that state of fear where everything seems to be so large and concentrated because you are making yourself do it, forcing yourself to mechanically do it so the fear won't get you.

They opened the front of the craft. We started to charge in the water. All of a sudden I thought, "What the hell is going on here?" It was General Westmoreland and his whole brigade of generals. They were all lined up on the beach, saluting the Cav on the way, saluting the Cav on the way into Vietnam. The only thing missing was the hula girls with the leis. What a letdown.

We were well indoctrinated with the Nine-Rule Card, which I still carry: Treat the women with respect, we are guests in this country and are here to help these people. We had a strong indoctrination in "help." It was still a kind of Kennedy . . . incredibly idealistic. We never had too much indoctrination about the Vietnamese according to their culture, their traditions, how different they were going to be. They were shockingly different from the moment we got there. We had never experienced people like that in our lives. We all had a tremendous big-brother ego, everybody gave the kids something to eat.

The end of October, the Plei Me Special Forces camp, which was heavily reinforced with ARVNs, was coming under attack by a regiment of North Vietnamese. The siege went on for a week to ten days before the 3rd Brigade of the Cav was called in to bail them out. This was the first serious involvement between North Vietnamese and American troops. The 3rd Brigade of the Cav—General Custer's old unit, the 7th Cavalry—came into the area thinking there was going to be a fairly decimated regiment of NVA, and instead two other regiments of NVA began to chew them up. This was early November. This started the battle of Ia Drang.

I went up to Ia Drang the end of the first week of November. I was eighteen turning nineteen years old. I had gotten myself transferred from helicopters to the infantry. As a crew chief and door gunner, they had been putting me in charge of I don't know how expensive a piece of machinery, and I didn't care how gung ho being a crew chief or door gunner is in an air-mobile concept, it's not the infantry. I had joined the service to become a paratrooper so I could play service football, and I thought paratroopers were Airborne infantry. So when they told me they're sending me to helicopter school, I said, "What?" I can't take care of a car and here they are putting me in charge of helicopters. They were a sweaty, dirty mess. I didn't like the responsibility.

I punched out a staff sergeant, so they granted my request. My only infantry training had been in basic training, but I had expertise on the M-60 machine gun [used in helicopters]. I remember leaving E Battery and everyone saying, "You're crazy." I was eighteen and said, "No, no, give me the gung-ho life," right? I showed up over at B Company and reported to the first sergeant. The first thing he said when he looked up at me as I gave him my new orders was "You're crazy." Then I knew I was in trouble.

I was assigned to a platoon, pulled a couple of days of KP, a couple days of shit burning, and the next thing I know the Cav's 2nd Brigade is being sent up to Pleiku because the 3rd Brigade is in trouble.

We got to the old Special Forces camp airstrip at Pleiku, which was famous because it was the first place Americans got fired upon. I was doing my best to keep up my front in this whole new atmosphere of the infantry. Someone said to me, "Oh, man, go over to the airstrip. There's a whole pile of boots there. Go get yourself a couple of extra pairs of boots." I was the only one who went across the airstrip to check out the pile of boots. I started noticing men's names in the boots and I said, "Oh,

these are somebody's boots. I don't want these boots."
Then I noticed piles of fatigues with lots of blood. And
then I noticed a couple of connex boxes, and on the
other side of the connex boxes was my first experience
with body bags . . . I had seen large piles of dead bodies
already, VC bodies dropped from a sky crane for inspection, but I had never seen the body-bag thing. I had
never seen a dead American. It hit me like a ton of
bricks because all of a sudden I realized what the hell
was going on and where they were coming from. They
were coming from Ia Drang.

We were air-assaulted out of Pleiku to LZ Falcon,
and from there we went out on a search-and-destroy mission to find the North Vietnamese who were butchering
the hell out of the 7th Cav. It was a drizzly, rainy day.
The mountains were about five hundred feet high, rounded
wooded mountains. There were lots of little valleys and
it was brown, red-clay country. We were supposed to be
going down the valley along the ridge line, splitting the
difference between peak and valley.

We had started marching about 6 A.M. and it was
now about 3 P.M. We had been walking the whole time
except for a ten-minute break to eat some C-rations. I
was carrying three days' worth of Cs—that's about nine
cans a day. We carried them in black socks strapped off
our packs. I was also carrying C-4 explosives, my M-16,
about sixteen clips of bullets and a couple of grenades,
about forty pounds all together. Walking nine straight
hours through mostly woods. Not much climbing, just a
lot of ridge walking, which can be a pain in the ass because you're walking on a slant all day. Somebody decided we were going to cut through the valley, radioing
in our position as if we were walking around the valley,
so we took a long break on the ridge line and they started
calling in our position from the map as to where we were
supposed to be. This was the whole company—three light-
weapons platoons, approximately 140 men.

After a good half-hour break we started coming down
from the ridge line into the valley to save ourselves a lot
of walking time. It was getting late in the afternoon and
they didn't want us to get to our predetermined campsite
in the dark. Everybody was tired.

As we came into the valley, the first thing that happened was we got some fast fire from the right. This was the first time I had ever been fired on. I froze. I completely froze and dropped behind a tree. The right flank started moving toward the fire, and as that happened, the enemy started dropping mortars in our middle and firing from the left, too. I realized I was supposed to do something, but the only thing I knew how to do was follow the guys around me and they were meeting fire with fire. But no sooner did they advance toward the fire and widen the perimeter than the enemy started opening up on the left and the rear, so we pretty much stayed where we were and some guys were returning the fire. They kept popping mortars into our center to keep our perimeter wide—wider than we could defend. It became a battle of trying to get back into a tight perimeter and fight off what was becoming a hell of an ambush.

It took a long time before some choppers came in. They would've come to support us, but it was raining. It was a gray, drizzling day. The cloud ceiling was very low, but they tried to bring in some ammo. I ran out of ammo real quick because I fired too much too soon. Resupply came in twice, but both times they dropped it out of our reach into the wood line. The choppers were making low runs, taking fire, then dropping boxes of ammo out, over the sides, hopefully into the center of our perimeter. Actually, we didn't have a perimeter. It was too disjointed.

I started noticing that some people knew what they were doing and some didn't. There was a lot of hiding going on.

Night came and we were out of ammo. There were lots of flares, which brightened the sky for us. The enemy started screaming. They must've had bullhorns, and as it got dark they started calling to us. I was afraid to hear them yell, "Kill GI, kill GI." They kept screaming at us. I found this staff sergeant, Starkweather, a Korean War veteran, and I started using him as a role model because he seemed to know what he was doing. He started yelling back at them, "Fuck you. Fuck you, you bastards. Come and get me." I thought, "Wow, he's fighting and I'm not." I started hearing a lot of painful screaming from our own wounded because there were a lot of people hit. I always had a bad habit of being afraid of wounded guys. A wounded guy crying, I didn't know what to do.

The thing that bothered me most was that as we started to come into a perimeter but didn't make it because they kept dropping mortars in, we kept leaving wounded guys out there that were crying, asking for help. They kept asking for medics and some of them started screaming, "Shoot me. Kill me." I got very confused in returning fire. As it got darker . . . the wounded guys . . . I started knowing that . . .

The enemy were in a woods and we were in very thin clumps of sparse trees. Our middle section was a wide-open space, a little smaller than the size of a football field, where the enemy kept dropping in mortars. As the woods thinned, there were clumps of twenty-to-forty-foot-tall trees with some underbrush to the right.

The NVA were firing and yelling sporadically. It got to be like torture—just popping here, popping there and dropping mortars in. There were still some of our guys returning fire. The choppers made two runs. I remember seeing ammo go off into the woods, which meant that the North Vietnamese got our resupply, and one time it landed on the left and our troops did get resupply and they returned fire for a long, long time. A medic crawled out to some wounded and he got shot under flare illumination. The NVA were still picking off people, the guys who were wounded, and both were screaming. What happened next was very fast. They made a rush.

When they made the rush there was a lot of shooting. They shot all our wounded, killed them. During the course of the fighting all the horror of people being wounded, parts of their body being blown off, became a blur. I think I stopped seeing that after some guy got shot in the midsection and doubled over and he caught all kinds of blood and crap coming out of him. I sort of got . . . it either blurred or I didn't see any more of that or I just concentrated on what I thought I had to do and kept looking for a direction to take and I kept finding it in Starkweather.

I didn't have any more ammo. I had a rifle. I held the weapon down by the flash suppressor [barrel end] and had my hand through the forward sight, ready to use the weapon as a baseball bat. And for some reason Stark-weather told everyone who was within hearing range of him to "put down your weapons and don't resist. Don't resist."

There were forty North Vietnamese who took us pris-oner. They were in brown uniforms and they were all full of leaves, leaves coming out of their pockets, out of their helmets, they were all camouflaged in leaves. The flares had stopped. I could see but not clearly. One guy had his bayonet out and was ready to fight, but Stark-weather told him, "Don't resist." The alternative to Stark-weather was to resist and get killed or don't resist and see what happens. I don't know why he took the gamble be-cause they were just killing. They killed the wounded as they came out of the tree line. The left column of the perimeter was still engaged in an exchange of fire and the right rear column wasn't . . . I don't know where they were.

Twelve of us were taken prisoner. We put our hands on top of our helmets and were immediately stripped of all our web gear. Then everyone got twined by the wrist, and we were led in a column back into the wood line where they came from and immediately up the ridge line in the cover of darkness to the end of the valley (which is the end of the ridge line that we would have come around earlier in the afternoon). We went up to the top of the hill. It was the head of two different valleys. They had a base camp there, which was cut out underneath and cam-ouflaged by all the trees. Underneath the camouflage was a cut-out open area with lean-tos. They took us down the side of the slope. They put us in a little clearing area which resembled a latrine. They made us take off all our clothes and tied our wrists to ankles, which became a very difficult position to maintain on our knees. There wasn't very much you could do. I fell over on my side for com-fort. They had guards on us all night, but they didn't bother us during darkness.

The next morning, I think they were enlisted men who found us all taking comfortable positions. They dragged a couple of prisoners to trees and tied them up by their necks—not enough to strangle them—with their wrists and ankles still tied together. It was enough to make me stay on my knees all the time. They kept us apart and wouldn't let us speak to each other. Anytime anyone was caught talking to another prisoner, he got slapped around. I didn't remember anything about the Code of Conduct. I don't remember feeling loyalty to anything.

They questioned only two guys. One was Starkweather because he was the oldest and ranking man. They sent officers down to see us. When Starkweather was questioned, he didn't know anything, because none of us did.

The NVA abused me and Starkweather and they took one guy, whose name was Elvin Evans, a white guy from Maryland, up to a hilltop. Evans never came back again. He was presumed dead, but everybody . . . I never got another bearing on him again. Starkweather had a silver wedding ring on his finger, and when they questioned him they wanted to take this piece of jewelry. Starkweather wouldn't give them the ring. The officer left and later this soldier came; he seemed like a sergeant. What they did was take Starkweather's hand—one guy grabbed a thumb, another guy grabbed a pinkie and they started cutting at his hand with a knife. They kept hacking between the fingers at the joint. They started to penetrate the skin and it started to bleed. When it started to bleed drops, Starkweather let them take the ring off.

Then there was just mild bullshit going on: little slaps on the face, little taunts in the balls with sticks, a game where we got pissed on. It was a latrine area, but they would come over and piss on us. A guy took a knife to my throat and pressed enough to puncture the skin. I spent the whole time praying. It was a very concentrated experience because I prayed a lot. I kept thinking that it wasn't happening to me. I kept praying that it was going to be over soon. But it kept dawning on me as it went into the second day that this was longer than I expected and that something almighty wasn't going to happen.

By the fifteenth the weather started clearing and I heard a lot of jets. It was very early on the morning of the sixteenth that we were found by a company from the Cav's 1st of the 12th, which was patrolling the area. The NVA had left during the night while we were sleeping. We were still all tied up and there was nothing we could do about it. A Lieutenant Anthony was leading this com-

pany on a sweep and his point man spotted us. Anthony
came forward with a squad because he thought it might
be a setup. They pulled a perimeter around us to make
sure it wasn't a trap and asked who the ranking man was.
Starkweather spoke up.

Anthony wanted Starkweather to identify himself. It
was crazy because we were all naked, tied by our wrists
to our ankles and "We're just out here for the hell of it,"
you know. They didn't untie us until they asked questions,
but as soon as Anthony knew he was making a fool of
himself, they quickly untied us.

I then got a little crazy because they wrapped us in
poncho liners and our knees were all fucked up, our skin
was all crawly and my neck all scabbed, blood all over my
chest. Starkweather's hand was all pused up and they
didn't give us any medical treatment. They called for
dust-offs [medical evacuation helicopters] down in the
valley, and all I could think was "It's going to happen
again. It's going to happen again." We were dusted out
really fast and taken to Pleiku, but there wasn't any room
there, so we were taken to Qui Nhon. We were there till
the twenty-first, then they brought us back to the Cav.

Ia Drang went on until after Thanksgiving. The Cav
fought there for another two weeks, chasing the NVA all
over the place. Eventually the NVA just dropped into
Cambodia. The Cav lost about a thousand men. They
were talking in terms of twenty-eight hundred NVA killed
and nine hundred to a thousand Cav. We couldn't do anything until about three months later. It took that long.
We pulled perimeter guard, road sweep, patrols, took the
holidays off. Morale was real low, the shock was real
heavy, and I relate to the experience from the naïveté and
gung-ho-ness with which we arrived till all of a sudden it
was ghost time. Everybody was spooked. It took a long
time to put the Cav back together again. It hit us extra
hard because most of the units were stateside together. It
wasn't like later on in the war, when there was a constant
turnover of individuals. We were friends of each other's
families, dined together, entertained together, argued together. The casualties taken in the fighting really got to
us and uprooted us. That also incited fighting in a way
that when somebody was hit or killed, it made the others

that much angrier, wanting revenge. They would just walk that much further into ambushes and traps.

When I was trained in counterinsurgency from an indoctrination and helicopter point of view, we were never schooled in Che Guevara. Air assault didn't mean shit in Ia Drang Valley. The joke of Ia Drang Valley is, If you can't bring a chopper in to give air support, what good is it? If they can't fly because it's too humid or because the weight they are carrying won't let them get off the ground or they'll burn up too much ammo to go out and resupply and get back to base camp, what good is it? Then you're down on the enemy's level and they are the masters there.

Toward the end of my tour, when I started knowing what I was doing in the jungle and started knowing what to do under fire, it was just about time to go home. If that happened to me—if I was just getting good in the jungle and really knew what to do and I was going home—what good is it? I'm going to be replaced by a guy who is as green as I was when I got here, and by the time he gets good at it he's going to be replaced by a guy who is green. It's no wonder we never got a foothold in the place.

Ia Drang was our first big battle. Afterward I wouldn't take it out on all the Vietnamese we were in contact with, but I knew something was going on. In spring we captured some VC suspects and gathered them around. As I walked by one of them, I gave him a thigh in the chest and he grabbed hold of my leg. All of a sudden I was trying to be aggressive or hateful and he didn't buy it. He grabbed hold of my leg and I punched him. I punched him about five times with all of my might and he wouldn't let go of my leg. Soon as I stopped punching him, he let go of my leg and looked up at me with this wide grin on his face. He didn't crack his lips at all, but looked up with this blank expression—it was all for me to read. I felt really strange about that. I started seeing that look everywhere I went. I was really angry with Vietnamese men. I started hating ARVNs because they were so unreliable and a couple of times in ambushes the ARVNs disappeared. I hated Vietnamese men. I never had any trouble with the women. I was always flirting with them. I never suspected the women.

David Ross
Medic
1st Infantry Division
Dian
December 1965-July 1967

The New-Life
Hamlet

I was involved with pacification programs. I would do anything from assist a dentist to play dentist. When major operations came up, I would go out on the operation as a medic. We were also part of a reaction team, and if any unit got hit hard and needed additional medical backup, we'd go out on that.

The first thing that really hit me was just after we arrived in Vietnam, during our initial reception period. We *were told not* to bad-mouth Ho Chi Minh, since the Vietnamese mistakenly thought he was the George Washington of their country because he had thrown out the French, but they didn't understand that he was a communist and would bring them to a sticky end.

Our base camp, Dian, was fifteen or sixteen miles northeast of Saigon. It wasn't a very exciting place; it was really flat, and as the monsoons were coming in we'd get horrendous windstorms. Because the area was very dusty, you'd occasionally get "dust devils," which were miniature tornadoes twenty or thirty feet across that could really dirty up your quarters, your tent.

There was a village called Ben Suc which was in the

Iron Triangle area, on the Saigon River north of where we were, and essentially it was considered a communist hamlet. We had pulled Medcaps (medical-aid missions) there probably a dozen times. It was one of those places we went back to a number of times. I learned to speak a little Vietnamese and I got to where I felt I knew some of the people.

Ben Suc was a very nice old village in a beautiful setting by the river. The graveyard was interesting because the tombstones were really old and in different shapes and sizes. They would have Buddhist or Taoist symbolism and some Christian symbols, too, for people who were Catholic. The whole place had a sense of antiquity and yet very much here-and-now.

We started out one morning on these forty-foot-long miniature LST boats. We went up the river in a convoy of about sixteen and landed at Ben Suc. The infantry was dropped in ahead of us and they met some fairly light contact. It was more like a fading or holding harassment action, rear-guard action. There were some people shot and killed on both sides, but it wasn't a battle.

We brought in Chinooks, Hueys, Skytrains. Trucks were brought in, Rome plows, bulldozers, and ultimately what happened was we took all the villagers out and relocated them into what was called a New-Life Hamlet, which for all practical purposes was a concentration camp. We were told that the purpose of these was to keep the Viet Cong out, to prevent reprisals against these good Saigon allies, when in fact these people were the communists and the camps were to keep them under control.

They were just flown out, so I didn't know where they ended up. We had been to that village a dozen times before. Nobody had ever shot at us, nobody even bothered us. We would come in, do our medical stuff and leave. People were happy to see us. We brought medicine. Medicine was very hard to get hold of out there. A tooth abscess could actually cause death in that environment because there's nothing to stop infection.

We would usually have a couple of people assigned for security. We're talking of anywhere from fifteen to fifty people who were going to put on a real show—it depended on how many doctors we were taking. Essentially we would organize the villagers and run them through an assembly-line procedure—there were so many people who needed treatment and such inadequate time to do it in the way it would normally be done. One doctor would diagnose, another doctor would give injections, and then we would set them off with a tag that said what time we should test the effectiveness of the anesthesia. A couple of other doctors would do the actual surgical phase. A couple more people would do the post-op and interpreters explained how to take the medicine. Given the medical need, it was conducted pretty professionally.

But we burned the village down. Any kind of holes that were found in the ground were blown up. There were a couple of weapons found, nothing that significant. A fair amount of rice was destroyed . . . and the graveyards were bulldozed. The whole thing was turned into a big parking lot.

What I remember most about the village was this one old woman. We had taken care of her once when she was in great pain. She came back and brought other members of her family, and the third time we were up there she invited me over to their place to eat lunch. So when we'd go up there I'd always have lunch with these people. And now soldiers were taking her and her family and a couple of pigs and their chickens—they didn't have that much—and loading them on a Chinook. She ran up and put her arms around me and wanted me to do something about it. There wasn't anything I could do. And that's when I started having second thoughts about the war. I still can see her face clear as day. I have no idea how her story ended. She reminded me a lot of my mother, always watching out for the kids, scolding, but very loving about it . . .

Search-and-destroy had gone on since day one, but this operation, Cedar Falls, was more search-and-clear, getting into major population relocations. The Iron Triangle area was a longstanding VC sanctuary and we were really going in to clean it out. They had tunnel complexes in there that—my God, you'd go down a little rathole and find a surgical operating theater with enamel walls and mercury-vapor lamps and the newest equipment from France as good as anything we had, all just down a little rathole covered over with a cooking pot. They had a lot of food and weapons caches in the area. There was a whole underground troop billet. They really built a maze in there. This area was the base from which they operated against Saigon. So the idea was to clear the civilian population out and essentially make it unusable by Charlie as a sanctuary. The irony was that the major thrust against Saigon during Tet came right out of the Iron Triangle not long after we had gone through all these operations. So we'd go out searching, do a lot of destroying, but we missed a few spots.

We began doing Medcaps in the relocation camps. They had very stylized types of architecture consisting of two-by-fours, a sheet of metal or fiberglass, basically just long buildings. The villagers would use cardboard or scrap wood or whatever they could get their hands on and try to block them off into family units. They were overcrowded. The sanitary conditions left a lot to be desired. You didn't have formal plumbing and a formal water supply. They were kept clean enough and I was not aware of any epidemics, but they weren't the kind of place you'd want to live. Buildings were set up on a concrete slab, then you'd have dirt and barbed wire and gates and that's it. There weren't trees for the kids to climb in and gardens for the people. They would just sit around and talk or cook and pass the time. It was pretty much USAID (U. S. Agency for International Development) food. We fed them wonderful things like bulgur, which they had second thoughts about even feeding their pigs. We shipped to Vietnam, which had been a major rice-producing country, tons of rice from Louisiana. They'd just truck in sacks and sacks of food with the old USAID "handshake" logo. Sometimes they would bring food out in plastic bags that had a picture of an ARVN riding a white horse, saluting or waving a Vietnamese flag, and the horse trampling a VC flag. The writing on the bag translated: "Your government has liberated food from the Viet Cong, who has stolen it from you. We wish you good health," or something like that. People used to read the bags and start laughing because at best it was probably the stuff that the ARVN stole from the people when they moved them.

When Americans are talking about Vietnamese or

people in India or somewhere similar, it's not like we're looking at them like they're our next-door neighbors. If someone came to our neighborhood and burned all of our houses and most of our possessions and put us in flying saucers which we'd never seen before and zipped us across the universe, setting us down somewhere in tent city in the middle of a sandbox with wire all around us, I guess we might not be too excited about it. Most of us were never able to see the Vietnamese as real people. I remember President Johnson in one of the psy-op [psychological warfare] flicks we saw saying that the communists weren't like us—they didn't have feelings. But I always remembered that old woman or remembered after a B-52 strike going into this area where there was a little girl with her leg . . . traumatic amputation . . . and . . . still alive. Her mother dead. The whole place turned upside down, a few people still screaming, some people wandering around with the look of the dead, a totally shocked daze. I wondered how people would feel in Pittsburgh if the Vietnamese came over in B-52s and bombed them. And while I feel some real sympathy for the POWs who were airmen, I pick Pittsburgh simply because it's a steel city and it has the image of the real hard-working honest American man. I'm trying to imagine a bunch of steelworkers after their wives, children, fiancées, parents, grandparents, have been blown up or are running around screaming in agony and some Vietnamese pilot comes swooping down in a parachute. I don't imagine they'd give him a very friendly reception.

The thing I remember most about Vietnam was the kids. I think almost everybody liked the kids. I never saw kids that smiled so much. It didn't matter if they were up to their chins in shit, they just kept on smiling. We did a lot of work in schools. We'd go into schools and teach them how to brush their teeth. We'd go out to the camps and the kids would always come around. Or we'd go out into a village and find a wild pineapple and start slicing it up. All of a sudden you had five or six kids sitting on your knees, all eating the pineapple and . . . We kind of really hoped a lot for the kids.

There was another thing I remember, too. We were going through a rice-paddy area in armored personnel carriers, and of course track vehicles going through a rice paddy isn't . . . The amount of labor they put into maintaining the rice and the paddy berms and the irrigation system and everything—it's all by hand. They don't have the equipment. It's all built a basket of dirt at a time and things have built up over generations. We're just ripping through there on the tracks, tearing the whole damn thing apart. This farmer out there is stomping on his hat and and beating his hand against his head. I guess, really, the bottom line is that all his stocks and bonds and his future and his Mercedes and his dreams he hoped for his kids, we just drove through there and in three or four minutes made a helluva mess of it.

There was another old man who was fishing. We had an ARVN interpreter with us and we asked him to ask the guy how the fishing was. The guy said he was getting mad, he usually has fairly good luck, but he's been fishing all day and hasn't caught anything. One of our guys says, "I'll fix that," and he pulls out an old Mark 80 grenade and chucks it out there and *vavoom*—all these fish came up. Well, that old man was just happier than . . . he was out there with his big hat picking up all these fish and bowing. He thought that was a pretty good show. It seemed like we'd do something real nasty and then we'd try to do something nice. It's like everything we did that was positive we canceled out with a negative.

One of the big problems was that there was no Ho Chi Minh Trail in the sense of some big interstate highway where enemy supplies were coming down in open-armed trucks. There were hundreds and hundreds of miles of two-foot-wide jungle paths with people bringing a couple of tons each on modified bicycles. There were small roads with rickety trucks bringing a load here and there. We used to talk about searching for COSVN, the VC's central office in South Vietnam, as if it was some kind of Pentagon East for the communists. In fact, it was nothing more than a few tents that got moved around here and there.

The VC would be the farmer you waved to from your jeep in the day who would be the guy with the gun out looking for you at night. They would come together and man a small offensive or probe attack, drop a few mortar rounds and go home and call it a night. We took more casualties from booby traps than we did from actual combat. The big problem was you couldn't find the enemy. It was very frustrating because how do you fight back against a booby trap? You're just walking along and all of a sudden your buddy doesn't have a leg. Or you don't have a leg. Even today, if I'm out walking someplace and there's grass, I find myself sometimes doing a shuffle and looking down at the ground. I realize that I'm looking for a wire or a piece of vine that looks too straight, might be a trip wire. Some of the survival habits you pick up stay residual for a long time.

Chairman Mao once referred to guerrillas as "small fish swimming in the greater sea," and what we tried to do, or what the government's real policy in the pacification program was, was to dry up the sea. If you could get the civilian base out of the countryside, then theoretically all that would be left would be the enemy soldiers. So it was approached on a number of levels. The first level was winning the hearts and minds of the people. They had all kinds of great names for it—REVDEV, for revolutionary development—and anytime anything unpopular happened, they just changed the name of it. They had the New-Life Hamlets and then after that they had the New New-Life Hamlets.

So what we were trying to do was either win the village over or, if we couldn't do that, move the people out, burn the village, put the people in concentration camps and designate the area a free-fire zone. Since you had theoretically moved all the civilians out of the area (but of course a lot of them just snuck out into the woods and came back when you left), everything that was "out there" was the enemy. So this gave us the right day and night to lob artillery shells out in that direction, and of course you still get more civilians. You figure whatever percentage of soldiers there are to civilians, the civilians really take the licking.

I was over there until I was late nineteen, early twenty years old. I volunteered, you know. Ever since the American Revolution my family had people in all the different wars, and that was always the thing—when your country needs you, you go. You don't ask a lot of questions, because the country's always right. This time it didn't turn out that way.

I had a friend who was an ARVN policeman in Tu Duc and his brother was a Viet Cong. We all talked over at their house one time. That was a real spooky thing because the guy was real friendly and likable. Once we got used to the idea that we weren't gonna be a problem for each other we were able to talk about things. The ARVN had a big family and basically he needed the money and his brother wasn't quite that attached. The ARVN didn't want to shoot anybody or cause any problems, he just wanted his salary and to raise his family and be left alone. The brother was a little more idealistic and wanted to fight because he didn't see that the Americans should be involved in Vietnam any more than the French.

Karl Phaler
U.S. Advisor to Vietnamese
    Navy
River Patrol Groups 42
    and 44
Mekong Delta
December 1966-December
    1967

Free-Fire Zone

I was an adviser to a group of Vietnamese coastal patrol
forces. There were a couple of hundred Vietnamese
sailors in our detachment and two groups of American advisers. We were based out of a little village, and most of
my patrol area was from the Cambodian border to the
southern tip of Vietnam on the Gulf of Thailand. Most of
the area was the U Minh Forest. We'd accompany Vietnamese forces into the interior of the U Minh, check out
villages, search tunnels and things like that. Most of the
U Minh was a free air-strike zone. B-52s would dump on
it at random and at will. The VC were short on medical
supplies, so they would restrict their hospital facilities to
combatants. They would take women and children and
old people who were injured in the bombing and put them
in sampans and send them out offshore. My boats and my
people would pick up these injured people, full of American shrapnel, and take them back to the province hospital, where there'd be no medicine for them because the
province chief was selling it to the VC.

Most of the medicine that was sent to the western part
of the country never got there. Hell, half the damn stuff

was diverted on the Saigon docks and driven directly to
Cambodia. Medicine was worth something. Who's going
to pay the most for it? Not the people you're supposed to
dispense it to. Not your own forces—they're not willing to
pay for it.

One day when I was on patrol outside the U Minh, a
sampan came out. In the back of it was an old *ba*, her
head wrapped, her breast blown away, blood seeping
everywhere. And under some reed mats was this beautiful
little girl, about eight or nine years old, just a lovely child.
The reed mats covered her from the waist down. I knew
right away I didn't want to see underneath the mats. Her
face was contorted in pain. The sampan came alongside
our boat. She looked up and saw me, this American—
"Ong me" in Vietnamese. This was early in the war, so I
was probably the first American she'd ever seen. She
started smiling. And what she had was one leg mostly
blown away and shrapnel. I got some morphine into her
and got the bodies back to the province hospital and
worked with the Quaker medical team that was there, a
couple of doctors and nurses.

I got her into surgery. Stayed with her. They had to
take her leg off. I'd been told by the people that brought
her out that she had no family anymore. The whole family had been blown away and she was the only one left.
So I felt a little bit of responsibility for her. There was no
one to take her back to.

I was by her bedside when she came out of the anesthesia. She looked up at me and smiled again. Magic Man
was back by her side. And then she looked down at her
covers and she reached down and she felt, and the most
ghastly look came over her eyes. All the magic in the
world had just gone away—her leg wasn't there anymore.
And I just didn't know how to handle that. I had blown
her leg off. Carried her off to have the rest of it ampu-
tated. And somehow on the way she'd gotten the idea I
was her friend.

I know I didn't actually do it, but we did. I've never
been able to distinguish these things really well. One of
the problems I had all through the war was that I was an
American, I was party to all this, I was responsible for it.
You can't say I'm just a cog in a machine. If I wasn't re-

sponsible, who the hell was? Who was going to be responsible for it if I wasn't? Who did it to her if I didn't? Some idiot out of Guam thirty thousand feet up on a radarscope? Bullshit. That's no good for responsibility. He never even knew what happened with his load. I knew where his ordnance went. I was so blown away I went back and jacked a full clip into my piece and I was going to get the son of a bitch that had made that targeting call. I knew who the Vietnamese major was that was making this targeting. The Americans were, theoretically, approving it too. There was an American colonel down there.

There were some evil sons of bitches wearing my suit. They were people who would execute civilians for the sheer joy of shooting at running objects. You would always run into these intelligence types who would draw little red lines on the map and say, "On this side's friendly and that side's enemy. Put your ordnance over there." Bullshit. There's farmers on both sides of that line living in their ancestral fields who didn't know a goddamn thing about a war. It's like some of these slime balls who'd fly around in the back seat of a Bird Dog shooting farmers in rice paddies, come back in grinning . . .

When I was in this state of paranoid confusion over my small child who was crippled so severely, I ran into one of the Quaker nurses. She soothed and calmed me and kept trying to tell me that I ought to be constructive. Going out and doing more destruction wasn't going to help. I said, "Well, what can I do?" And she started talking to me about what happened to the kids when they left the hospital, which was what bothered her because there weren't foster-care facilities or anything like that. When the kids get out of the hospitals, they just go out into the streets. They didn't have family anymore. Little girls hang around until they become whores and little boys became thieves and pimps immediately.

The bombing campaign was well enough under way in '67 so there were massive migrations of people. The cities were beginning to swell. There wasn't any housing. There were cardboard tenement shacks everyplace. Where it used to be spacious tree-lined streets, there were now slums. And so this nurse put me in touch with a group of Vietnamese nuns in Rach Gia who were trying to provide some sort of aftercare for the children that were discharged from the hospital, the ones that survived the hospitals where the medicines were being sold to the VC. I talked with the Vietnamese sisters and they had some land south of Rach Gia, but they had no money. I asked the sisters, "Well, about how much money do you need?" It worked out to be about ten thousand dollars. I made about four hundred dollars a month. "I'll get it for you, Sisters." I hadn't the faintest idea where I was going to get money like this. I'd been writing for a couple of years to Art Hoppe of the San Francisco *Chronicle*—a fellow Harvard man, by the way. He's a little bit older than me, but I had always admired his writing style, and when I got to know him later I was immensely gratified that yes, there was a fellow sensibility.

But I wrote to Hoppe and a friend of mine who was then a prominent businessman in San Francisco, asking both of them, "Look, I'm not trying to put the arm on you or anything, but here's what's happening. Do you have any idea how I could raise ten thousand dollars?" Well, the businessman, bless his eyes—he's still up in the Bay area and still a tremendous human being—he sent me a thousand bucks. And Hoppe said, "Look, I'll get you that money. The way to do it would be to print one of the letters you're sending me. Can I do that? Now, this might hurt you."

Not that I was fed up with the war. I was talking about what is. I was talking about American steel dismembering Vietnamese children for no apparent purpose. I was horribly distressed that having dismembered the children, we couldn't at least . . . The responsibility, damnit. Remember I said I was responsible? I wanted somebody else to help. We ought to be responsible. I wasn't enough to stop a war. I couldn't go back to Washington and tell Lyndon, "Look, you're hearing lies filtered and purified fifteen times. Everything you're hearing about the war is crap. Stop it." I wasn't going to stop the war. What needed to be done was some after-services. There ought to have been someone helping to order the carnage around a little bit. If we're going to inflict so much misery, I felt at least we had a moral obligation, which is the most compelling kind I know, to do something to alleviate the misery that we'd inflicted. Like care for broken children, for starters.

Art ran one of my letters in his column in the San Francisco *Chronicle* and he was syndicated. He was in the Long Beach *Press-Telegram*, the Des Moines *Register* and other papers I never heard of. Checks started rolling in from all over the country.

He printed my letter with my name, rank, address and PO number. I don't know that any American officer in the combat zone had a nationally syndicated column published about what we were doing at that time. Certainly early '67 was not a popular time for expressing critical sentiment in the armed forces. You were quite a bit out of step if that's what you were voicing, at least publicly. In addition to the money coming in, the Navy came in. They ordered me to Saigon to the basement of COM-NAFRV headquarters [Command Naval Forces Vietnam]. The upshot of that was I got chewed out completely and was considered a troublemaker, just for trying to help the orphans. I was reassigned out of the Delta up to II Corps in Tuy Hoa and ordered never to return to the Delta.

However, before they did that to me, I worked together with a guy and I wish to hell I could find his name—if he could ever find me, I would love to see him again because I owe him. He was a guy working at Chase Manhattan branch in Saigon in March, April of '67, and I had all this money to change. From all over the world checks were coming in from different banks and cash and drafts and money orders. If he had changed it for me at the official rate, I wouldn't have had too much money. But he got me the black-market rate. And thanks to that son of a bitch I think I finally wound up shipping fifteen to twenty thousand dollars down to the nuns in the Delta.

And something else, another little word that I would like to get out to all of those people, in the farmhouses of Iowa, the swamps of Georgia, the suburbs of L.A., that sent me their five and ten bucks for the kids. It really didn't go to the whorehouses in Bangkok. It honest to God went to the nuns. And they built an orphanage. I never saw it, but I worked with people that came out of Rach

Gia and they said, "Yeah, it was built." I understand it
even survived the Tet offensive. And one of the things I'd
like to do someday is get back to Rach Gia.

I went up to Tuy Hoa and commenced standard combat operations again—coastal patrol, night landings, infil-
trations. The province team I was assigned to was
commanded by a black army colonel who was a tremendously impressive professional. The national elections
were scheduled for September, October of that year. The
elections were accompanied by a massive assault on the
province capital of Tuy Hoa, and at one point in the middle of the night it was feared the town would be captured.
The province advisory team, forty to fifty Americans,
were all billeted on a little sand spit right down by the
beach. The Vietnamese did not understand why the
Americans wanted to live right there on the sand where
people crapped and everything, but Americans love
beaches. The town was taken. Everything in the south was
blocked off. We had the sea to our backs, and then we
received word that a reinforced battalion was moving
from the north along the coast. And we all shit because
there was no way out. There were no Vietnamese forces,
there was nothing available for them.

That night when the colonel got word that the battalion
was coming down along the beach, he called me on the
horn down at my base. I was with my Vietnamese. I lived
south of the Americans on the Vietnamese base. He
wanted to know if I could get some swift boats in to evacuate them if necessary, and could I do anything with my
Vietnamese to deal with the battalion coming down the
beach?

The word was "a reinforced battalion," whatever that
meant, right? Five, six hundred guys, who knows? I had
one hundred Vietnamese sailors and six or seven Vietnamese officers. Out of these hundred sailors, maybe fifty
were actually fit to go someplace. And the colonel wanted
to know if I could do something about this battalion. Well,
I wasn't going to get anywhere by going to my counterpart
Vietnamese lieutenant and telling him, "Hey, guy, it's you
and me and twenty sailors go up and kick ass on five hundred main-force VC." So I told him it was a platoon.
The only way I'd get that sucker into combat was to con

him into it and then lead him into it and shame him. You didn't ever follow him into combat, you walked first, and if you did it with enough style, he might follow. You don't lead, you con. I took my counterpart and about thirty sailors, loaded up in a couple of junks and sailed a couple of kliks [kilometers] north of the American compound. We did a line abreast, one man deep, thirty-foot intervals, going about a half klik inland. It was just the scrawniest goddamn defense. All we had was hand-held weapons, nothing. I got Spooky on line to help us out. Spooky is a C-47 airplane with Gatling guns. I got him up and, oh, it was nice to hear because we started making contact and had some pretty heavy automatics against us. I remember in the middle of the night when I really thought we were all going to get eaten, Spooky came up and called me, saying, "Hello, hello, this is Spooky zero-two with forty thousand rounds of happiness." And, oh, happy to see him.

Anyway, between Spooky's presence and the fact that we were there, they stopped and regrouped and reanalyzed the situation because there wasn't supposed to be anybody between them and the American compound, and you know how the VC war-game everything. Thank God they didn't come through us and check later. They backed out. For which I was decorated.

My citation was originated by the Army colonel commanding the advisory team, not by the United States Navy. At the same time I was on the Navy's troublemaker list, the Army was commending me for bravery. I found it very difficult to fully assimilate. How could I be a hero and a goat at the same time?

Jonathan Polansky
Rifleman
101st Airborne Division
I Corps
November 1968-November
1969

Lang Co Village

THE place where we stayed in the lowlands was a little
fishing village called Lang Co. A beautiful, beautiful
place, on the coast of the Gulf of Tonkin. It was a peace-
ful little village, a combination of French and Vietnamese architecture, cement buildings and different shades of
blue, little concrete houses.

We were stationed on a bridge to protect the village
and the railroad from being blown up. That was probably the finest time I spent in 'Nam because I met a lady
there who I fell immediately in love with. We'd spend
our days together every day. I was pulling night guard
duty, so I had nothing to do during the day. We would go
across the tracks and lay out by this big waterfall, me just
getting into this woman, who had been married to an
ARVN who had been killed and had a child by him. We
would talk for hours and hours. She spoke English pretty
well. It was so strange how the conversation would be so
close to a conversation that you might have here. We'd be
talking about the children and about her and me. How
much we enjoyed each other. What we might be doing if
we were in the States. What it was like where she grew up

59

in Saigon before she moved up here. She had come all the way up north with her family. Her father was a scholar and was running the school.

One day a young lieutenant approached me: "Do you want to teach school?" I said, "Yeah, sure." So he said, "Okay, pick out somebody to go into the village with and talk to the hamlet chief." So I grabbed this guy J.J. from Chicago, a big black guy with a big gold tooth in his mouth, bright eyes. We had gotten pretty close. We talked to the village chief and to the assistant of my girl's father. He told us it would be okay, we could work in the classroom with the kids during the day. We couldn't teach them English, but we could certainly work with phonetics, minimal English words and things like that.

The next three months we worked with the kids, teaching English every day. The classes were made up of kids from five years old all the way to teenagers. Me and J.J. would work out little skits to present to the class, like playing baseball with words. We would stand across the room from each other and throw the word back and forth. We'd pronounce it for the kids and they would go along with us. The kids would be roaring, they loved us, to see these two jerky Americans, these two animated young fellas. It was a pleasure beyond belief because each day after class we would go through the village and as we'd walk through we'd hear the little kids whisper to their parents, "Schoolteacher, schoolteacher," and we'd be invited into the houses for soda and tea, and all the kids loved us. They'd come up to us in the street and grab our arm: "Come in here."

After a while I started feeling really, really fine and I stopped carrying my weapon into the village—which I almost got court-martialed for. All of a sudden I didn't believe the war was going on. I thought I was a Peace Corps worker in this country, dealing with the classroom. I was finding my own little made-up methods to try and relate a little more to the kids. And after the school day was over, I would find myself in the houses with the parents, enjoying talking to them, being invited to the hamlet chief's house for dinner and being catered to. That really brought the roughness off me.

And all this time the relationship with this woman is

growing and growing. All of a sudden I found myself happier than I had ever been in the States. I felt like I was accomplishing something. A month ago all the terror and everything that was going on around me, and here I had found this little place where I could really be of some use and I was really appreciated for it. I was really enjoying what I was doing and being treated finer than I was ever treated at home. I had this woman to love. She wanted to come back to the States with me. She wanted to escape the country and the situation and the war. She wanted a good life that she felt was going on over here, compared to having to sleep in a bunker at night. She would tell me her dreams of what the United States would be: big streets, big buildings, all the food that anybody would need to eat, safety for her baby, not having to sleep in a bunker in a place where she felt lonely. She told me about her relatives whom she thought she would never see again. She made her living selling Cokes and whatever else she could get.

While we were guarding the bridge, the VC never bothered the village. We left the bridge to go to the Ashau for three months. Completely pulled out. After three months we came back. The village was flattened. There was not a soul in sight. It was flattened by VC destruction. The village was completely burned because all the people were American sympathizers. The only persons left were old bums. The interrogators grabbed them and tried to find out what happened. I couldn't believe it— the village had been so picturesque, the most beautiful little town. Destroyed. Everything was destroyed. Every living thing was gone. I walked into the schoolhouse. I started crying and crying. It couldn't come together for me, after three months in the mountains just thinking about this village. I had totally forgotten about home by that time, after eight months in country . . . after heavy fighting those three months in the Ashau. It just couldn't come together for me.

Lee Childress
Sergeant
206th Assault Helicopter
   Company
Phu Loi
June 1967-May 1968

Chrome Dome

Good old Chrome Dome. I named her that because she was bald on top of the head, and like most gooks, you couldn't tell whether she was twenty-one or forty-five. There's no middle age. She had one bad habit that I understood and realized: she wouldn't steal anything from you but gum. It was one thing you couldn't keep around the hootch all day.

Christmas 1967, they allowed the Vietnamese to come on post. I had mailed a letter to my wife telling her that we were going to have this little function and kids were going to come, and my wife sent me some toys and—I'll never forget it—a great big salami. I had her mail me some pictures of snow because they had no idea in the world what that was. There was nothing in Vietnamese for the word "snow." I spent Christmas with the kids and Chrome Dome. She really warmed up to me because the communication was through the children. I played with the kids and with the toys. I can remember cutting salami and giving it to all of them. They didn't even know what to do with it. They could tell by the smell that they were going to eat it, but how do you eat it?

We spent that afternoon together, and on the twenty-seventh our own artillery killed them all, took those three kids, and fuckin' Chrome Dome showed up to work the next day just like nothing had happened. And you know how gooks were with living with that every fucking day, right? Chrome Dome was a changed woman, but you really couldn't tell.

She had gone into my hootch and she went down to another soldier's living area and took a piece of spearmint gum. He shot her point-blank through the chest and killed her. Even now, every time I see spearmint gum it blows me right out of the fucking saddle, man . . . For a fucking stick of gum. We got in more trouble for killing water buffalo than we did for killing people. That was something I could never adjust to.

But there were some great guys. Benny "Boo" Bagwell, that's what we named him. Really a fine guy. He came from Gillian, Ohio, scared shitless—made the plane rattle on the way over, that kind of a dude. But he found it there and really became that center-pillar sort of guy. You know, all the macho motherfuckers kind of bellied up, and I was one of those belly-ups, right? And the guys that seemed to be just the opposite were the ones in those situations that seemed to have the strength.

One time we got wiped out. My hootch took a direct hit and I was so paralyzed with fear that I couldn't move. And Bagwell—this would never be funny for anybody else—Bagwell slides up to me and with his rifle butt hits me on the side of fucking helmet and says, "Come on, Sarge. They're writing U.S. Army in the sky. Shit, let's move." 'Cause Bagwell had his shit together in that situation and I didn't. That night I listened to a guy die for about three hours, and I was just . . .

Today I go down the street and I see things in a way that nobody else sees them. I look at my own kid and it scares me. 'Cause it's a baby, and babies are alive and they're beautiful and they're perfect, and they've got arms and legs and feet and toes, and their mind is like an empty plate that hasn't had all these things happen to it. And I think, "If you ever saw what I've seen. If you'd spent the time that I spend every fucking day of my life, going over and over and over again the *why?* and the *why?* and I always know there's no answer." There's no answer anywhere. And that really scares me sometimes.

The first time you were under fire, you thought, "How the fuck can they do this to me? If only I could talk to the cocksuckers firing at me, we'd get along, everything would be all right." I just had the overwhelming feeling that if I could talk to these people, that they really are the same as I am, that it's not us that are doing it, it's some other system and we're just pawns in this fucking thing, throwing the shit at each other.

Samuel Janney
Recon
1st Infantry Division
Dian
July-November 1968

Getting Loaded

I'D never gotten stoned before in my life. We were at Song Be and we'd taken a bunch of incoming mortar rounds, so they put our platoon on the bunker line to guard the POL dump—petroleum, oil and lubricants. We're taking incoming rounds and if an incoming round lands in there, forget it.

I was in a bunker with two other guys. They said, "We're going to bring some other guys back here to get stoned. Do you mind?" And I said, "Hell, I'm from California." You hear about the people who didn't get loaded the first time they got stoned—whoa. We did about seven bowls that night, and I woke up the next morning with my feet down in the bunker and just laid out straight back. They'd taken my brain out that night and passed it around and played with it. They had a lot of fun with me that night. That was my platoon. And that was the first time I'd gotten loaded with them. I'd probably been in the unit for two weeks at that point. It makes a big difference being part of the group. They definitely initiated me.

Douglas Anderson
Corpsman
3rd Battalion, 1st Marines
Nui Kim San
February 1967-February
    1968

Doc

I was about to be drafted, so I went into the Navy Reserves. I was a hospital corspman. At that time so many hospital corpsmen were being killed that they put the reserves on active duty. I went through six months of medical training at Great Lakes and from there I was transferred to Camp Lejune in North Carolina, where I went through field medical school, the Marines teaching Navy people how to stay alive in a jungle situation, which was very ironic because it was the middle of winter and about fifteen below. We're stomping through the marshes and the ice training for Vietnam. They had little model Vietnamese villages set up and Marines who had been in Vietnam telling us what booby traps were, how they were made, what to look for and what we would be up against.

If you got orders that said "Fleet Marine Force," that meant you put on the green uniform. Yeah, I joined the Navy to get out of the infantry and ended up in the infantry. I was assigned to 3rd Battalion, 1st Marines, Lima Company, which was about two kliks south of Nui Kim San, the town right below Marble Mountain. It was about five kilometers from the ocean and three kilometers south of Danang.

We were mainly engaged in squad-sized patrols, five or six men who would go out five or six miles from the battalion staging area. If we were going to patrol outside the area for any length of time, they would usually send the platoon. We ran into old-style Viet Cong—black pajamas, bare feet and M-1 rifles.

We would get ambushed, one or two men hit, and they'd run before we could get in an air strike or choppers. It was fighting on a small scale my first three months that taught me some fundamental things and gave me a chance to learn the ropes. A lot of the corpsmen who went over were immediately engaged in large infantry actions and killed because they didn't have time to learn some basic skills—to be able to tell, for example, the direction the fire was coming from. Frequently it was coming from two or three directions in an ambush. I learned how to find cover in flat sandy areas where you wouldn't think you would be able to find cover. You stayed below the horizon line. Small lumps in the earth can provide more cover than you expected. And I became quite good at crawling.

I'm six foot three. Yeah, I'm a good target. I'm skinny —maybe that's why the rounds missed. I got a lot of rounds thrown at me. I saw a tree splinter in front of me once, and I just stood there looking at the tree, wondering why I didn't get it. One of the things that amazed me is how many bullets can be fired during a fire fight without anyone getting hit. This is a really extraordinary thing.

I learned that you can save a man's life with what he has on his person; you don't need a first-aid kit to save him. It's nice to have a first-aid kit because you have an airway, morphine, tourniquets and battle dressings. But you can stop bleeding with a belt, you can stop bleeding with a piece of string out of a poncho. You can tear a piece of clothing off a man for a battle dressing. You can stop a sucking chest wound with the cellophane off a cigarette pack. You can use his chin strap to secure things. I learned that first aid is a matter of primitive wits.

Fortunately I learned to hang around with the fire team and move with them. The fire team is the machine-gun team, the machine gun and two riflemen. As I became closer to some of the Marines, I could get them to work with me on the casualties. They would give me cover fire when I needed it. They knew very well how to take care of their corpsmen. There was no lack of cover fire and there was usually a fire team with me when I went after a casualty. There were several occasions when I did have to go out alone, which were the most horrifying experiences I've ever had in my life.

There was one ambush where I had to crawl about fifty meters to get to a man and no one else could move because we were pretty well pinned down. He was the point man. The rest of us had to pull back because the fire was so heavy, so the point man was stranded. The fire team laid down a sheet of automatic-weapons fire that was working its way right in front of my nose. They worked me along until I got to the man, and then kept covering me while I tried to treat him. Unfortunately he was pretty well dead by the time I got there. I was scared to death. The enemy was very close because the rounds were coming close. There was a man in a spider trap maybe thirty meters away who kept popping at me. Another Marine managed to get close enough to cover for me and he almost got hit. There were bullets kicking up sand all around me during the entire thing. When I got to the man I had to lay on top of him, grab his clothing and roll him over to the left to get him out of the line of fire. I succeeded in getting him behind a clump of earth, and I calmed down a bit and was able to treat him. He had bled to death internally by this time. This guy's name was George Custer. He was seventeen years old. If your parents signed certain kinds of papers, you could get over there and die at seventeen.

It's taken me twelve years—it'll be thirteen in March—to assimilate the gap between what I thought I would see and what I did see. First of all, I'm not a heroic type of individual. I don't believe the things I did over there. I don't believe that I got up and ran under fire as much as I did to get to people. I don't believe I made myself do those things. But I did. But what really bothered me were some of the things that I saw that were not compatible with the ideals that I'd been brought up to believe in, in terms of being a member of the military and fighting for a country that heriocally helped defeat the Germans and the Japanese and was supposed to be the good guy and all of that.

I saw cruelty and brutality that I didn't expect to see from our own people against the villagers. It took me a while in country to realize why it was happening. In this type of fighting it was almost impossible to know who the enemy was at any one time. Children were suspect, women were suspect. Frequently the ARVNs themselves were on two payrolls. Their army was heavily infiltrated with Viet Cong or people who were politically ambivalent, who could change sides as easily as changing clothes.

When, for example, we would patrol an area of villages for a number of weeks and continue to lose men to booby traps, and the people in the villages who pretended not to know anything about these booby traps walked the same trails that we did day after day without stepping on them, it became obvious that these people were well informed by the VC where the booby traps were.

One must understand that it's very easy to slip into a primitive state of mind, particularly if your life is in danger and you can't trust anyone. It was difficult for me to assimilate both sides of the picture, that maybe some of these villagers really were enemy. In one case I saw a young man, probably eighteen years old, push an old man into his family bunker inside his hootch and throw a grenade in after him. We'd been hit a lot that week and pressure had been building up. It wasn't anything that happened that day. But I remember this guy distinctly because he had a tattoo of a little red devil on his left arm and he had his shirt off when he threw the old man into the bunker and threw the grenade in after him. This is something that I blocked from my memory for twelve years. There are several of these memory blocks that are coming back to me now that I had just put right out of my mind. And I think it's probably my association with other veterans that is bringing these things up.

The most intimate relationship I ever had with a Vietnamese was a very weird one because I was asked to guard a prisoner one day. The rest of the platoon was too busy and they had caught a Vietnamese prisoner after a fire fight. He was about forty-five, he could have been fifty years old, and he had one hand missing. He had an old wound where his hand had been neatly chopped off. This led me to surmise that he had probably fought the French and probably had been caught as a thief at one time in his life and had his hand cut off, because many of the legionnaires fighting for the French were Algerian and this was a typically Middle Eastern form of justice.

I tried to figure out how he fought and realized he must have rested his rifle on the arm with the missing hand and fired. They couldn't tie his hands, so they tied his feet and gave me an M-16 and I pointed it at his head. This black platoon sergeant came over and beat him up. He was really furious because we had just had a man killed, and started poking him in the genitals with a bayonet, telling him he was going to castrate him. I remember this old guerrilla sitting there knowing he was going to die that day and just staring straight at me. The sergeant went away and left me to guard this prisoner. I had the M-16 trained on his face and my hands were shaking. I think I was very close to crying. He was looking right into my eyes and psyched me out. He knew who I was. He knew that I did not want to kill him, but he knew that I would. His eyes kept flicking over in the direction of another M-16 that was lying several yards away, and I knew what he was thinking. I knew that he was thinking that if he could get to that M-16, he might be able to kill me and escape. And I remember it was probably the most horrible five minutes that I spent, being totally conscious of my emotions.

Afterward they brought out an intelligence officer and a Vietnamese intelligence officer. I don't know whether they were Navy, Marine, CIA or what. But they both spoke fluent Vietnamese and they proceeded to torture the prisoner by holding his head underwater for increasing lengths of time until finally he broke and staggered into a hut and pulled out the rifle that he had hidden and incriminated himself. After that they tied his legs together with a chain and tied him to the back of an amtrack and the Marines dragged him for a couple of miles over the countryside until all the flesh was torn off his body.

I will never forget the man's face, and I will never

forget his eyes, and I will never forget holding the rifle at his face. I had treated this man for an arm wound. Patched him up so they could drag him across the countryside. I'll never forget how old he was. There was something about the internal solidity of this human being that I will never forget. I feel that's the closest relationship I ever had with a Vietnamese. Something went on that changed my life.

The further we got from Danang, the more peasant-like the people became and also the more involved they got with the Viet Cong. It was well known that the VC would come into the vills at night and even sleep. The villagers did not like us, they were hostile to us, except in some of the areas like Nui Kim San, where they found that they could make a great deal of money out of us. They set up laundries, whorehouses, they set up various means of corruption, they sold marijuana. They discovered middle-class capitalism, basically. Anytime you saw a Honda in the village, you'd know the middle class had set in.

I saw, strangely, American kids particularly from the South who had been brought up in religious Baptist families have a lot of trouble reconciling what they were doing, even though the communists could very well be conceived of as the anti-Christ, according to certain Baptist sects. They were having a lot of trouble killing people, basically. I saw some fairly sensitive kids begin to know themselves because of this and begin to discover contradictions in their thinking. And unfortunately this cost some of them their lives because the minute they would begin to think, they would move just a little less quickly under orders and pause just a little bit more before shooting at somebody.

I remember one night patrol. We were walking over an area of sand dunes. A VC armed with a weapon ran across the trail in front of our point man. He was a new guy, his first night patrol. The VC stopped, looked at him and kept on running. The point man could have very easily shot him, but what he said was "Halt, who goes there?" I remember the squad leader saying, "Did you really fucking say that? Did you really fucking say, 'Halt, who goes there'?"

In my unit there were few Hispanics, there were a lot of blacks. There were two categories of blacks: Southern blacks and blacks from Chicago and Cleveland, Northern blacks. There was as much difference between the two as chalk and cheese. It was incredible. This was during the time that Muhammad Ali refused to go into the service and became a hero. The blacks in the battalion began to question why they were fighting. Honky's war against other Third World people. I saw very interesting relationships happening between your quick-talking, sharp-witted Northern blacks and your kind of easygoing, laid-back Southern blacks. I began to notice certain radicalization processes going on there. Many Southern blacks changed their entire point of view by the end of their tour and went home extremely angry.

The black/white relationship was tense. I saw a couple of fistfights. It usually happened when somebody got mad, and the first thing that happens in an argument between a young white redneck from Louisiana or Mississippi and a black from Cleveland or Chicago is names start flying and the first word that comes out of the white man's mouth is "nigger." And the fists start flying. I saw this happen in the field, as a matter of fact. The lieutenant had a considerable amount of trouble breaking it up. When you see racial incidents developing and weapons lying around, it gets pretty tense.

Also, the VC, not being dumb, were putting propaganda pamphlets along the trails that we'd find all the time, encouraging black soldiers to refuse to fight. I'm sure that the war had an incredible effect on black people. The context of this is very economic in a way because both for poor whites and poor blacks the service was one of the few alternatives to get out of an absolutely miserable, dull situation in the South.

Under fire the strangest kinds of camaraderie would develop. It had nothing whatsoever to do with patriotism. It did have a great deal to do with taking care of each other. Because when you're out there, politics notwithstanding, the basic idea is to stay alive, and in a situation where we were fighting an unconventional war, which confused most of us, the main point was to stay alive.

The very idea of the search-and-destroy operation is

one of enormous logical fallacy. You send a patrol out in order to get it ambushed, in order to mark a target with a smoke rocket from a helicopter so jets can come in and napalm the area. In other words, you have to get ambushed before you can find the enemy. Now, this immediately gives them a chance to inflict damage and then get out of the way. The VC were smart enough to know that it was going to take two or three minutes at fastest to get a Huey out there, so they could kill a couple of people and split before anybody ever got there. We proceeded to mark the target where we thought the fire had come from. Meanwhile the VC were eating their hamburgers in Danang. It happened time after time. An incredible drain.

I know one artillery shell cost fifty-five dollars in 1967. If you were to add up just how many artillery shells were expended during the war, it might mean something. That's not to mention five-hundred- to two-thousand-pound bombs, rockets, smaller ordnance, tanks, what it cost to put someone through an emergency room in a hospital and give them medical help or send them to a hospital ship or send them home, or how much gasoline and oil was used, or what it cost to feed people. I think at the height of the war, when Nixon was skulking around Cambodia and trying to keep it quiet, they were spending how many hundreds of millions of dollars a day on the war. You can't tell me that doesn't have something to do with the present state of inflation. Meanwhile large corporate entities were making money off the war hand over fist.

I was in the field about nine months and I began to get the shakes. I don't know if someone reported me as having the shakes or not, but anyhow I was transferred to 1st Hospital Company in Chu Lai. I sat back there and was drunk for three months. I could put away a six-pack before anyone else. I began to drink extremely heavily.

I remember an incident in the field where I thought I couldn't take it anymore. I told this friend of mine, this black guy named Ryan, that I was going to throw a grenade around the corner of this hootch and stick my leg out. I wanted to go home, I wasn't going to do this anymore, I didn't know how to reconcile what I was doing.

I was standing there shaking and crying, and he's telling me, "You're stupid, man. You're stupid. You're going to blow your leg off. You're about the dumbest son of a bitch I've ever seen in my life." He talked me out of doing it.

Once before, I had gotten an easy wound. I don't even think it deserves a Purple Heart, but it was done under such dangerous circumstances that perhaps it could be seen that way. I was on a patrol and walking right behind a guy who stepped on a very cleverly constructed booby trap. There was a slope into a ravine that we had to go down in order to get where we were going, and the VC knew that when we got to this slope we would slide down because the dirt was loose. So they rigged a trip wire where it would catch us as we slid down the slope. It was one of the damndest things I'd ever seen. And Charles Wright—he was one of the guys who always wanted to be John Wayne, a little bitty skinny guy from somewhere in the South—tripped it. It wes a Chicom [Chinese communist] grenade, fortunately, so it didn't do him too much harm, but it took off part of his calf. I was real proud of that medical job, by the way—I saved his life. The blast from the Chicom set off a smoke grenade that was on his belt, and yellow smoke was going everywhere. It also made one of the grenades on his belt start to hiss. I could do two things: run or try to get that grenade off his belt. I knew that the fuse was five seconds, so I was probably going to die. But nevertheless I struggled to get the damn thing off. It probably took me a whole minute to get the damn thing off and throw the whole belt away. Fortunately, the grenade didn't go off, but in the process I blistered both palms of my hands. This sufficiently impressed the squad leader that I deserved the Purple Heart.

I started having a lot of trouble when I got out of the field. I began to drink all the time. There was lots of beer, that Filipino beer with formaldehyde preservative in it. Horrible hangovers.

One time there was a bunch of officers watching a movie in the battalion area. I walked right on the movie screen and took out my cock and took a piss right in front of all the officers. I was very drunk, but it doesn't take much to realize that was a gesture of pure expressive hostility, for which I was chastised. I was then sent further into the rear.

I was sent down to 1st Hospital Company in Chu Lai, where I proceeded to drink even more. They put me to work in an office typing because evidently I was one of the few people around who knew words of more than one syllable. I think this was the point where I became what you'd call an alcoholic, which took me a good ten years to shake when I got back. Most of the surgeons in the Hospital Company were alcoholics at that point too.

I remember New Year's Eve 1968 the VC rocketed . . . First of all, everybody in Chu Lai must have been drunk because the people on the perimeters had entire magazines of tracers in their .50-caliber machine guns, crossing them back and forth in the sky for fireworks effects. That night the VC dropped a rocket on two big oil tanks, and we were all drunk, standing on the roofs of our hootches throwing beer cans and screaming "Happy New Year!" while these two big oil tanks were burning. The captain in charge of Hospital Company was so scared he was hiding under his bed with a pistol. And we were all on the roofs screaming and yelling and throwing beer cans, screaming "Happy New Year!"

It's a funny thing. Up until the time I was pulled out of the field, I kept myself pretty much together. I had become calm in a weird way. I could walk around during a fire fight as long as I knew where the fire was coming from, or crawl or do whatever was necessary at that point. The people had begun to trust me. They knew if they got hit that I would come after them. I wouldn't just lay back there and cry. I would come get them. People would give me the goodies out of their C-ration packets. If there was an air mattress to be had, the doc got it. People would give me things. They treated me like gold. And I know that if I had ben hit and there was no way to get out of there, they would have grabbed me up in a poncho and carried me a hundred miles if they had to. There was that kind of feeling. This was above and beyond any kind of politics.

Donald Smith
Demolitions
101st Airborne Division
Phu Bai
October 1968-June 1969

Wings

WE had one operation on top of this LZ that had been abandoned by the U.S. They left all their ammunition there. So what happened? Charlie came up, took all the ammunition, all the hand grenades, pulled the pins and depressed them under sandbags. You lift the sandbags and the spoon flies off the grenade and it goes off. About two weeks later we came back. We arrived about two in the morning. The first two helicopters were blown right off the LZ. A couple of guys got it. A total of thirteen guys were killed in just a few hours. So they called in EOD [Explosives Ordnance Disposal]. We landed and went to work. We must have went through thousands of sandbags. We found a lot more hand grenades.

We probed underneath each bag with a knife. If we felt something we pulled the sandbag up and gave the old grenade a good kick. The best way to do it is with a swipe of the hand. You hit the deck, swipe them away.

After we worked the first day and got most of the stuff done, the weather changed drastically and it got very cloudy and rainy, so foggy that they couldn't airlift us out that night. It was a pretty high mountain. I have a feeling that the weather was clear everywhere except on top of the mountain. We had to stay there that first night, so we built a little bunker, me and my partner. The bunker collapsed. We weren't very good at making one. So the CO said, "Come over and stay with us," and we stayed. The next day we got up and did some more work. The weather was just as bad. It stayed that way for a week and a half. We couldn't get out. We were all stuck on top of that mountain.

We got hit with our own artillery one night. I was laying there, sleeping out in the open. It was slightly raining. I remember that just as I got into this little niche on the side of the hill, I pulled some landing planks over so I had a little shelter. All of a sudden on top there is this big *pshhoom.* I realized a 155 artillery round had landed right on top of the mountain. I took one look at that and said, "Uh-oh, I know what's going to come now. We're going to get hit with a barrage." Our artillery had gotten the grid coordinates mixed up. But that didn't last very long. The lieutenant was yelling over the phone, "No! No! Wrong! Wrong!" And they got that straightened out.

One guy walked off the mountain. It was a week after his ETS and he was still stuck on the mountain. He said, "To hell with it, I'm walking home." He got about halfway before they finally picked him up. He was doing fine.

One day clouds miraculously broke and there was this bright blue sky. The lieutenant radios in, *"All right, we've got a beautiful clear zone. Let's get the Chinooks in."* And there is this hemming and hawing back at the base camp: How many Chinooks do you need? What is this? What is that? And so, all right, the Chinooks are on the way.

Just as they came overhead, the clouds came back again. Closed up tighter than a drum. The CO was yelling over the phone, "You fucking assholes. We've got to get the EOD guys out of here. They're short-handed."

This Huey pilot said he'd do it. You could hear him buzzing over the top of the hill. You could just see the underbelly in the fog. And he says, "I can't see. I can't see. I can't see anything. It's not good for helicopters to be flying in the fog. I'm going to make one more pass." We said, "All right. Wait. Wait. We'll light some flares."

So we took the little night flares and made a round circle for the LZ.

He comes by and says, "I saw it! I saw it! I think I can make it." Everybody cheers. All of a sudden he comes down out of the fog and lands. He says, "I'm not leaving. I'm not flying through that again. I'm not leaving until it clears." The CO says, "You gotta get them out of here, man. You made it down. You can make it back up." The pilot says, "You don't know, man! I'm not going anywhere in this fog."

Finally they convinced him. So they loaded me and my partner and some other guy who was hurt, and the pilot said, "All right, hold on." We started going straight up. It was just foggier and foggier and foggier, and I said, "Oh, my God, this is horrible. What's going to happen? We're probably going to crash into another mountain." We held on. We just kept going up and up and up, and finally we lifted above the fog. You could see for miles. Oh, man! We made it! I looked back and there is that hill with a big layer of fog around it.

I got out of Vietnam the sixth of June, got home the eighth. All of a sudden I found myself at one or two in the morning standing outside Oakland Air Force Base in my dress greens. I was out of the Army.

I wish I would have had a barracks to go to or an EOD unit to settle down and relax and talk to people that could listen to me and understand, and then program out of the Army that way. I wish it wouldn't have been so abrupt because it did fuck me up. Not only was I getting out of a traumatic situation, but I was getting out of a way of life for almost three years. All of a sudden I was on an aircraft going to Chicago. O'Hare Airport.

I was going to rent a car and drive home. I thought of all those plane trips I took from Fort Riley to O'Hare visiting my parents. And I thought, "This is the last time I'm going to have to do this again." How anticlimactic it was. Nobody met me at the airport. Nobody knew I was coming home.

I rented a car and drove home. There was nobody there. I just sat out on the front doorstep of the house and looked around. It was a nice warm day. "This is wonderful," I thought. "This is home." I'll never forget that picture of myself just sitting on the stoop, out in the country, just sitting, whistling, just looking around, listening to the meadowlarks, bright sunny day. "This is home. I'm here."

I thought of when I left Vietnam. Sergeant Smith and Sergeant Carlton drove me to Phu Bai Airport and just shook my hand and said, "See you, Smitty." I had just spent two years with these guys but, you know, they're lifers. They understand. We exchanged goodbyes and that was it. I never had any contact with them except once, three months afterward, I had letters. I have some friends I want to look up sometimes, find what happened to all the people, too, but I . . . What's the use? Might find things you don't want to hear.

June 10 I had to start school. I was really buzzed sitting in the classroom. In my mind I could still hear the sound of choppers overhead. I'd daydream so much. I remember staring off into space. Looking out the window. Waiting to see if a helicopter would come and take me away. I used to dream about that a lot—I was going to be airlifted out of there. "I'm going to get airlifted." In fact, the only sounds that really freak me out now, even after this amount of time, are bangs. Loud bangs—something that sounds like a detonation. I can't take that. And helicopters, any helicopter that goes by with the right pitch on those blades. Whenever I hear that I just look up at it. Especially when I'm out in the woods, in the park with my dog. I just think, "At any moment that thing's going to land. I'm going to see some blue smoke or green smoke or something else, yellow smoke. That thing is going to land and pick me up, take me away. Who knows where."

I've never been in a helicopter since.

3

Peaks
and
Valleys

Herb Mock
Rifle Squad Leader
25th Infantry Division
Dau Tieng
November 1967–November
1968

Fire-Base Burt

THE night of January 30, I was having a fantastic night in this crap game in the track [armored personnel carrier], won sixty-five bucks, and they were mortaring us. I didn't think nothing about it. It was just standard operating procedure to be mortared. 'Cause I was hot-streaking, boy, rollin' them sevens. I crawled out into my bunker as they started mortaring us again. It got real, real heavy. I knew nothing but shit was going to hit the fan.

What it was is they give all their men mortar rounds and line them up on the mortars, and as each man went into battle he dropped his round into the tube and charged, so that by the time he gets there all the mortars have hit and he's right on top of you. We lost one track on the road, hit by an RPG [rocket-propelled antitank grenade], and another track on the perimeter got hit with one too.

Well, they come on us, and Don and all of them got in the bunker with me. Lieutenant Kelly got in the bunker because it was about the only one left. They were firing at us from the woods, trying to RPG our tracks. So 2-2 [2nd Squad, 2nd Platoon] ended up the only squad left to hold this side of the perimeter. And this whole area was no man's land. A duster [truck with multiple cannons mounted] tried to pull up and hell, it never even got to the perimeter. They blew that son of a bitch up. The first squad had to abandon their bunker because it was filling with hot metal from a destroyed track. It melted, killed one or two guys that were in it. The driver was in it, and they never found nothing of him. The metal was running into their foxhole and they had to get out. It looked like a smelter or something, just running in a stream.

Helicopters started landing more ammunition. Jets were bombing in the woods. They were dropping anti-personnel deals. They'd hit and BAWWHAM. I mean the ground would shake . . . bombing, man, right on top of us.

The enemy kept getting in with satchel charges [explosives]. We ran out of ammo. This was like from midnight to 5 A.M. It was about five hours we fought. So I had to run from my bunker across this fucking no man's land to a track to get ammo for the .50. I already burnt two barrels up. I burnt one up with a thousand-round burst trying to cover Hildebran so he could run back in. I had to run across the no man's land and bump into gooks with satchel charges. Knocked them flat on their ass. They were carrying explosives to blow up them artillery guns. I hit them with a box of ammo. Just run over them. In fact, one I had hit, hell, I didn't even see him. We just kind of bumped into each other. And I was a damn sight bigger than he was, with two big boxes of ammo in my hands. I couldn't carry weapons for the simple fact that I needed ammo and I couldn't carry a rifle ready to shoot. So what was the use of carrying the son of a bitch?

Anyway, me and Don made five or six trips over there. Finally ended up setting up a .50-caliber. We couldn't get it working right and we had been fighting for so goddamn long, got so irritated, ended up in a goddamn fistfight. Man, we were surrounded by these motherfuckers and me and Don were fighting over who was going to shoot the .50.

Sergeant Alexander came over and cussed us out: "Goddamn it, what the fuck are you doing?" We got up. "Aw, I'm sorry," I said, and started shooting this .50 that

I had set up 'cause I had done burned the .60 up. Melted that motherfucker.

I was standing up in the open portion 'cause I could never squat down or lay down and shoot a machine gun. I like to stand up and let them have it. So I'm standing up just peppering the fucking tree line and all I could see was red tracers—mine. And Don and Kelly said, "Goddamnit, Mock, sit down, motherfucker. Goddamnit, get down here." "Aw, fuck you, man," I said. Don said, "Goddamn, they're fixin' to blow your head off." I said, "What do you mean, motherfucker? Those motherfuckers can't even get a shot in." Don says, "Yeah, motherfucker, come here." I squatted down and he says, "Now look up." I looked up and saw tracers—green tracers. Don said there was a set of green tracers on both sides of my fucking head. Of course I never saw them while I was standing up. So I decided I wasn't going to stand up no more.

We ended up fighting the rest of the night. We got three hundred fifty or sixty of them. The next day you just found their bodies laying all over. General Westmoreland flew in. All the news outfits and everything. It was the most hilarious thing. As these son of a bitches came out there, the GIs started lying. The newsmen would walk up to just anybody and say, "What did you do?" "I singlehandedly killed three hundred thousand with my Bowie knife." And man, they'd write it up.

There was a sergeant that led an ambush patrol. His RTO, this Mexican, was a damn good man. When the attack happened, somehow they got off their ambush and got into a bomb crater, and man, I mean these fuckin' gooks were crawling up to the edge of the bomb crater all fucking night. That sergeant laid down there and cried at the bottom of the crater. The RTO took over, that Mexican boy, and kept them alive. Kept fighting while this motherfucking E-7 cried. Anyway, the next day that fucking ambush patrol come in, and before the officers can get to that goddamn sergeant and put the whammy to his ass, he talked to one of these dudes from one of these magazines. "Sgt. Hero"—that's how they wrote him up. And it came down that he was to be recommended for a Distinguished Service Cross. But his RTO did the work. The sergeant was supposed to be court-martialed, but because he told this newsman . . . They believed any fucking thing anybody said. All they wanted was a great story. But oh, man, the Army couldn't go back on that. And instead of being court-martialed . . . Our first sergeant said he wasn't going to recommend him for no medal. The brass told him they would hang his ass if he didn't. The main honchos said "the E-7" was going to be recommended for it. Chickenshit.

One of them old boys from CBS or NBC says, "Goddamn, I wish I'd been here." And Eberwine looks over at him and says, "Yeah, son of a bitch, goddamn, I wish you'd been here too!" This shut his ass up. Eberwine, he was in one of the tracks that got wiped out.

Scott Higgins
Supply Officer
Headquarters, II Field Force
Bien Hoa
October 1967-October 1968

James Hebron
Scout Sniper, Fire Team
  Leader
1st Battalion, 26th Marines
Khe Sanh
August 1967-February 1968

Size-Twelve Boot,
Size-Ten War

SCOTT HIGGINS: I went over there in October of 1967
and came back a year later. I was stationed at Bien
Hoa, twenty miles northeast of Saigon, at Headquarters,
2nd Field Force, which was the commanding unit for the
III Corps area around Saigon. I worked about four
months as compound coordinator, supplying all the housing, food, water and electricity for the compound. Later
we moved out near USARV between Bien Hoa and Long
Binh. It was a heady experience for me at age twenty-

one. I had received an officer's commission through
ROTC at Gettysburg College. I went over there against
the war because I thought it was a mistake, but that still
didn't excuse me. If I was called I was going to go. I suppose it comes from a certain kind of patriotism many people had back then.

Five of us who had been in supply officers' school at Fort
Lee, Virginia, were selected for Vietnam immediately
after six weeks of officer's basic. It was an "emergency situation," they said. I arrived at the 90th Replacement Battalion in Vietnam, stayed there a few days
before being called by an artillery unit. A major interviewed me and told me I had a choice of two jobs. One
was searchlight platoon officer. All I could think of was
as soon as you turn on the light, everybody knows where
you are. The other job was convoy escort platoon officer
in III Corps. I said, "Look, I just got out of college, went
through six weeks of supply school, and here I am. I will
probably wind up getting a lot of people killed in both
those jobs, including myself. You've got the wrong guy." I
really felt I was, plus I didn't want to get my ass shot
off. We kept at it and kept at it and finally I convinced
him. I went back to the 90th Replacement Battalion and
got a call three or four days later from the commandant
of Headquarters Company, 2nd Field Force. They needed
an assistant club officer. My first job was to go down to
Saigon and hire bar girls. That lasted about three weeks.

James Hebron: I went to Vietnam in August of 1967
and was assigned to the 1st Battalion, 26th Marines—1–
26, as they say—at Khe Sanh. I just turned eighteen
when I got to Vietnam, because you can't go into a combat zone until you are eighteen. I had joined the Marines
when I was seventeen, having graduated from high school
a year early. At that age I was super-naïve. I was influ-
enced by combat as written by noncombatants, i.e.,
Stephen Crane, author of Red Badge of Courage. A combination of that plus bravado, you know: Marine Corps,
blood, rape, kill, plunder, that kind of thing. It was just
fantasy until I got orders for Vietnam. I had been in Okinawa since January and had to wait until my eighteenth
birthday in July before I received my Vietnam orders.

I had twenty-two hours before I landed in Vietnam. Individually placed. That was one of the cold things about it. I guess it's better for replacement, but I never got the sense of unit camaraderie. It took so long to develop it. There is a kind of chemical reaction one feels, a kind of sixth sense, like when a close friend speaks and I know what he is going to say before he finishes the sentence. That kind of tightness should be developed in combat units to delay any kind of problems in a hot LZ. You know from the way the guy is behaving what is happening, you sort of read between the lines. It takes a long time to develop that. It just doesn't happen if you are going in as individual replacements. It just isn't there. It's like being new on the block—everyone who was new had to walk point.

HIGGINS: I went to the Saigon bars and talked to the girls and decided whether they had pleasing enough personalities and looked at the bands to hire for the officer' club in Bien Hoa. The first three weeks I was on the job I would get up at ten in the morning and take a jeep down to Saigon, go around these bars checking out the groups and the gals, hire a few and then come back. In the evening I'd be in the Bien Hoa officers' club.

Saigon was an incredible city, an incredibly active, bustling town. There were probably fifty thousand prostitutes by the time I left. Some unbelievable French restaurants were still there. Supposedly you could walk into this elegant French restaurant with a .45-caliber pistol on. There were still some vestiges of French occupation there.

At Bien Hoa there really wasn't very much to do. The club officer was a captain, I was a lieutenant. We had this old villa on the most expensive street in Bien Hoa. At that time Bien Hoa was considered a safe town. There wasn't any curfew. It was one of the larger towns, with about a half million people—hell, it could have been a million. It was a big town.

We had a big Air Force base there. The government had rented at astronomical fees the finest buildings on the wealthiest street in Bien Hoa, Cong Wei Street. There were old, high-ceilinged cement buildings that the wealthy in town lived in. French architecture—the French had a

major impact on the town. We went in and either confiscated the buildings or negotiated some sort of deal. I
saw some of the rental agreements and they were amazing. For the officers' club we were paying some landlord
forty thousand dollars a year for the use of this magnificent
old building. We had literally taken over the whole street
and had put barbed wire around the whole thing.

My initial experiences the first couple of months over
there were sort of unrealities, living in this compound, in
a room with a high ceiling fan, and in a villa. Each officer had his own room or we doubled up at that time.
It depended, but there was no lack of space.

HEBRON: I was a private, PFC. I wasn't told a damn
thing. What I thought it was going to be and what it
turned out to be were so totally different. There was no
romance at all in it. Absolutely none. That was stripped
bare immediately. The high sign was when I reported to
Khe Sanh. This lieutenant swept open the tent; I just saw
the hand. I thought it was a "Welcome aboard" hand. I
went to put my own hand out. He said, "Get the fuck in
here, Hebron." Jesus Christ, I hadn't fucked up, I hadn't
done anything wrong or anything else and he was treating me like that. I said, "Oh, shit." I was also out of
shape at that point because I had just spent six months
partying hard in Okinawa. They gave me a flak jacket,
pack and all this other shit and, you know, I wasn't used
to humping all that gear in that heat. I had to go up to
the LZ and wait for a ride up to Hill 860 and commence
humping.

We had a base camp on Hill 860, company size, Bravo
Company. There was another company sitting on Hill 81.
On 860 I had to start walking point man. Lieutenant Pete
was my troop commander. I was really dragging ass. I
was really out of shape. The equipment we carried was
very heavy. I had no idea how to walk in elephant grass,
either. There is a certain style to do so it doesn't wrap
around your feet and make you fall. I was just trudging
through and falling down and really getting bleary-eyed.
I was hoping for a fire fight so that we could stop and
rest. I was broken and beat, but we kept going, "Let's
go, Hebron, this isn't New York City, no sidewalks here."

Good troop commander, but I don't think he exercised good judgment by putting someone that out of shape on point. The new-man-on-the-block rule applies regardless of conditioning or anything else. The whole experience is so different from anything you think it is going to be. You watch John Wayne movies—and it just wasn't the case. Not at Khe Sanh, anyway.

HIGGINS: I also had a carpenter and was supplemented by a number of other people who came in to work on special projects. We had to maintain all the billets and frequently things had to be done—fans had to be fixed, repairmen had to be brought in. It was almost like running a hotel. It was a different kind of hotel. The officers were sometimes very unreasonable in terms of what they wanted. I was a lieutenant, I wasn't the hotel owner. Since this was the headquarters of the whole III Corps, the people were high-ranking. Lieutenant colonels, colonels—we had three generals. General Weyand was my commanding officer, who later became Chief of Staff of the Army. So it was a special kind of arrangement. I think because of that there were more resources available to me, and that's why I could have an interpreter, for instance, and a carpenter. Those kinds of things were not available in other sorts of situations. There was a tremendous misallocation of resources over there. It always bothered me.

There were a lot of deals being done on the side. I think a lot of them happened through people who in situations like in headquarters had a certain amount of flexibility there and through people in supply who ran the PXs. I saw some of that. There was a tremendous amount of trading. To give you an idea of the misallocation of resources within the war, I tried to get hot-water heaters and I found these hot-water heaters in Bien Hoa from some guy from AID [Agency for International Development]. I traded this guy some steaks that I had gotten.

HEBRON: Food was a big thing at Khe Sanh. All you got there was two C-ration meals a day. That's all you could eat, no matter what—two C-ration meals a day. Somehow some of this law and order broke down a bit as the siege started. They had this big supply—mounds and mounds of C-rations there—but a lot of them had been damaged by the shelling. That hadn't been a major area of attack, but of the three hundred rounds that hit us the first day of the siege, one or two of the shells are bound to hit some supply area, just by the law of averages. The office post was guarding it—you know, the office post against us. So a few people got up there with a rifle and said, "Listen, motherfucker, I'm gonna get some C-rats. Okay?" That C-rat stock went down rapidly when we all started eating. For about six days we had about four C-rat meals a day. We were getting so we shot canned bread around.

It got to be more miserable by the minute. The guys had shirts on they had been wearing since October (this was late January), and our packs were all black in back. This was from lack of resupply. Doggie straps—that was the thing we used to dream about, shoulder straps. Army wide ones to support that weight. Packs were getting tremendously heavy in this war. You carried more ammunition—new weapons can fire that much more ammunition, so you have to hold that many more rounds—plus new flares and whatever else. They were really heavy and the old pack straps cut into your back. My clutch belt must have weighed forty-five pounds with a K-bar knife on it and .45 pistol and you name it—it just had tons of shit. It was a real coup to get your hands on doggie straps.

They gave me a size-twelve boot over there. My foot is still fucked up from that today. They gave me a pair of size-twelve jungle boots and I wear a size ten. My foot slid in it. I tried stuffing it with paper, but part of the problem is how you walk. If you are right-handed, you carry your rifle in your right hand. So if you are going down a hill you lean to the left side so you can bust caps [fire rapidly]. So the left side of my foot developed a blister, then a callous and then a planter's wart. That's the kind of shit we got. Size-twelve boot and size-ten war.

HIGGINS: I traded the man from AID a case of steaks for the water heaters. My job there was always scrounging around, trying to find water tankers to ship in or truck in water. It came from wells near Saigon. I had gotten the steaks from some private engineering company out in the field that needed cement, and we had a whole lot of cement. The whole black market in the Army was to get what you wanted. This was a totally different war. We needed a water tower, so I stole a water tower, this enormous water tower that I found in a compound in Bien Hoa that was not being used. I brought in a sky crane, picked this thing up and took it over to where we were, and I have no idea who it belonged to or whatever. We needed it, so we took it.

HEBRON: On Hill 881, 881 meters high, they gave us five-gallon water jugs to go down to the base, 881 meters down, and lug up the five-gallon cans of water. That was the most terrible fucking humping I ever did in my life. That was really a ball-breaking hump. We had no water and no food. From October 15 through April there wasn't any hot chow in Bravo Company. Five months, then they said, "Open Hill 881," and it became seven months.

That was only part of the detail. Khe Sanh really got to be a motherfucker. We were mopping Hill 881 from October 15 until December 26. We didn't have any time. They were going to bring hot chow up on the Marine Corps birthday, November 10. First sniper fire opened up, so they voted and the fucking choppers had to buy off. In the meantime they dropped some ice cream in the landing zone and it just splattered all over. We all dove for it and had it all over our faces.

Christmas Eve, Christmas Day, New Year's Eve and New Year's Day were cease-fires. That's when cease-fire took effect. Supposed to. I always say "supposed to" because it never really did. Christmas was the darkest night of the year. It was very, very dark. We got shelled that night, but we didn't return the fire.

HIGGINS: In Headquarters Company you always had access to materials, or men for that matter. I needed men to put in pipes for this water system we were putting in, so I borrowed some men from some guy who wanted something else. He wanted some men or food or something, and we gave him that in exchange for his men. Everybody wanted a piece and that's the way that things got allocated. You could get in a helicopter and go down to Vung Tau beaches if you wanted to, if you knew the general, and there was a lot of that. You could go on a couple of R & Rs if you knew the R & R officer. I went on two R & Rs. You could get an air conditioner. You could do those kinds of things. The war was out there and around you, and some of your friends were getting killed or wounded or whatever, but you, on the other hand, could carve out an okay existence. There was decent food. There were Red Cross girls.

HEBRON: I didn't brush my teeth for two months in Vietnam, the reason being that though they sent toothbrushes out in SP packs, we had to use them to clean our rifles. There were certain things that came first. I remember when I was going home I had to go to a dentist's office in Danang. I walked in and sat down. I had the scuzziest clothes in the world on. I had just left the fucking combat zone. So I hadn't brushed my teeth in a couple of months and I was real dirty. I bathed in the meantime, but I still had these old clothes to put back on. I couldn't pick up any new clothes until the following day. I get in the dentist's chair and the dentist tells me, "Get the fuck out of here and go brush your teeth." I was mortified, you know. I thought these guys were used to seeing this kind of stuff. I mean, I hadn't been initially embarrassed by it, although I saw some guys walking around looking pretty strac [neat] with spit-shined boots and shit in Danang.

So I walked out and I was embarrassed as hell. I walked around for a bit and then I got really pissed. I got really cold, and I went back there and I said, "Goddamnit, I don't know where you people have been, but I just came back from a war, up in the combat zone. I had no toothbrush up there. I had no place to brush my teeth."

HIGGINS: The sergeant who was in charge of the PX came in from Saigon in a jeep. He was part owner of the hotel down there. After five or six years, when he went back to the States, he was stopped by the FBI and had about ten thousand dollars in cash on him, undeclared. The last I knew he was on trial in a major gambling scheme that the sergeant major of the Army was involved in. I think they covered his ass, pretty dramatically.

They had slot machines in the NCO clubs in Bien Hoa, and he was getting a skim off the top and was kicking some of it back up to the sergeant major. In addition, I think he had his own deals. For instance, selling cigarettes on the black market was a big thing. He did that in enormous quantities, so I am told. There was a lot of graft over there. There was a lot of money-changing.

HEBRON: We don't talk much about Americans killing other Americans on purpose, not only in fire fights. A friend of mine put sixteen rounds in a staff sergeant's back in Vietnam. The staff sergeant received a Purple Heart, was put in a green bag and packed home. No autopsy or anything else.

The staff sergeant was just an incredibly short-tempered, evil man. They would go out humping for eighteen days, come home, and he'd hold a full field inspection or some shit. You had to unload, clean your weapon, stand a full field inspection, and you only got three hours' sleep that night. That's what I'm talking about, you see. Sleep is the most valuable thing in the world over there. If anybody fucks with your sleep, you want to take their ass off.

HIGGINS: Sometimes there was no question about it that people in headquarters got privileges that people in the field didn't. One guy literally stubbed his toe and got a Purple Heart. He was jumping from his trailer on the night of Tet. (High-ranking officers and some of the generals had their own trailers.) So he jumped out of his trailer and stubbed his toe and got himself a Purple Heart. Isn't that incredible? I mean, he didn't even write it up as stubbing his toe. "During the course of enemy action, he was injured. Injury sustained to his foot, abrasions on his leg" and so forth. It was bullshit. What he did was stub his toe. When the story went around, everybody . . . But who's going to question that, you know? I mean, if it doesn't stop at the top . . . And there was a lot of that. A lot of Air Medals went out that way, the kind you get for hazardous duty, for acts of valor in the air. A lot of officers would go out and just fly around and put themselves in for Air Medals or a Service Cross.

* * *

HEBRON: I'm not sure that anybody in combat came home without traumatic effects. I remember a guy who turned down his Purple Heart. In my platoon outside of Khe Sanh there were only four of us left alive. I received a post card from this guy, Jimmy Kirk. It was very poignant. When he was dusted off at Khe Sanh, he lost all his equipment and belongings. He wrote back to the squad and said, "Divide up my packages among the squad and send my mail to this address and let me know who gets killed or wounded. By the way, I lost my foot." It was one short paragraph, not asking for pity or anything else.

Artillery was coming into Khe Sanh. People were literally getting blown into the trenches, crushing us. We were getting hurt. This one guy was standing on top of the bunker talking to me. He was kneeling over and going along to tell the trenches to pass the word along. All of a sudden a round goes off thirty-five feet away, BOOM, and he gets blown right on top of me. Shit like this was happening all fucking day.

This one guy, Clare—ballsiest motherfucker. I'd been in Vietnam for seven months and had been in a number of fire fights and everything else at that point, but his really amazed me. I'd never seen anything like this. He was walking on top of the fucking trenches, on top, not ducking or anything. He said, "Keep your head up and make sure nobody is coming over the wires." Ballsiest motherfucker I had ever seen. He guided an observation post back in during the shelling. He got a Bronze Star for his actions that day and deservedly so. We used to call him Tarzan. He was from California. Only had one front tooth. Every time we'd clean up a patrol—and our patrols were really exhausting—and he was out there, he'd reach the crest from where you could see the camp was and let out a Tarzan yell. Making Johnny Weissmuller sounds five octaves higher. He wasn't college material, as they say. He was really into war. He was a lance corporal at the time, soon to be made corporal. He wound up getting killed about three or four weeks later—February 25, the day I landed in New York. He's up for the Medal of Honor, too. I don't know if he ever got it or not. He was in the ambush that killed my platoon, wasted them. He was up for the Medal of Honor for his action that day.

It was a U-shaped ambush, from what I understand. He had broken open a good portion of it and a lot of people were getting out of there. He refused to evacuate himself and got a couple of other guys out who couldn't make it. He was hit a number of times at that point and was firing one-handed. He used a pop-up flare to take out a couple of gooks. He had done everything. This guy had firmly stated that he wanted to become a Medal of Honor winner. That was his whole raison dêtre for being involved in the Vietnam War. He was a crazy fucker, ballsiest son of a bitch I ever met. There was nobody there to write up his Medal of Honor papers. Half the battle is getting a good writeup, and since the officers and everybody else were dead, he doesn't stand a very good chance.

HIGGINS: Tet was the last day of January 1968, three o'clock in the morning. I will never forget it. It was a complete surprise. I was asleep. I wasn't on duty. I had a few days a month where I didn't have to do anything, there were enough officers to go around. To give you an idea of how everybody thought Bien Hoa was so safe, we built two-story billets, six of them, housing about two hundred officers. We built them close to Route 1, right on the road, and they were laid out one behind the other, classic army style. I was up on the second floor. We had no bunkers.

It was 3 A.M. I jumped out of bed, grabbed my flak jacket and my underwear, grabbed my .45 and my helmet, which I put on, and ran out the door. What woke me were these 22-millimeter rockets that started to come in. *Whoosh, crack*. That scared the living hell out of me. You could smell the graphite.

HEBRON: I'd seen a lot of war pictures as a kid growing up, as we all had, I'm sure. I was impressed when I found out there were four divisions of NVA surrounding Khe Sanh. They put barbed wire behind our position. Lieutenant Colonel J. B. Wilkinson, our battalion commander, came out, walking around the lines, asking us if we needed any water or anything else. I got goose bumps. I

said, "Holy shit. This barbed wire behind us and this lieutenant colonel coming out here asking us if we need supplies or anything else—it looks like these guys are writing
us off." Last request, all that kind of thing. I really didn't
have a hyperactive imagination. I mean, the men were
out there asking us these questions. That really made us
feel weird. We were understaffed also. In one area we
had eight guys guarding one hundred fifty feet of perimeter.

HIGGINS: You learn so much so quickly at such a young
age. That is part of the readjustment problem for a lot of
people coming back. There's some trauma, but they've
had their whole value system changed.

It's a confusion about the value system, thinking that
the world was one way, living on one set of rules. It's a
rude awakening to find that it was done on another set.
Your sense of reality is changed too. I mean, here I was
in a fairly safe area. We got hit that one time at Tet, we
got hit once again. They blew up the ammo dump twice.
The first time they blew it up, I looked out and screamed.
I didn't have my glasses on and there was this mush-
room; I thought they had nuked the place.

After that there was always this feeling of kind of an
edge that wasn't there before. Once in a while I used to
have trouble getting to sleep at night. I would be lying
there and I'd think, "We're going to get hit again tonight."
If we got hit, my fantasy was, one of those 22-millimeter
rockets was going to come right down through the roof
and right onto me.

When I came back stateside, I used to have a lot of
bad dreams about that, and it's funny because I had
thought I had dealt with it pretty well, but I had night-
mares for two years. I roomed with this guy whom I met
when I first went into the Army, and we were back at
Fort Lee, Virginia. Hell, he used to wake me in the middle of the night and I would be down on my hands and
knees, holding onto the bedpost in my sleep.

When I came back, I was trying to find out what was
important to me. All of a sudden, what was going on back
here didn't seem that important. It didn't seem as important as the life-and-death questions that were going on in

the war. Not that I want to go back to it, but there seemed to be a total misunderstanding of what it was back here.

HEBRON: We had a very long fire fight, about twelve hours, between December 26 and January 1. We had just come off Hill 881, and they set up our company as a blocking force in a hammer/anvil kind of concept; the others were sweeping the enemy toward us. We made contact early one morning and were busting caps all day. It seemed like it would never end. Constant adrenaline. That's why I think people find it hard to come back and adjust. Everything seems so damned boring.

There's the old saying that I wouldn't do it again for a million dollars, but I wouldn't take a million dollars for the experience. Also, that sense of power you have, a tremendous sense of power—an eerie feeling when you're walking out the gates and locking and loading your rifle. You see people blessing themselves, whatever superstitious or religious hand movements or symbolisms, all evoked many times. That sense of power of looking down the barrel of a rifle at somebody and saying, "Wow, I can drill this guy." Doing it is something else too. You don't necessarily feel bad; you feel proud, especially if it's one on one, he has a chance. It's the throw of a hat. It's the thrill of the hunt. If you just keep it at that and don't go closer and try to anthropomorphize them and take pictures, it is pure symbolism at that point. Everything is symbolism that you're living on.

Herb Mock
Rifle Squad Leader
25th Infantry Division
Drill Sergeant
Fort Polk, Louisiana
1968-1969

The Drill Sergeant

AFTER '69 it was just a joke. Fort Polk had been a pretty tough basic training base. It was a hellhole. But it just got totally ridiculous, the things you had to do to the trainees. Now, you know they were going to fight. Psychologically you have to psyche people up, and I don't care, psychologists can say whatever they want to, if you're going to psyche somebody up, I can have you breathing fire if I want to, but I got to be able to do it. You run them around in the morning singing "Airborne Ranger." Every time their left foot hits the ground, they yell, "Kill, kill!" When you get through, you're breathing fire. It's just drilled into you. And when they went to the mess hall: "One Cong killer. Two Cong killer." No shit, man, I thought the general was going to have a hemorrhage when he heard that: "Oh, we can't do that." It was almost like to say, "We're going to train 'em and we're going to send 'em over, but we don't want 'em to hurt nobody." That's exactly what the attitude was. "Now we're going to teach you how to protect yourself, but we're not teaching you how to kill." They wasn't teaching them to win, just teaching them to be there. There was nothing to it, nothing at all. The sorriest fucking training.

We had a couple of drill sergeants who didn't go to 'Nam, but they were old-school DIs [drill instructors]. And the old-school Army was a little tougher. I'm not saying you ought to take everybody in a room and beat the dog shit out of 'em, but you know, if someone gives you some trouble, I don't think it would hurt to go in there, put a couple of knots on his head. Wouldn't hurt at all. In fact it does wonders for the morale of the outfit.

You have got to have harrassment. It plays too much of an important part. Because the type of harassment you get in basic is very simple. Easy type. But the type you get in war, where you're laying next to a guy you been with eleven months and you're just like brothers, and all of a sudden his brain's spattered all over your nose, that's a different type of harassment. And the worst part about it is, nine times out of ten when it happens the enemy will be gone. You can't even fire a shot. You can't take your anger out somewhere. You're left frustrated. That's harassment. If you can't take the training, you damn sure can't take that.

Jonathan Polansky
Rifleman
101st Airborne Division
I Corps
November 1968-November
1969

Shanghai'd

IN May of '68 I was working a small job in a mail-order house. I went home one afternoon, walked up to my bedroom and saw a letter on the bed. My father yelled, "Jon, you got a letter. I think it's from the President." I remember picking up that letter, looking at it and just sitting down, not believing it. I had to report in seven days to Whitehall Street [in New York City].

We had the physical examinations and were told to report back five days later. Thousands of us. We came with nothing. They marched us down into the subway, took us to Penn Station, threw us all on trains down to South Carolina. When we got there they gave us those little cards that are preprinted, saying, "I am fine and I am in Fort Jackson, Carolina." They told us, "Sign your name and address on it."

Well, my father, of course, was pleased as punch. He wanted to see me go. I was sort of kicking around. He thought that would shape me up, make a man out of me. He was a sergeant in the big one, so he was looking forward to me trying to . . . There was really no conception of the war. My father and I never really spoke about it. I grew up with total lack of current events. I was never interested in the newspaper, and if I did turn on the tube it was to watch *Superman*. The question of not going into the Army never entered my mind because not many alternatives were available.

I remember that when I did go down on that second trip to Whitehall Street when we were all dragged away, a friend of mine, Eulis Connors, this black guy, had punctured his arms with all kinds of needle tracks, and the first thing he did was say, "I'm not going anywhere." I remember watching him and wondering why he was doing it.

I remember walking out of Whitehall Street with thousands of guys on the way to the subway. As we walked down the street, all these young kids with long hair were screaming and yelling at us and we had to walk through them. I didn't know why this was really happening. I didn't feel sympathetic toward them or myself. I knew something was happening, but I didn't know what the fuck it was.

The sergeants lined everybody up in a long line and told everybody to count off in fours. Everybody counted off by four all the way down the line. "Every number four take one step forward." I looked to the left and right of me and stepped forward. "You are all Marines." They were drafting Marines. All of a sudden my heart went up in my throat. I turned red and started perspiring because this was threatening. All of a sudden this tall black guy who was standing next to me takes a step forward and says, "SIR, I WOULD LIKE TO BE A MARINE." The sergeant looked at him and looked at me—I weighed about 110 pounds—and said to me, "YOU, get back in line." And I stepped back, really, really shaken.

This fellow who I met and got to like was made leader of the Blue group. They had separated the thousands of us into color groups. The sergeant said, "We're making this man here the leader of Blue because he looks like the soldier type." Everybody bought that.

When we got to the processing camp at Fort Jackson, this guy really couldn't handle it. He had made the decision that he didn't want to be in the Army. The first night he came up to my bunk and told me he was leaving. I was shocked. They had already shaved our heads, gave everybody the same uniforms and gave us numbers. The next time I saw him was three or four days later. He had welts on his face. We never got a chance to talk to him. He was back for about three or four days, kept in kind of a quarantine. He always had a sergeant with him. After three days I heard that he had split again. The sergeant would say, "That man, you remember that man. That man's a runner. You don't become a runner."

The next thing I heard, he was in a psycho ward. He had just sort of flaked out and gone over the edge. And all I kept thinking about was this guy with this big smile and the sergeant at the induction center saying, "I'm making this man leader because he looks like a soldier." It was kind of hard for me to put together. I think probably as much about him as anybody I spent nine or ten months with in 'Nam. And I wonder where he is now.

I remember being on the plane as we were about to land at Cam Ranh Bay. It's the same kind of thing as on a chopper going into an assault. There's very little eye contact with others because you don't want them to see fear in your eyes and you don't want to see the fear in theirs. All I knew was I was landing in Vietnam and I didn't have a gun. And I didn't know why. And I didn't know when the door opened on that plane if you were supposed to do like in the movies—hit the ground and belly down the gangplank. Would there be somebody to give us ammunition? Would there be anybody to tell us what to do? What in heaven's name would happen? And why weren't there stewardesses on this plane?

Walking down off the plane, looking around, the first thing I smelled was shit. Somebody was burning shit from the latrines, as was the sanitary process there. I took a whiff and said, "Oh my God, how am I going to make it?" It was hot. The heat wave hits you. They got us into columns and started marching us. I couldn't believe I was marching just like back in South Carolina. We had arrived late in the afternoon and it was getting dark. After they gave us bunks, they let us off for the evening. I went walking and saw this outdoor screen and movie. So I went closer to see what the movie was. It was John Wayne in *The Green Berets*.

I was shocked and elated when I found out I was going

to the 101st Airborne Division because what it meant to me was "The 101st, they're going to be in a lot of fighting." And that scared me. The tales and the movies and the patch with the Screaming Eagle on it. But I was so excited to write home to my father and say, "I'm in the 101st Airborne Division. Screaming Eagles."

James Bombard
Rifle Platoon Leader
101st Airborne Division
Phan Rang
December 1967-February
1968

The Screaming Eagles

W<small>E</small> arrived at Cam Ranh Bay at night. As the doors of the aircraft opened, the first thing that startled everyone was the heat. NCOs entered the aircraft and said, "Welcome to Vietnam." I don't think anyone who was on that aircraft was ecstatic about being there.

The operation was in full scale. It was the middle of the night, but the airstrip was well lit. We were bused to what they call a repo depot, or replacement center. It was around one o'clock in the morning. They were getting planeload after planeload of troops from the States, processing them in and assigning them to various units. They were having transportation problems getting troops to various units. There weren't enough planes to transport them.

When I arrived in Phan Rang, war was not there. It was a rear base camp of the brigade, along with an airstrip and the home of a lot of other units. Big Air Force base there. The thing that struck me the most was a big sign, with a big Screaming Eagle. If you know the 101st, it's very proud of its insignia, and it's a very proud, elite unit.

When I first arrived the cadre was still Regular Army.

Good or bad, it had the aura. At the time they had the Airborne mystique drilled into them, the spirit, or espirit. But as my tour wore on, we were getting in non-Airborne personnel and it was only a time before the unit lost its jump status.

We got to the forward brigade base camp and enlisted men went to a separate tent, the officers to another area where the brigade adjutant was a major. He stood about six foot six and was baldheaded. He assigned us to our different battalions and I happened to draw the 502nd. This Texan came up to greet me. He was tall, rawboned. "Y'all," he says. "Real *good* for you to get into this outfit. This is the best outfit in the Army, y'all." And I just kept looking around and thinking, "These Texans talk funny."

The veterans looked much older than they really were. Maybe it was because they were so grubby, but they looked older—they were boys with men's faces. The green kids looked younger and were scared, but what I found was after the first fire fight they were all veterans. They lost that greenness immediately. Usually the first fire fight consisted not only of a fight but also so many days in the jungle putting the skills of a soldier to use— walking in the jungle, being scared, setting up defenses, perimeters. It was thinking about survival, and all of a sudden, BOOM, you were a soldier, you were a veteran.

We moved into Saigon during the Tet offensive and fought into the Cholon area. I didn't think that Saigon would be that intense, but it was quite intense. In the racetrack was extremely heavy fighting in which I did not partake, but a sister battalion did and they took heavy casualties. A number of people I had gone to jump school with and knew very well were killed. A guy named Bo Calloway was killed. He was a Texan. We had gone to jump school together and Ranger school and officer basic together. To see your friends killed, hear about them being killed, it was . . . A little piece of you gets killed each time.

I can remember sitting at McCord Air Base before I went to Vietnam with a friend of mine, Hunter Shotwell, he and his wife. He was a West Pointer and had been to Vietnam before the build-up as an adviser. He was from Massachusetts. He had a beautiful wife and a little child, it was beautiful. I said to him, "Hunter, why are you going back? You're going to get out of the Army." He wanted to be a lawyer. He wanted to set his life in motion. And he said, "I'm going back because I am a soldier." I said, "But you're leaving the military." He said, "But I believe in the nation and I believe that this is my duty. I went to West Point. I am leaving, but I must shoulder the responsibility of leadership." Hunter was a patrician and from a good family. Hunter and I and his wife proceeded to have a few beers and we were pretty mellow when we left together that day. We had served together in the 82nd, we were very close. He had been a hockey player and I was a hockey player, and we had a lot to talk about. He represented everything that was good about the country, the future of the country—it was bright, he was bright, he was handsome. He was everything that our generation stood for.

Right after the Tet offensive I found out that Hunter Shotwell had been killed. And I couldn't help but feel that had been such a loss, such a waste. I had seen other people killed, I had experienced the loss of many friends closer than Hunter was to me, guys I was in the field with . . . But somehow his death to me was the most significant, the most moving. Somehow I saw that he had served, he had shouldered his responsibility and yet he had done it again. The nation shouldn't have asked him to do it again. He represented to me what was good and right in the nation. And he was destroyed. I thought of his little child and his wife, what that did to them. And with that death and many like his, with each death a little bit of the fiber of what was good in this country was being destroyed. That's what bothered me.

I didn't see Hunter Shotwell get killed, but I felt like I had. There are many people close to us in the field who were killed. Doc Brown. I remember Doc Brown was a medic who always read philosophy and never took a bath and would always tell everybody to clean up and wash for infection: "Do as I say, not as I do." He would read Saint Thomas and he was a confirmed atheist and he would philsophize. But in the field he was tremendously skilled as a medic and also very daring, and he was killed the day I was wounded. He was moving to a man and he was wounded and killed. Here was a man who was an intellectual, a philosopher, a thinker, and he was there. Probably not agreeing with what was happening. But somehow, again, the good was being destroyed.

I think we lost a lot more in Vietnam than the troops we lost. We really didn't lose too many battles. When we met the enemy we usually won. What did we win? We lost more than we won, especially the aftermath of the war. Having served in Vietnam, having served in the infantry, having been wounded, feeling the bullet rip into your flesh, the shrapnel tear the flesh from your bones and the blood run down your leg, and feeling like you're gonna piss in your pants and it's the blood running down your leg. To put your hand on your chest and to come away with your hand red with your own blood, and to feel it running out of your eyes and out of your mouth, and seeing it spurt out of your guts, realizing you were dying . . .

I had been hit the second time by a direct hit from a mortar. I was ripped open from the top of my head to the tip of my toes. I had forty-five holes in me and I was bleeding everywhere. I can remember saying to myself, "My God, I'm dying." And at that split second, I was calm. Completely, completely at peace with myself.

I can remember them putting us in a helicopter and the wounded getting wounded again. They were shelling the helicopter. They shot one down and we were running out of ammunition and we were surrounded. They were shooting the shit out of us. This was in Hue. It was the Tet counteroffensive. We were trying to relieve Hue. The city of Hue.

Robert Santos
Rifle Platoon Leader
101st Airborne Division
Hue
November 1967-November
    1968

My Men

I was drafted in March 1966. It wasn't my intention to go into combat, but to go to Officer Candidate School, and quit a month before OCS ended. It wouldn't be held against me and I'd have less than a year left. But the way it worked out, a friend did that ahead of me and he went to 'Nam, anyway. So I decided that based on what I had seen and my own feelings about myself, I should complete OCS.

I went over to 'Nam with two other guys as part of an advance party for the 101st Airborne, mainly to handle logistics and to make sure all the equipment was there. The rumors were that advance parties were being wiped out. When my company got there, they were under the impression that I had already died, which was a really weird feeling, to meet the company commander, who I didn't get along with, and the first words out of his mouth are "I thought you were dead." My response was "Too bad, huh?"

The 101st were mostly West Point officers. I was the first guy to come there from OCS, and was not well received. They had a camaraderie. Most of the lieutenants out of West Point graduated from the same class. They graduated through Airborne school, Ranger school, and all came there as a unit.

We were part of the Hue liberation force in the Tet offensive. The North Vietnamese Army had taken the city. So the Marine Corps, the South Vietnamese, the 101st and the 1st Cavalry went in from different angles to liberate the city.

I was twenty-one. But I was young in terms of commanding men in combat. I didn't know anything. I was the kind of lieutenant that they'd say, "Oh, shit, here's another green lieutenant." That's what I was. You don't know what to do, your mind races over the training you've taken in how to deal with these kinds of situations. I was naïve and really took what they said at face value.

We operated for maybe two weeks with only minor contact. I was working the whole time, spreading the platoon out, doing it right. I was lead platoon on our way into Hue. We came past the paddies, the trees, came around the green. I looked up and saw an NVA flag flying over the next open space. I couldn't believe it. I just . . . I guess I just freaked. I got on the horn right away and called the CO. I was stuttering and stammering: "I see it. I see the flag! I . . . My God, they're finally there."

All I knew at that point was "My God! I'm scared shitless. Holy shit. This is the real thing." I never expected to see a flag. I expected to get shot at. But they were so brazen. They were there. Dug in. The CO said, "Move out." I've heard that before: "Follow me." But I was in the bottom of the infantry. He didn't say "Follow me," he said "Move out." I said, "Now I know what 'Follow me' means—Lieutenant says 'Follow me.' " And that's what we did.

The strange thing about war, there's always humor. Prior to that, when I was walking around I was your typical "asshole lieutenant." Everyplace I walked something got caught. You know, guys could walk right through a bush. My helmet would fall off, my pack would get snagged. And although no one ever told me, I had a reputation as the wait-a-minute-lieutenant. "Hold up, hold up, the lieutenant's caught." Here you're trying to lead men in combat and be a tough guy. Most of the guys were bigger than me. I weighed like 130 pounds. And really, always getting snagged was embarrassing.

I remember walking through the rice paddies that opened up and the small stream and the green on both sides. We were walking down the right side, near the trail, and there was another company on my left flank. All of a sudden all hell opened up. You have to understand, I've never been a Boy Scout, I've never been a Cub Scout. The closest I came to that was going to my sister's Campfire Girl meetings. I grew up in New York City and Long Island. Watched a lot of movies and read a lot of books. I never fired a weapon. I never got into fights with my buddies. My RTO was from East Wenatchee, Washington. Grew up a hunter. They opened up fire and Wes started going down. You make a connection real quick that someone's being shot and someone's getting hurt.

The first thing I did was yell, "Follow me," and I turned to the right to run for cover. There was a bamboo thicket. I couldn't walk through a jungle, an open field, without tripping. Somehow I made a hole through those bushes that everyone in the platoon could go through side by side. Got on the other side—my hat was on my head, my rifle was in my hands, I'd lost nothing. There were guys from another platoon that didn't know what they were doing. Everyone was running around crazy.

I said, "Come with me. Follow me." And I didn't know what I was doing. I knew I was supposed to go toward the enemy. I was trained not to stand still. Don't stand in the killing zone. Don't get shot. Move. So I moved, and as I ran forward I heard these noises. Kind of like *ping, ping* —no idea what that noise was. I finally jumped down behind this mound of dirt that turned out to be a grave, which I didn't know at that time. So I jumped behind this mound of dirt with my RTO and we're all kind of hid behind this stuff. I said, "Just climb up, tell them we're in place and we're hooked up with the left flank and the enemy is in front of us." And I started playing the game. I got up and ran around yelling "Move this machine gun over here" and "Do this over there." I mean, all this noise is going past me. I still didn't know what this noise was. *Ping.* Just a little weird, something new. I finally got back after running around, sat down next to the RTO, and he said, "What the fuck are you doing?" I said, "What do you mean?" He said, "Don't you know what's going on?" I said, "Yeah, goddamnit. I know what's going on. Who do you think I am? He says, "Don't you know what that noise is?" I said no. He said, "That's the bullets going over your head." I never knew it. I mean, if I'd known it I probably would've just buried myself and hid. But I didn't know it. I just didn't know it.

The NVA were in the thicket. There was a stream between us and them, and they were dug in on the opposite side. And they nailed us. They had us pinned down all over the place. Everything that day was done by the book. Just incredible. I don't know how I survived that day, because lieutenants had a very short life expectancy and the reason is because they're jerks and they run out and do stupid stuff by the book. That day we took our first casualties in our platoon. Sergeant Berringer, I think his name was, next to me got shot in the arm. And I remember the training again. Here you were a medic. Look for the bullet's exit. So I found the exit and patched him up with his bandage. Then I realized that there's also an entrance. So I took my bandage out. This is a mistake. You're not supposed to take out your bandage and patch someone else up. But I had to do it. I turned around and called the medic, but he was all freaked out. The bullet that went through Berringer's arm killed the guy next to him. It was a very traumatic day for all of us.

I had told that guy's squad leader that morning, "Tell him to stay behind with the gear and the chopper will bring him forward later." But he wanted to go out. To this day I still think you can tell ahead of time when someone's going to die. Whether they know it or not, I'm convinced that I can tell. It's not something deliberate. Kind of a blankness comes over their face. It's not like they're already dead. It's like a distance and a softness to their features.

But he died and it was a really bad day. We found out how heavy a dead guy could be. The biggest guy in our platoon couldn't pick him up and carry him. So I picked him up, took about three steps, and I couldn't go much farther. But by that time the big guy realized that he could pick him up—It was just mental. We were freaked. And eventually we got out of that mess.

From that first time we made contact we proceeded to keep sweeping in toward the city. The way the 101st operated, we sometimes moved as a battalion, but generally the company split off and we did that whole anvil/hammer bit. So although you were working in the battalion operation, you were functioning as a company and sometimes as small a unit as a platoon.

I think it's funny how you can rationalize everything while you're there. Everything is justifiable in terms of survival, which is unfortunate. I can criticize people today, like at law school when I went there, for being so competitive, so survival-oriented. They were called "gunners," would do things just to make sure they got a better grade. Seems to me today's perception of how unimportant that all is . . . Whereas you go back there and you're justifying killing someone. I'm not sure which one's worse—whether it's unimportant or the means by which you compete. It's really crazy. But we would chase them every day, they'd shoot at us and we'd shoot at them, never making contact. And then every day, almost like clockwork, in the late afternoon they'd stop and make a stand and we'd fight. Went on for months, literally for months. Even after the city was retaken, they still operated in the area.

We overran a base camp on the way into Hue. We called it a base camp, but it probably wasn't but a staging area—there were packs just like ours lined up on the ground. It's a really freaky thing to think you're chasing someone and then to suddenly show up and there they are taking a break for exercise or going inside a barracks for a class—I don't know what they did. But psychologically it really shook us because shit, they're just as disciplined and efficient as we are. They're so confident they can just walk away and leave their stuff like it was a field exercise, training. Maybe it was. Maybe that's what I was to them. But this time we were using live fire. We opened up their packs and they had sets of civilian clothes, military clothes, personal effects. I really wondered if they were at war, except to know that we fought with them every day.

North Vietnamese, that's all I fought. I went into Hue

and saw the civilain bodies lined up. I know I didn't kill them. Americans don't shoot people from a distance and then line the bodies up. So when you walk in and find them lined up there on their stomachs with their hands tied behind their backs, you know it was the NVA who did that. I know no Americans did that because we were the first ones to enter that portion of the village. They killed the water buffalo, everything.

It was civil war and we were in there and they were killing us as we killed them. I mean, the poor victims who had relatives in the North and relatives in the South . . . The only equivalent I can imagine was I was sent to the Detroit riots with the 101st before I went to 'Nam. Coming back, my biggest fear was going to Fort Dix, because even though I wanted to be close to home, I didn't want to be stuck on riot duty. I said, "I'll be damned if I come all the way back here from Vietnam to go on riot duty and have someone throw a bottle or a brick and split my head open." What's your reaction going to be? Pull that trigger? Shoot my own countrymen?

Patriotism is just loyalty to friends, people, families . . . I didn't even know those guys in Vietnam until I got there, and it wouldn't have mattered if you came to my platoon tomorrow—if we got hit, I would go out and try to save your ass just as I would've done for anyone else I'd been with for a month, two months, three months. Instant bonding.

One thing I did find out after I went to Hue and came back, which I didn't know at the time because of the cultural gap, was the significance of the pine trees in the middle of the jungle. Every time someone died that was relatively famous, they'd plant a pine tree in his honor so his spirit would live on. I had a teacher who was Vietnamese when I went to school after getting out of the service. His father was a poet laureate of Hue who had a tree planted for him. I never had the heart to tell the teacher, who was a friend, that I used to sling a poncho on those trees. I mean, I thought it was a great place to sleep because the pine needles were nice and it was always clean. I didn't make the connection that there was something special about the area. We used the needles to help start our fires. Dig little holes in the hedges around it

—dig in. Sacrilege. In some sense his father's spirit gave me shelter, which is kind of ironic.

It was really a break for us to go to rice hovels because we hadn't cooked for so many months. A little boy came out and wanted some C-rations. When they want C-rations, you know they're hurting, the food's just terrible. He was going to share his dinner with us and he brought out some fish. The hottest damn thing I ever had. I can still to this day remember them being fuming hot. We shared our food and we asked him where he lived. He pointed to this house in the clearing. He said he was there with his sister, and we said, "Well, why doesn't your sister come out and join us for dinner?" And he said, "She can't. The VC will see her with us, they'll kill her." We said, "What about you? They'll see you." He said it didn't matter because they know he's getting food.

So it's just like everything else: you leave and they're back, and people have to live with that. They have to deal with the fact that we're going to be gone and leave them behind. But what struck me that day when I was looking at that kid—and I didn't know how old he was, but he had to be under ten—was that all his life he knew war. And then when we're gone he's going to know that Americans may have come through and raped his sister. The VC may have raped his sister because she allowed the Americans to do this. And if the Americans had conceivably seen her with the VC, they would've . . . the whole thing was just . . . it was certainly a statement. It was a tragedy and it was so horrifying. I tried to think of what I would be like if this took place in my hometown. This may have been a turning point in my life, at least in the terms of the war.

When we operated around Hue we didn't stay in the populated areas. We were in the mountains and in the dry season and wet season in different places. I remember having to cross a river at night to set up a blocking force for what we called a major invasion the next day in what we termed VC-controlled territory. The VC controlled one side of the river and the ARVN's controlled the other side. We always operated with the South Vietnamese; we figured there must be VC sympathizers there. And the ARVNs we worked with refused to cross the river. Now, that told me two things: either they were waiting for us to get shot at or they were telling me, "Look, this isn't worth it. They don't bother us and we don't bother them." And that was a great way of living. Survival, right? But we were forced to cross that damn river.

I had to send my platoon across. To say I was pissed and confused would not be adequate. But we did it and it happened all the time. Whenever you went on an ambush with the ARVN they made so much noise that no one would ever walk through your ambush site. So it was safe. You never got hit, but then again, you never carried out your mission either, which was not clear to the American soldiers. And what became confusing was the ARVNs didn't want to fight for their country. Why should we? If you want us to go out and defend ourselves, don't stick us with those guys, because they're going to run away. They're not going to fight.

There were a couple of units, the South Vietnamese marines, the rangers and the paratroopers, who would stand and fight for the most part, but working with regular ARVNs or the Popular Forces or police—that was a liability.

Also, whenever you worked with them you were subject to S-5 [U.S. military intelligence] coming down and asking how you're doing. They were trying to win the hearts and minds of the people, which I could never fully understand because I didn't think there was anything to win. I thought we should just leave. There was confusion from a military standpoint and, of course, from a psychological standpoint.

I remember going on an operation and being attached to the 1st Cavalry. We had full security for a mine-sweep team down the road. Well, out there was a command-detonation mine team. As the truck went over the bridge, that mine team detonated the mine. My men were in the truck. I watched the VC run into a village, and after taking care of what we had to take care of, we went after them.

There was nobody in the village, only an old couple, and there's all this VC literature. It made no sense, absolutely no sense to me. Why this village was there, why this old couple was there, why they were killing . . . I

mean I know it made sense, but I just couldn't put it together. I did the whole thing I learned in training. You go
to the fire and scrape off the top ash to see if there are
hot coals underneath. Everything was warm. The pots
were warm, warm embers underneath. And my men were
obviously upset. One of our men had died and a couple
others were wounded, engineers as well. They just went
right up in the air and that was it.

When the explosion went off. An object was moving
through the air towards us. I'm thinking clear. How long
will it take? Not very long, I thought. But it was like a long
time coming and it was high in the air and this dark object was moving and I was watching it. I was transfixed
by it. It was almost hypnotic. Here were two seasoned
combat veterans standing there in a crouch watching
something come through the air at us. I thought calmly,
"It's gonna hit me." We watched it and we watched it
and we watched it. It came closer and closer and closer.
And at some point I suspect we both realized that it
wasn't a bomb, it wasn't . . . it was part of a body. And
we stood there, he and I, about three feet apart. It landed
between us. It was a boot with the leg in it sheered at the
top of the boot. It landed fucking upright and it was like
a goddamn movie.

But we didn't shoot at the village. I had seen these two
guys running and then when we got to the village and
found the old couple I knew it was obviously utilized by
the enemy. I was trying to deal with my men and find out
what I could do. So I decided to—from purely military
standpoint—try to close my men psychologically. We
would burn down the hootches except the old couple's,
who remained for one reason or another—we left their
property alone. We just burned down, denied the enemy
that kind of shelter, although they could build them again;
they were just grass and weeds. In the process of burning
down the village a major from the 1st Cav came by. I
never wore rank in the field and he was looking for it. He
says, "Who's in charge here?" I said, "I am." He said,
"Who are you?" And I told him I was Lieutanant Santos.
He says, "Were you doing this here?" I said, "Yeah. We
were looking for the men that detonated the mine. They

ran into this village. We came in and looked for them. This is a VC village and . . ."

It's not so much that we missed them as the frustration of having been blown up from a distance and the old people standing there saying, "No VC here, no VC." And everything around them says someone just left. What do you do? My responsibility would be, I think, somewhat complex. I had to uphold the traditions of military America, all that crap. I had to worry about my men. And I felt that responsibility goes down rather than up. I owed no allegiance to America. I owed no allegiance to the S–5 or the 1st Cav and all of that crap. I had to make sure that these thirty guys—which were never really thirty; eighteen or twenty-two—had to keep their head in line. And the men burning down a few grass huts which would kill no one and hurt no one but deny the enemy shelter in the rain, which they had no problem finding, was worth it.

That was very confusing. We thought we did what we had to do and they would understand that. But apparently we upset the winning of the hearts and the minds of the people. I told them, "What are you talking about, hearts and minds? Look what they just did to us. I mean, I should risk my men every day so you can come in and tell me that these people belive in America?"

These S–5 guys were from base camp. They operated out of planes, dropping those propaganda leaflets. Those leaflets mean nothing to you when you pick one up next to a dead American. They operated in a vacuum. They operated more in a vacuum than I did. I went there with some ideals. These guys were just stupid.

I ended up going there . . . It sounds corny, but this is what I felt when I went into the service: that if I didn't go, someone else would have to go in my place. I couldn't possibly be responsible knowing that someone else may have died because I didn't want to go. It was a question of having enough confidence or being sure enough of my convictions that it would be the right thing and that my job would be to permit someone else not to go. So I went.

At the nitty-gritty it was only survival. It was only to come home and see your friends, your family, not to shame them, not to hurt them. Come back to America.

And it wasn't like "America the great, the land of the beautiful." I mean, I didn't grow up in an area like Pennsylvania—it's beautiful out there—but I came back to Long Island and New York City. Traffic, people, noise. I just wanted to come home. And I think that the one thing that people lost track most of was their families. I mean, you realized that you die . . . My philosophy is, and I used to tell people this, they'd come to my platoon and I'd say it was the best platoon in the battalion. Probably the best battalion in the brigade, the best brigade in the division and all that bullshit.

I said, "Only two things can happen to you. You can get wounded and go home early. Or you can die. And then you really don't give a shit. You're just dead. I'm planning to go home, and I think when it's your turn to go home, the best way to go home is whole. If you stick with me, stick it out and learn from the guys who are here, you won't get wounded. You won't die. If you stick the whole fucking year out here and go home, that's the worst possible thing that can happen, and that's what you should look forward to." I believed it. I really believed it. And that's what we did. We really tried to do that.

You didn't want to get close to anyone over there. I was trained not to get close to my men. I was trained to keep a distance. And it wasn't simply because they would lose respect for you, but because you would never be able to control them, you would never be objective in your decisions if you had friends. You'd stay with them, it's only logical. That was really hard, being an officer. I mean, it's just a title, being an officer. And it's a strange thing that the men hate you, but when the bullet goes off, they look to you: "What now, Lieutenant?" Everyone wants to say, "Get down. Let's not do anything." In the field you always look to the leaders. In the military it just so happens that they're preordained by rank—not necessarily by skill or competence or anything else for that matter. I mean, one of the things is realizing that because somebody has more rank or is older than you, it doesn't make him any smarter.

Another thing I learned after going to Vietnam. I grew up and was in the kind of crowd in high school that was the all-American bunch. But back there I didn't realize that having the last name of Santos made me different, until I found out later on that it had an effect on me in the Army in how people treated me. Having a Hispanic surname—I didn't even think about it. I just thought I was white like everyone else. I grew up in a clique that ran the school, the officers of all the clubs. We were the athletes, all that bullshit.

I mean, I was in the Airborne. Airborne guys are tough and all that bullshit, and they're the best outfit. So I looked around for some kind of support. Of course, I looked at the guys who I thought identified with me: "Oh, he went to college. Hey, you're an athlete. Hey, you're this. Great." Well, they're not all from New York City, much less from Long Island. They're from all parts of the country.

I found out that bullshit is not an indicator of what you're going to do under stress. It's so artificial, the world we live in. And in the service, tall, short, thin, fat, good-looking, homely, ugly—it didn't matter. Name, color—it meant nothing under combat. Bullets have no discrimination. And I think some of the smallest guys carried more weight than the biggest guys because they could psychologically do it. They could take more abuse physically, mentally, because they were stronger.

For me it really wasn't a limit of confidence. I was determined. And part of my determination came out of the fact that I was responsible for bringing these guys home. Eight of my men died over there and two got wounded. All I was determined to do was protect us. I wrote very few letters home because there was nothing to talk about. And I would watch the mail come in. The mail was dropped off at the CP [command post] and I'd watch. Let's say Jones got letters this week and then I noticed there was a break in his mail. I'd watch the guy to see if it had an effect on him, would depress him. And if in the second mail call he got nothing again, then I would go sit down with him.

Or I always had a three-man point and I was always number three because I felt I couldn't ask the men to do something that I wouldn't do. So I would be first. If I died, then they knew better to do it themselves. Right? It was kind of a sick psychology, but I think it was appropriate for my position by virtue of survival and fairness. But I'd go along on point with the guy and say, "Damnit, I didn't get a letter again." Kind of compassion by identification. And within a couple of steps, the guy would lay the whole story out on me, what happened, if it was important. If it wasn't important I'd just move on. But if the guy was really hurting, I'd stay.

I was like a father and a mother to these guys, even though they didn't know that. They carried more ammo or weapons than anybody else. A lot of times in between when you need it, it's just a pain in the ass to carry all of it around. But I wanted to bring back thirty guys. I didn't. I remember when they died. I remember their names periodically, but I can't remember all eight at the same time. But I do remember them. Still to this day.

I can almost picture my platoon, how tall they were, where they were from, what they did—I mean, who cried and who didn't cry. I had a lot of deep feelings for those people. I say "my men," but the average age of the platoon was around nineteen. We had an old guy, Coogan. He was twenty-eight, "the Old Man."

One time after I got wounded and was waiting in base camp to go back out to the field, this new guy came to me. His name was Peterson. He was a young guy—I mean, he was a kid. They sent him over to me. He wanted to talk to somebody. He didn't want to stay in country. His brother was in the Navy stationed on a ship somewhere, and he wanted to know if this could get him out of Vietnam. I explained to him what I understood the rules to be. I said to him, "As far as I understand it, you're going to be in the field. What company are you assigned to?" He said Charlie Company. I said, "Look, when you get out there, tell them you want to be in the 3rd Platoon. That's the best goddamn platoon out there. They'll take care of you."

He was really upset and he left. I called the field and said this guy's coming out—I wanted him in my platoon. I got out there about two days later. He was sitting down and they were trying to explain things to him. He was a kid.

It wasn't so much that he was younger than us, but he was a kid by our standards. We got old fast. We were exposed to so much shit and you find out so much about yourself—your good, your bad, your strengths and your weaknesses—if you're honest with yourself—so quickly that you might as well have aged. You might as well be eighty years old looking back or looking forward, however you want to talk about it. It's the only way to survive.

I had to know how everyone would be responding because of that old thing: the chain is only as strong as its weakest link. I would always keep my weakest link protected. I would never put my weakest link on point, never put him out on flank. At the same time I made everyone think that the weakest link was pulling his share. So it was very confusing at times, giving orders to the platoon and rotating responsibilities. But Peterson came in March, and I think it was by May—two months later—that Peterson was for all intents and purposes a strack [exemplary] trooper. I mean, this guy had confidence. We had built him. We had taken him in that sense, a guy who was crying and scared, no confidence whatsoever, and made him feel confident. He was in some contact, but the men protected him and kept him away from things. He was so sure of himself, and it was really a pleasure, like watching your kid grow up. Everybody kind of took him along as the kid brother.

Well, it was a day where nothing was going to happen. We hadn't had any contact in a while. He wanted to go on point. I said, "Who's on point?" They said, "Peterson." I said, "What's he doing out there?" He wanted to go on point. I used an unorthodox formation. I was in the middle, so the point he was going on was a right flank because there were people on the trail. We're out in an open area. We're relatively safe. Some of the in-house rules: If you get wounded, don't say a word, don't scream. Sit still. We know where you are. We know where you went down. We'll get there.

There's people on the trail and we were lax, I guess. Shots rang out and somebody yelled, "Peterson." So we immediately went forward. I ran over. I never asked my men to go forward without me. I always went with them. I was up on that trail. Peterson starts screaming. Two more shots rang out. Silence. I just stopped. Peterson's dead. And of course, no one could believe that. We wanted to go forward to get him. I said, "He's dead. Leave him be." We got pinned down going to the left.

The battalion commander was in a chopper right above us. He says, "I don't see you guys." I say, "You're not supposed to see us. That's what we're trained for, to conceal ourselves. I can see you. I know where the chopper's pointing and I'm going to give you a direction on it—a compass reading—to tell you where we are. I see two guys over there. That's them. Hit them." He says, "I can't take a chance. It might be your men." I said, "We're not anywhere near that kind of terrain. You're facing them. Just shoot out of the goddamn chopper, you'll hit them. We're behind you." He refused to do it. We never found those two guys.

We got to Peterson. Since we heard Peterson yell, we knew he was hit twice. The first shot was in the arm. The second shot was in the head. If he hadn't screamed he would've lived. There's no question, he would've lived. He freaked. He broke.

One thing I did over there I think to this day is valid, though I think in one point in time it was one of the most cruel things you could do to someone. After every time someone was wounded or someone was killed, you're psychologically most vulnerable to suggestion. I knew what I was going to say. I pulled the platoon together and told them that the wounded person, the dead person, their buddy, their friend, fucked up because he did something I told him not to do. He did something he was trained not to do. And by virtue of doing that he risked all our lives. Sure, feel sorry for him, but now you know why he died. You want to end up the way he did? You want us to feel about you the way you feel about him? Then go ahead and fuck up. But this is what he did wrong . . .

All I know is that psychologically we had to stay up. And this is when I hit them, when they were most vulnerable, smashed them down—and they might not have liked it, but they never forgot what I said. It was important.

That day when Peterson . . . I asked the platoon to move forward and I left them in the field and I sat down and tried to cry. It was the first time and . . . I moved my platoon forward because in basic training at Fort Hood our drill sergeant was sick one time from the flu. He made the platoon do an about-face while we heard him throw up—timed it so we wouldn't see him. We knew what he was doing. It stuck in my mind. And that day, certainly risking my life, I moved the platoon forward because I knew they knew what I was feeling. I had Peterson's personal effects, and there was a letter addressed to, I suspect, his girlfriend. He had flowers on the envelope. Nineteen years old. When he arrived he was eighteen. He was a young kid. He was our guy that we were going to take care of. We adopted him in a sense. We were going to bring him through. The one guy we didn't want killed. He didn't belong there any more than we belonged there. He belonged there even less.

See, I never cried in Vietnam. I cried that one time. I cried inside all the time. I was so unhappy. But I never cried. Not because you're a man or not a man, but as an officer you weren't supposed to cry, no emotion.

I didn't know of anybody in my entire platoon that wanted to kill, who ever killed before. There was one guy, Haynor, who was like a cowboy, young, brash: "Hey, this is an adventure." He saved my life and left the field wounded as a result of saving my life. He was the only guy I felt was like that. Man, it was just . . . you become tight or you don't become tight.

I remember freezing at night and wanting to crawl up next to the RTO—we spent ten months together and there was no sexual overtone or anything else. I was freezing. He was someone who had been with me every day, every minute, and I just wanted to hold the two bodies together. I couldn't do it. I couldn't do it because of the fact that I would show weakness. I would become too close psychologically and I would be really upset. What a lonely fucking place.

I was convinced my platoon had to carry more ammo, more weapons, and that I had to carry more ammo than anybody else in my platoon. Because once the company ran out of ammo and we were the only ones left with some, so we held the ground while the other platoons backed off. From then on I was convinced you had to carry it. You never know. What you did saved their lives, but they hate you for it. They're feeling guilty now, but they're living and they're going to hate me for saving their lives. If they're miserable when that took place, they'll hate me for making them miserable. You know, it's that —or I've earned their respect. I'll never—I mean, once or twice people will say something to me and you get the feeling that you earned their respect. But the whole time doing it, it's hard to make decisions that tomorrow . . .

We caught a VC rice harvest and were given a stand-down as our big break. The colonel came down, battalion commander, and said, "The general's coming down to give you a medal." I said, "Well, that's nice. What about my men?" He says, "What about your men?" I say, "Don't they get anything? You can't do it without them." And the lieutenant commander says, "Well, what should we do about his men?" True to form, the colonel said, "Well, sir, they could use some baths and haircuts." And he turned to me—the colonel had been an NCO and got commissioned and worked his way up—and said, "What do you think, Lieutenant?" I said, "Well, I think they could get laid and drunk, personally. A couple of men just died." You don't talk to a colonel like that, but that was my feeling—that was what my men wanted. They didn't give a shit about showers, we washed with rain water plenty of times, we never had showers. The colonel left, the general came. But shortly after the colonel left, two motor scooters came down with cases of beer on the back and women.

The lieutenant commander just looked at it all and said, "Okay, all of the guys get Airborne haircuts." Vietnam? Airborne? I had long hair. So I called all my men together in formation. I said, "All right, you guys, you heard what the captain said. You're getting Airborne haircuts. Now line up. Dress-right-dress."

They were grouching, "Fucking Vietnam. Say, jerk, what's going on?" So I marched them over to the barber chair that was set up. I turned around and pulled the old Sergeant Rock routine. If I had a cigar I would've put it in my mouth. "All right, you guys, you're going to get haircuts just like mine." The guys really thought I flipped. I sat down and told the guy, "Cut it just one snip. That's it." I got back up and I said, "All right, next . . . next

. . . next . . ." Just like mine. We just didn't want short hair. We always shaved. We were clean. We fought. But my feeling was that if it's going to make us happy, then give it to us. Just give us that one concession. And no one could say anything to me because I happened to have gotten a lot of medals when I first got there. I got a reputation of being a great soldier, leader, combat leader. My platoon got lots of medals. So we did whatever we wanted within bounds and we got away with it. You have long hair—no other platoon has short haircuts. That's stupid, really dumb to cut a guy's hair. Doesn't make you a better soldier. There's one way to go—and that's home.

Before I went there I remember thinking that if I lost anything, a finger, an arm, my face, my teeth, my nose, anything, I'd rather die than come back. And there are so many things that I thought were important before I went there. I want to do this, I want to do that. I missed this club, I didn't see this movie, read this book. By the time I came back all I wanted to do was see America. I wanted to travel, wanted to see what it was all about. I just wanted to see the rest of life. God, how you value things . . .

When it came to survival, we just avoided stuff. I didn't kick off ambushes when I could have. There was no reason to. Killing them meant nothing. It was just stupid. I mean, they saw us walk past them during the day, they could walk past us at night. I walked in a very distinctive formation. The VC knew who I was, and if they didn't shoot at me during the day, I wouldn't shoot at them at night. We just survived.

When I left the field after being there for ten months, I came to Bien Hoa–Long Binh for the first time. When we came to the gate at Long Binh I was still into carrying my rifle wherever I went. It was a very uncomfortable feeling not to have a rifle with you. We came to this gate, and I'll never forget it, the first thing we saw was a taco stand. Then I saw a soft-ice-cream truck—you know, one of those guys that drives around the streets in the suburbs. And then we got to MACV headquarters. We walked in and they had a water fountain, a cooler. You stand there and you just drink until your body is distended and you faint from all the water. And you're just staring because there are women with round eyes. I don't know where they came from, but they were there. I didn't ask. Didn't matter—I mean, I didn't give a shit, they were there. I couldn't touch them, couldn't talk to them.

Once I went on an in-country R & R to Danang and I had the personal effects of a man to deliver. I was in my fatigues and I went to where I was supposed to stay for three-day R & R. The guard said, "Check your rifle." I responded, "Wait, I want to keep it." Gotta check your rifle, so I checked it. I said, "Well, what are we going to eat?" They gave me directions. One day you're fighting and the next day you're in another sector. It was like living in New York City, where there's poverty and right across the street an opulent town house.

I went down to the river and there was a big barge and these naval officers going to the Marine Corps naval club. It was a special launch for officers. So I remembered from the books, the movies, to salute the flag. I went abroad and thought, "This is ridiculous. I want to be with my men." We never did things separately. We always drank together, ate together. My father was the same way. He was an officer in the Naval Reserve. I met him there in Danang.

The cab to the officers' club was called the Pink Elephant, appropriately so. My XO and I were there together. Jungle fatigues, clean-shaven. We'd been fighting for almost three months. We go in there and see a big buffet, just like my first day in country. The plates were china. No C-rations, no paper plates. This is a naval club.

We sat down and we looked at each other. We didn't say a word. We were shoveling the crap into our mouths. Both of us looked up simultaneously—the plates were clean. I mean, I don't even know what I ate. Clean. We looked at each other, and you didn't have to say anything —you knew. And then there were the stares. I looked around and there are all these Navy officers, Marine Corps officers and some Army officers. Dress whites. Dress uniforms. Women with round eyes. Danang. Blond, blue eyes. And they're looking at us not like you expected— "Ah, there are some men from the field"—but "What is that scum doing in here?" I couldn't believe it. They didn't want us there at all. The only person that was nice to us was an enlisted man who was a waiter, who came over and offered to take us out to the patio for dessert. I said, "Dessert? What dessert? Peaches?" He says, "Well, I recommend the vanilla ice cream with crème de menthe." "I'll take it." I never had ice cream with crème de menthe. My parents don't drink. I never had any alcohol around my house. It was delicious. We got thoroughly plowed and watched them dance. And of course, no one came over and asked us to dance with them. They were all escorted.

All these Americans—well, round eyes. I was just totally blown away. And it wasn't like a whorehouse. It wasn't like a Saigon bar or a club upstairs. This was really legit. I mean, I didn't think these guys were fighting. This was maybe how the French fought the war: all the officers standing around the hotel balcony while all the men swept below. They're drinking and talking about the old days, when the war was going to end real quickly and people would come out from Washington and sit on a hill and watch the war going on in the distance.

This was the war and these were the people who controlled the war. This was MACV. It blew me away.

We were told that you could call home. It was on the MARS phone line [military satellite radio]. This was probably a sick way of dealing with something—my uncle had died in Korea. I called home. I hadn't written any letters yet. This is right after Tet, after most of the shit was done. My mother answered the phone, which is not unlikely because my father is never home. He's out at sea all the time. I can tell she's pissed off. "Hello." She sounds like a drill sergeant. I said, "Mother, this is Robert. Now relax. Don't say anything. You have to follow military radio procedures. Now I'll say something, and when I stop I'll say 'Over.' Then you can speak, and when you stop you say "Over" and that way we can continue. Do you understand it? No, no, no. Try it again. Over." Okay, second try she got it. I said, "Look, I'm fine. I'm healthy. I have no problems. I've been taken in as a prisoner of war, but they're treating me real well, Mom." You could feel a thud. You could hear her heart. She didn't want to believe it. "No, no, I'm just joking, Mom. I'm just joking." She was all excited: "Where are you? Where are you?"

I told her Danang and I explained the whole bit to her. But I could never tell her up front—I always had to pull a little twist to it. It's my own personality. I always do the reverse, you know, the sick way of doing it, but it was in a sense kind of funny. I thought, "Ho, ho, ho, yeah, she'd think of the worst and then she'd be relieved to find out I'm alive."

Being the kind of guy that I was, not really following orders, I decided, since my first duty there was to deliver personal effects, to go to the fucking morgue. The military term for it was "G. R. Point" [Graves Registration]. I remember walking into it—it was in a hangar in this huge fucking building—I remember walking in and going past a room. It had these contoured fiberglass chairs, like a futuristic barbershop. I looked over and there were guys in these chairs. Dead bodies, all naked. They just had big stitches. I mean, they were like Frankenstein. A guy's face had been blown apart. They just stitched it, a job you wouldn't put on your face for Halloween. But what they did there was put them back together as far as stuff them and—the word escapes me—embalm them. Then they were going to go back and get cosmetic later on.

There was a guy trying to get a ring off a hand, because they stiffen up and everything swells and it's tough. This was like a Gahan Wilson cartoon. These morticians looked like they were embalmed themselves. They were inhaling these fumes, whatever they use to embalm them, and it does something to your skin. Talk about waxy-looking people. The receding hairlines . . . These guys really looked like they were undertakers. They were probably just a bunch of soldiers who got assigned burial duty. And I remember them saying to me, "Hey, take it easy. Nice talking to you. Maybe you'll come around again. See you again." I said, "I doubt it. I hope to God I never see you. And if I do, I'm sure I won't be looking at you. I don't ever want to be here." And I left.

I said, "Look, that ruined my fucking day. They owe me a day." So instead of going back on Tuesday, I went back on Wednesday. I said, "If I get into trouble, I'll just tell them I missed the fucking flight. I tell my men to say that. What the hell."

Tuesday night the company was out in the field, the

mountains. My platoon lacked an officer. They sent another platoon out on ambush. This was the thing I didn't realize—my platoon was always sent out on ambush. We were always point platoon when it came to combat or contact. And I think part of it was because my last name was Santos. I had the blacks in my platoon. I had the guys who had been fuck-ups. I just thought we were really good. I thought we were kind of a Dirty Dozen. We had tough guys. We were good.

But they sent this other platoon out. The platoon made a mistake. Instead of holding their perimeter, they went into a horseshoe and were wiped out. I thought my platoon would have been pissed at me for not coming back, but their response was "Boy, we were glad you weren't here. We were really lucky. Because we knew what you would do, where you would sit or where you would dig in when we'd start setting up." My replacement was sitting there, and the first round that came in took him out. We never found him. We just found the book he was reading.

You can't translate it or explain it to people. I try to explain post-Vietnam syndrome by saying, you know, it's trauma. Ging through war is trauma. You lose your arm, you lose your uncle, you lose your mother, you lose your father, it's trauma. You go through a period of depression. I mean, it didn't just tell me I lost something. It told me a whole bunch of things about myself I probably never would've found out. I probably in some respects would be far more successful if I'd never known. On the other hand, I'd probably be less developed and less wise. But maybe that's the way I should go through life, ignorantly happy and successful. Instead I struggle and I do what's important and I always have to fight with myself to go out and push Robert. And it's a real pain in the ass.

One of the sad things about being an officer was that you never knew that doing the right job meant that you'd earn the hatred of your men. What you did saved their lives, but they hate you for it. I mean, often I've heard these people talk about how doctors think they're God. I was looking into med school after I got out of the service and I used to hear them talk about this shit, and I said to myself, "You really think it's going to be great. You really think this is going to be something. That you're going to

be God, you're going to cure people, save people, and
your ego is going to be so inflated and you're going to be
so fucking important." But they just don't realize how
lonely it is.

I never had the opportunity to directly save lives. My
responsibility was to kill and in the process of killing to be
so good at it that I indirectly saved my men's lives. And
there's nothing, nothing, that's very satisfying about that.
You come home with the high body count, high kill ratio.
What a fucking way to live your life.

Brian Delate
Helicopter Door Gunner
Americal Division
Chu Lai
March 1969-March 1970

The Party

BEFORE I went over I knew a couple of friends that came back. I asked, "What was it like?" and they didn't know how to explain it and I didn't know what I was asking. And when I came back I ended up being the same way. Almost mute.

I tried to explain to people. I'm a verbal person, so I really wanted people to understand what I had gone through. My parents gave me a cocktail party. They didn't know what else to do. They gave me a cocktail party like it was a graduation party. And they realized in the middle of the party, they both did and I guess that's why I love them so much, that they really had made a mistake.

I was starting to get loaded, and this lady friend of my mother's said to me, "Well, did you kill anybody?" She's got a martini and a cigarette. She had no idea what she was asking. She was somebody who I'd looked up to for years as a kid. I said, "You have no idea of the dimension of your question. You just threw that out like, 'Did you ever deliver newspapers as a kid?'" I started staring her right in the eyes: "Do you realize what you're asking? Do you have any idea of the nature of your question?" And I left, I just split and I thought, "Oh, man."

133

Kit Lavell
Pilot
U.S. Navy Light Attack
    Squadron 4
Binh Thuy
August 1971-April 1972

The Flying Black
Ponies

LIGHT Attack Squadron 4 was the only land-based squadron of Navy aircraft in Vietnam. We flew OV-10s, twin-engine turbo-prop planes that were primarily used for observation. We strapped rockets and bombs on them for close air support, a mission that really had not been performed in this kind of propeller-driven aircraft since World War II.

The original purpose of the squadron was to fly close air support for the Riverine Patrol Forces, the Brown Water Navy, which operated on the Mekong and its tributaries. The squadron came into existence in 1969. The Vietnamization program had been under way and the Vietnamese were running the show. And of course they weren't doing anything. They would never take the boats out, only during the daytime, during good weather. We did fly some support for ammunition barges, the convoys that went up the rivers, but we kind of made our own missions.

We were supporting the ARVN and American advisers, primarily working with the Army. We would work directly with units on the ground. In fact, I spent a lot of time pounding the rice paddies [infantry patrol] with guys on the ground throughout the whole Delta, to be able to learn their tactics and techniques.

We interfaced with an air-cavalry pack. They flew helicopters—Loches, Slicks, Huey gunships and Cobras. We'd integrate and work targets with them. We'd stay above, and when they ran into trouble we'd come in with the heavy stuff. We were a lot different than the fast movers, jets, which had very little loiter time on station and were very inaccurate. We would work within ten meters above friendlies. In fact, many times, too many times, I put in ordnance on top of friendlies that had been overrun. We did close air support like it hadn't been done before.

When we were fully loaded, I don't think we could get up above four thousand feet. It took us from the time of takeoff until halfway to the target before we could get up at altitude, and we quite frequently worked below that. We literally worked at treetop level. We flew around the clock seven days a week, night and day without stop, loaded with about three thousand pounds of forward-firing ordnance primarily. And we had Gatling guns, four machine guns, a 20-millimeter cannon and other things. We'd drop CBUs, cluster bombs.

Sixty percent of my combat missions were at night, mostly in bad weather, either in monsoon or even worse, in the dry season, when farmers were burning their fields and visibility was a half mile or less. The bad guys never came out until it was bad weather. Nobody else was flying. Many times it was a tremendous problem just to fly the airplane and find the targets because there were no reliable navigational aids in South Vietnam. We did not have sophisticated navigational equipment in our airplanes. We literally flew seat-of-the-pants and had to fly underneath the clouds. If the ceiling was one hundred feet, which it often was, we flew below one hundred feet.

On more than 80 percent of the missions we took fire. We would take AK-47 rounds all the time through the aircraft. Occasionally we would come up against something a little bit bigger—a .50-caliber would really do the job on us.

We had instant communication with anyplace in the Delta by scrambler radio. A call would come in during the middle of the night. The duty officer would take the call and sound the horn to notify all of the crews and pilots. We slept in our flight gear. The planes were all set up, all the switches were thrown, ready to take off. The front-seat guy would run out to the planes, turn the left propeller. The back-seat guy would get the coordinates, the frequencies and the nature of the mission. He'd jump into the plane, and as soon as he's strapped in, you turn the right engine and off you go. Pull the pins in the armaments and we would have wheels in the well six minutes from the time we got the call. The furthest place we'd go in the Delta was less than twenty minutes away, so inside twenty-five minutes we would be on station, ready to help out.

You can see in the dark. The Delta is crisscrossed with canals. I knew every single village, town, hootch in the Delta, every canal, every tributary, every little squiggly, every little creek, every little light, just by flying over it day in and day out. You constantly drilled yourself; that was your insurance. You had no other navigational aids. You had to know the terrain. We would fly quite a bit at night for practice.

Occasionally you'd fly over an area and take fire. You'd call up the guys on the ground and they'd tell you which enemy unit it was and quite often you'd get clearances to put in an air strike on them. Sometimes we used to do what we called chumming. One plane would turn off its lights and one plane would leave its lights on and he'd go down and buzz the area and take fire. The guy with his lights off would then roll in on the target.

The Delta has always been a kind of no man's land, especially the western part, the part they call the U Minh Forest. There were always a couple of NVA battalions down there and VC units. They had their headquarters in the U Minh. For many years the South Vietnamese government would never go into that area. They finally opened it up. The 9th ARVN Division and the 21st ARVN Division were stationed in the U Minh. And we used to go in there quite a bit, flying support for them.

It's all triple canopy, three layers of trees and jungle growth. It was virtually impregnable. But a lot of the area was defoliated and a lot had been subject to B-52 arc-light strikes. It was peppered and pockmarked and looked like the back side of the moon, the damage we've done to the environment there was just incredible. You look at it from the air and it was just amazing. I mean, *you* try to estimate the amount of ordnance that was dumped on these places.

But we would fly quite a bit, around the clock. Somewhere in September of '71, we got involved in a major operation in the U Minh Forest. For a period of 168 hours we scrambled. Every combat mission was a scramble mission. The 21st ARVN Division engaged several battalions of VC and NVA, and it was a bloody fight. You'd go out and fly the mission, come back in, you'd hot-turn around—wouldn't even turn your engines off. You'd refuel, rearm and go right back out. After your third flight in probably less than three hours, you'd be back. You'd go back to your hootch, hit the rack. In about four hours they would have gone through all the other pilots in the squadron and it was your turn again. We did this for one week. Took a lot of battle damage in our airplanes, expended a hell of a lot of ordnance. We set a record at that time for KBA [kills by air] by an air unit in Vietnam.

Quite a few of the Vietnamese that could speak no English knew at least two words—Black Ponies. We were called the Black Ponies. ARVNs would never call Vietnamese air power. They didn't trust them. Vietnamese flyers dropped a lot of short rounds, killing friendlies. They were flying fast movers, the Sky Raiders. I can't say the pilots weren't that good, because there were a lot of good pilots. But to us it was a one-year tour of duty. You fly so many combat missions. To them that was their life. They'd flown for years, thousands of combat missions. But none of them had a real sense of commitment. There was always another day for them. They don't fly at night or in bad weather. They would only fly in good weather. And quite often they'd never fly on weekends. They used to take their spotter planes and fly up with their families to Dalat for a picnic on weekends.

We once got involved in flying support for one group in an area that was a free-fire zone. We were unaware of what the nature of the target was, and quite often these targets were dreamed up by the province chief if people didn't pay their taxes or whatever. We flew this cover mission for an Army operation that literally devastated a village. The Loch pilots were throwing hand grenades in windows and shooting all of the animals. We sat up there at three thousand feet in case they took any heavy fire, just watching and listening on the radio. I was just totally amazed. I realized as I was watching this that there was no real military objective. They didn't receive any return fire at all. Supposedly it had been a staging area for the VC or something. It was a "VC village." They asked us to roll in on a couple of targets. We said we were running low on fuel, and left.

I almost got court-martialed once. I couldn't get clearances from anybody and it was a holiday, Christmas or whatever, and the ARVNs were literally getting their asses kicked. I couldn't get clearances from anybody. I took it upon myself to put an air strike in. It just went ahead and did it. It was bad weather and we took a lot of fire, but we saved the guys from being overrun.

We got back to squadron and the skipper was talking about writing us up for some kind of commendation, and the next word I heard was they were going to ask us to go to Saigon and explain why we shouldn't be court-martialed for breaking the Rules of Engagement. We talked our way out of that one. But occasionally we would have to break the rules, though they were fairly strict.

The Army, on the other hand, I think abused them systematically. They were a lot closer to the ground, the helicopters, and would go in with hand grenades just to stir up activity. I'm sure most everybody in that area, including civilians, who could arm themselves were armed. And putting myself in their position, if somebody comes in over the treetops in a helicopter and drops a grenade in my house, I'd shoot back too.

Generally, I like to think of myself as a professional. Whatever I set out to do I try to do the best job I can. I'm very motivaed that way. I studied a lot. I really knew my airplane, I knew the missions, I knew the tactics, I knew the people. I engrossed myself entirely. I'm a workaholic. I can go for long hours without sleep. So when I wasn't flying, I was involved in other duties in the squadron. I just immersed myself in my work and gave myself very little free time. And when I was free, I just drank.

Having a family myself, missions where I had to fly into villages or populated areas troubled me an awful lot. Especially in working with orphans, I saw a lot of kids that were obviously war-injured. And seeing captured prisoners and seeing the results of what you've done have a tremendous effect on you. I started to see the difference between pilots and the other combat people. Pilots saw the war from a different perspective. It's man and technology, really, part of this peculiarly American characteristic, the idea of a challenge imposed by yourself and using technology to overcome that challenge. It was a technological war.

After a while, I got so fed up with everything, I spent a lot of my time at a Catholic orphanage in Can Tho. Toward the end, I was spending all my spare time there. I spent more time than I probably should have and I neglected some of my duties. But I got to know the kids. It was called the Providence Orphanage. There were about four or five Catholic nuns and it fluctuated between 160 and 190 children. It got to be one of the most touching things you've ever seen. They would lose ten or fifteen kids a week through disease and malnutrition. But we managed to cumshaw a lot of stuff for them, and we built buildings and facilities and helped take care of the kids. That made life human for me.

We'd organize United States assistance drives for clothing. My wife was a nurse and she'd send supplies. I met her while I was in the Navy, in flight training. Barbara and I have a child, who was born in February 1970, so it was very difficult to leave a year-and-a-half-old child. My wife didn't even know how to drive when I married her.

I thought of my wife and child an awful lot. In the back of my mind I always remembered that I had volunteered for this. Not only had I volunteered, I had taken extraordinary steps to get into the squadron. I questioned my own judgment for doing that, many times. I did it for a number of reasons. I did it because I like flying, and that's the ultimate test, and for things that, I guess, a man could understand. A woman would probably find it more difficult to understand, especially a wife when you're leaving her.

She was real upset, but she tried to contain it as much as possible because she knew the effect it had on me. We never talked about it. In fact, I didn't, until the last week, make any preparations. I did the checkbook, the bills and everything else . . . because we didn't want to confront it until we absolutely had to. Finally, about two weeks before I left, I started to teach her how to drive. I had absolutely no patience. I was a flight instructor, but I couldn't teach her how to drive. So I finally wound up taking her to driving school.

A family separation is very difficult. The wives back here formed a close-knit association, and whenever a pilot was lost or an accident happened, the commanding officer's wife and some of the other wives would get together and make phone calls and get together to keep the morale up.

I tried to keep myself as busy as possible to not feel homesick. Knowing that you can't go back for months, it's very difficult and you have to psyche yourself up. You have to wrap yourself up in what you're doing, otherwise . . . You can't afford to feel homesick. You've got yourself to worry about. Psyching yourself up for flying combat missions is a chore in itself, and to allow yourself to think about your family affects your performance.

My first combat mission was to fly air cover for a Miss America show at Can Tho. We were flying a couple thousand feet above the area and we had gotten a call that some rounds were being taken on the perimeter. I was in the back seat of the plane, and in front was a guy who's got to be one of the craziest people I ever met. He said, "That's where they're at, down there. Watch this." And he turns off his lights and went down—while the Miss America show was going on just a couple of hundred meters away.

As he rolls in, he turns his lights on. We were at three hundred feet, in a very, very shallow gun run. All of a sudden we start taking fire. Green tracers are literally crossing our canopy from two different sites, one on each side of us. We're just a couple hundred feet off the ground. He pulls the throttle back, which slows your air speed and exposes you to fire for a greater period of time, but it also gives you a greater chance to do some shooting yourself. He opens up with his machine guns and strafes the area. We made a couple of passes. That did stop the tracers from coming. He nailed them.

When I saw those rounds coming, I was scared as hell. It's kind of hard to believe that there's somebody out there wanting to kill you, but you begin to appreciate that fact after a while. Especially after you take a couple of rounds in the aircraft.

When you talk to a pilot, you get a completely different perspective on the war. That's why the POWs fared as well as they did. You're talking about people who are highly trained, very well educated, generally very patriotic, don't have any questioning of their orders or their situation. In my case it was a lot like that except because we had to live on the ground and live with the Vietnamese and see what was going on, I think our pilots were more sensitive to the situation, unlike B-52 pilots stationed in Thailand.

I had some grave reservations about the war before I got there, and when I got there and talked to a lot of Vietnamese, I became very disillusioned. But I did what I did because you almost have to. It's like being a football player. If you don't give 100 percent and you hold back and play 96 percent, that's when you get injured. It's a matter of psyching yourself up. That's the way I looked at it. Plus I had other people dependent on me, not just my wing man and the people I flew with, but also the men on the ground.

For the pilot it's a set of coordinates. It's an altitude, it's a distance, it's flipping a switch, it's all these things that are so abstract. Even the bullets coming up from the ground are abstract. You tend to focus on yourself. You depersonalize the enemy and you depersonalize the civilians. You depersonalize the whole war, you almost have to. It's a game, almost, and that's how it's viewed. It's hard to imagine there's actually a man down there shooting those bullets up. You don't see the effect of what you do. Except the closer you get to the ground, the more that changes.

Gayle Smith
Nurse
3rd Surgical Hospital
Binh Thuy
November 1970-November
1971

The Nurse
with Round Eyes

I wanted to go toVietnam to help people who didn't belong there. I objected to the war and I got the idea into my head of going there to bring people back. I started thinking about it in 1966 and knew that I would eventually go when I felt I was prepared enough.

One thing that I hadn't anticipated was that it made a difference that I was a woman with round eyes who could speak English. I think there were about twenty American nurses at Binh Thuy. There were a lot of American nurses in Saigon. I went up there for a vacation. Can you imagine? A vacation in Saigon. I was desperate.

We were shelled close only once at Binh Thuy. But we could always hear it. Every night we could hear it, three or four miles away. The hospital compound wasn't big, but engineers were behind us and Air Force on one side and the Navy and dust-offs on the other. It was the Air Force that used to get hit. And then one night it came in a few yards away. Let me tell you, I moved that night. It was like thunder and landed right beside me. That was halfway through my tour.

Actually, I was queasy the first three months because

142

James Bombard, Vietnam

Above: Douglas Anderson
Upper right: David Ross,
                    Vietnam
Center right: George Lawrence,
                    Vietnam
Below: Lee Childress, Vietnam

Left: Thomas Bird
Right: Admiral William Lawrence
and daughter Wendy
Diamond: Samuel Janney, infantry training

Upper left: Luis Martinez, Vietnam
Center left: Scott Higgins, Vietnam
Upper right: Robert Rawls (with cigarette), Vietnam
Below: Robert Santos receiving Silver Star, Vietnam

<u>Above:</u> Brian Delate
<u>Center left:</u> Gayle Smith,
Vietnam
<u>Center right:</u> James Hebron

Above: Herb Mock (with machine gun) and Don Hildebran, Vietnam
Lower left: Stephen Klinkhammer
Lower right: Warren Nelson

Upper left: Kit Lavell, test pilot
Upper right: Jan Barry
Center right: Dennis Morgan, Vietnam
Below: Lynda Van Devanter, Vietnam

Above: Al Santoli (kneeling, left) CRIP
        Platoon, Vietnam
Center left: Donald Smith, Vietnam
Center right: John Muir (hands crossed),
        Vietnam
Lower left: Jonathan Polansky, Vietnam

I had visions of somebody opening my door and throwing in a grenade. I had trouble sleeping the first three months because of that. Then I got used to the idea that there wasn't anything I could do to prevent that from happening, so I may as well forget about it and get some sleep, and if I woke up the next day, that was good.

I came into Vietnam at Long Binh. There was a replacement camp there, Camp something-or-other, I can't remember the name of it. On the bus from the airport to this camp, the first thing I saw was some Vietnamese guy peeing on the side of the road. And I thought, "Oh, geez, this is a backward country." And the next thing I saw was Coca-Cola signs. I thought, "This is very strange. This is a very unusual mixture." I saw barbed wire all over the city.

The first night I was there, the compound next to ours was shelled. A couple of guys were killed. I went over and there was a big hole in the barracks and it just dawned on me that . . . this was it. I was here, in the middle of a war. It was all around me. That day I went down to Binh Thuy and it was probably the first and last time I cried. I realized I was halfway around the world from home and I couldn't go home if I wanted to. I thought to myself, "What have I done? Here I am in the middle of this godforsaken country. I might get killed. I can't see my parents." I have to say I did cry a couple of times after that, but it mostly was because of my patients. It was when they died.

Boy, I remember how they came in all torn up. It was incredible. The first time a medevac came in, I got right into it. I didn't have a lot of feeling at that time. It was later on that I began to have a lot of feeling about it, after I'd seen it over and over and over again.

But an interesting thing happened in that it was very painful for me to keep seeing the same thing happen. And instead of doing I don't know what, I got *to* it. I turned that pain into anger and hatred and placed it onto the Vietnamese. You know what your head does, the way you think to survive . . . is different. I did not consider the Vietnamese to be people. They were human, but they weren't people. They weren't like us, so it was okay to kill them. It was okay to hate them. I see now that they're people just like us. But at that moment . . .

Toward the end, I was sitting at dinner once with some Navy fellows, pilots, and I was telling them how I felt. And they said, "Boy, you want to go up with us? You can sit behind one of the guns and we can kill some water buffalo if you want." And I thought, "Gee, I don't want to kill any animals." It was okay to kill people, but it wasn't okay to kill animals. But I didn't consider them people, so . . . And then I was tempted to do it and I thought, "I don't have a lot of time left in the country, and if I go up there and start shooting, I might get shot back at and I might get hurt." I didn't want that to happen.

I never knew what the word "hate" was until . . . I would have dreams about putting a .45 to someone's head and see it blow away—over and over again. And for a long time I swore that if the Vietnamese ever came to this country I'd kill them. Or maybe the only thing that would stop me from killing them was that it was against the law in this country to kill people. I had thoughts . . . I just was . . . I remember one of the nurses saying. "Would you be interested in working on the Vietnamese ward?" And I said, "No, I think I would probably kill them." So she said, "Well, maybe we won't transfer you there."

It's weird, isn't it? What you do, the things you do. You know, if I thought of a child dying, that's the way it was. That's war. Children die. You kill them, they kill you. Women kill you, you kill them. That's it. There's no Geneva Convention. There's no rules. There's nothing.

It was apparently not uncommon for Vietnam vets to come back angry, and when some became upset, their method of coping was to become violent. And they all had guns in Vietnam. They used them on each other over there. Guys came into the hospital after gunfights among themselves, especially when the town was off-limits—you know, when guys couldn't get downtown to see the girls. They would start shooting up each other. Practically every night there was somebody getting shot. One night this guy went off the handle and took his gun and went into the shower. Another guy was taking a shower, and he shot and killed him and ran. The MPs and one of the officers that was in charge ran after him, and they shot him in the legs. He turned and shot one of the MPs. Shot him in the head. And the guy still kept running. One of the officers was shot in the right side of the chest.

I was working. They called me to go to the emergency room when they came in. We were trying to resuscitate all three of them at the same time—and the one that lived was the guy that had done the killing. For the first time I saw what damage a .45 could do. It was incredible—it blew an enormous hole in his chest. We put in a chest tube on one side. I saw all this blood pouring and pouring out of the tube and I said, "Wait a minute. Roll this guy over." The chest tube was coming out of his back. It just went right through him.

When dope would get scarce, when heroin would become scarce, there were a lot of gunfights over that. It was incredible among the enlisted men. The officers were mostly doctors and nurses, and we knew enough to stay away from stuff like that—because we knew we had to stay on the ball, because we had to take care of everybody.

There was a lot of drinking going on among doctors and nurses. But you don't want to get drunk because you know you have to perform and you don't know when you're going to be called upon. You have to be on your toes.

They busted our compound once for heroin, just heroin, not for acid or coke, not anything else, just heroin. And they said, "Anyone who doesn't turn themselves in will have to go to LBJ." That's Long Binh Jail. They put bunk beds in the hospital, there were so many of them from the enlisted people that were on our compound, and they all had to do with hospital work, working in the laundry or supply or as medics. I had a medic die right in front of me—just from taking heroin too long. Pneumonia was the end result. It was two weeks before he was to go home and he went home in a box.

These guys would come to work stoned all the time. My medics would shoot up my patients, my patients would . . . I caught them in the bathroom shooting each other up. Once I tried to stop it. Then I realized that he was a lot bigger than I was. I thought, "My medics, I can't do anything about them because they're stoned all the time—not stoned, but they're on heroin—and the administration isn't sending them away." You could report

it to their CO and nothing would be done about it. I
guess there were too many. I don't know.

Who knows? There was bad stuff going down. Like the
food on our compound being sold to the Vietnamese and
the restaurants, and I didn't have enough food for my patients. They wouldn't let us give the patients seconds. I
tried to report that and nothing was done about it. I mean,
you guess why . . . I'd get in more trouble with the Army
and I thought, "What the hell, I might as well put in my
time." I knew I was going to hate the Army. But what
surprised me was nothing comes as close to organized
crime. I thought organized crime was the last word in bad
guys, but I swear, the Army has them beat. You just pay
off the right person and that's it. That's what goes down.

I knew my patients were shooting up. They would
come in and we would have to rule out gastroenteritis or
appendicitis because they were sick from heroin or were
withdrawing from it, so we had to be careful. And so I
told them. I got to that point. I never thought I would
care or not if somebody was on drugs, but it got to that
point. I said to them, "I have enough to worry about with
patients who have been wounded in battle or have had
accidents without worrying about whether you are going
to run out the back door and take heroin. You want to do
it, just don't do it in this ward, because frankly I don't
give a damn whether you die or not. If you do, that's
your problem; if you OD, that's your problem, not my
problem. I can't afford to worry about it. That costs me
too much emotionally." I had too much invested in other
people to divide myself with something like that.

Casualties waxed and waned. It depended what was
going on in the field. What I saw were young men coming
in, eighteen or nineteen years old. Some of them didn't
even have enough hair on their faces to shave and they
would be without a leg. Then you would hear of things
going on in the Vietnamization program—like an American pilot trying to teach a Vietnamese pilot how to fly. I
heard of one case where the Vietnamese pilot did something wrong and the American swore at him and the Vietnamese pulled a gun out and put it to the pilot's head
and said, "Fly us home." Then there were cases that
came to our hospital from dust-off ships called into a hot

landing zone to pull out wounded Vietnamese. We got them to our hospital and pulled off their bandages and there was nothing wrong with them. And when you see stuff like that it makes you want to put them back on the ship and throw them out at about one thousand feet. And I'm not sure that didn't happen.

I used to shake when I would talk about this. I would shake and I would want to kill them all over again. I'd feel my face get hot, I'd become incredibly angry. But, well, it worked out. Now I understand myself a little bit better and I don't have that feeling.

I remember when I got back not being able to listen to the radio, not being able to listen to the news. I couldn't stand to listen to the news. I'd be compelled to turn it off or walk out of the room and not listen to it because I knew there were things that might pertain to people in our compound being killed or people I knew being killed or other people being killed over there. And I felt I should be there still helping them until the war was over. So I just couldn't do it. That was the first sign that I had . . . that I knew there was something going on.

When I came home, I cried when I saw my parents, but that was the last time I cried for a very long time. The guys I was dating before didn't mean anything to me. My parents meant something, but I hadn't figured out what. And I just kind of went along. I went out with fellows and I thought, "Well, they're nice. So what?" I had no interest in sex, no interest in anybody. Then one day on the ski patrol I fell and hurt my thumb. It hurt really bad and I started to cry. It wasn't because I was crying about my thumb. It had come to a head. I was beginning to realize that the problem was I didn't feel anything about anybody anymore. I had no feelings, no feelings of love or hate or anything. Just nothing. And I didn't know why. I guess it was because I was emotionally exhausted. I had been through the highs and the lows and the fears and the hatred and the caring for a year and I had nothing left to give anymore. There was nothing that could compare with what had happened to me.

I dated somebody for that year and I began to realize that I cared about him, and as I began to care about him, I began to realize how much I hadn't cared about anything else. I was beginning to open my eyes and see what had been wrong before. I knew there was something wrong, but I couldn't put my finger on it. There was something wrong with me, but I didn't know what it was. And it was in a Vietnam veterans group that I realized that all my hatred for the Vietnamese and my wanting to kill them was really a reflection of all the pain that I had felt for seeing all those young men die and hurt . . . and how much I cared about them and how much I would stand there and look at them and think to myself, "You've just lost your leg for no reason at all." Or "You're going to die and it's for nothing." For nothing. I would never, never say that to them, but they knew it.

I just never said anything and they never said anything to me. But I knew it somehow. I remember there was a young man, he was nineteen and he had a full scholarship to the University of Pennsylvania. I still remember his name . . . He was in a helicopter crash. He had caught on fire and had burns over 100 percent of his body and his leg was a mess, all torn up. There wasn't any way we could save him. It was an impossibility to save him, but he was still alive. He came in around noontime and he was very alert. His eyes were swollen shut by that time. His face was all bloated up. I came on duty at three o'clock and the nurses gave me a report and they said , . . they showed me . . . they lifted up the sheet and I saw this incredible-looking person. They said, "We've been talking to him about how he's going to go back and about his scholarship and about him going home, but of course he's not going to make it. We've put him in oxygen to make it a little bit easier for him to breathe." And I thought to myself, "There's no one in my experience that I've ever run into that doesn't know that he is dying. Without exception, everyone knows when they're dying." And I said, "He knows. And he doesn't have much time left, so we better talk now." So they took me over to him and I introduced myself and I said, "I hear you have a full scholarship to the University of Pennsylvania." And he said, "Yeah, but I don't think I'm ever going to be able to use it. I don't think I'm going to make it out of this one." And I couldn't say anything. I knew and he knew and I just didn't know what to say at that point. I said, "Is there anything you want me to write to your folks or to your girlfriend?" And he said no.

We had morphine ordered about every two hours, which is very close for morphine, and I gave it to him about every hour and a half. I knew it was accumulating —but I just couldn't stand to see him suffer. So he died a few hours later. And he looked so bad the medics didn't even want to touch him or put him in the bag. I went over and did it. I'll never forget that as long as I live. What a waste, huh? What a wasted, wasted, wasted life.

Over and over and over. I used to see these people— they'd come in and give them Purple Hearts on the ward. And I'd look at them as they'd get their Purple Heart. At that point, it looked like it might be meaningful to them, so I didn't say anything. I never said anything, never said anything about what a waste it was. I would never dream of doing that, because they knew it and it would hurt like hell if they heard it anyway. But I would watch this ridiculous little ceremony, and they'd get a Purple Heart for what was left of them, and I'd think, "You're getting this? What are you getting this for? It's not going to get your leg back. It's not going to get your looks back. It's not going to make you avoid all the pain you're going to have to face when you go home and see your family and get back into society. It's all sitting in front of you and you're going to have to deal with it . . . and nothing will make up for that."

I remember one young man, he had lost his leg and he was walking around on crutches. He had adjusted pretty well. This was probably the first few weeks after he lost his leg. We didn't keep them more than sixty days. Our standard was: If you couldn't cure them or kill them in sixty days, you had to lose them somehow. And he went down and called his mother and told her he had lost his leg. He had been doing pretty well up to this point. I said, "What did your mother say?" He said, "Well, she cried." And I could see he was going to get a little teary-eyed, but he didn't want to because it was a twenty-two-bed ward. All the guys are looking at each other and they don't like to cry in front of each other. So I just gave him a hug, in front of all the guys, and that made him feel good.

A Notion of Honor

JONATHAN Polansky: I remember being in Oakland in the overseas camp waiting to go. That's when Johnson halted the bombing, in November of 1968. And everybody said, "Fantastic, maybe we won't have to go. Maybe it will be all over." God, what pipe dreams.

AL SANTOLI: In November of '68 I had already been wounded and to Japan and back. I was in the field when Johnson halted the bombing. We were angry in the field because we knew it wasn't going to end the war. We knew what would happen—the stepping up of enemy supplies. We started getting rocketed more. The shit hit the fan whenever they stopped the bombing. It wasn't the NVA that beat us, it was our own politicians. We had pretty well wiped out the main-force VC in our area and had the NVA beat after Tet. We chased them as far as Cambodia and had to stop at the border, which allowed them to regroup. This cat-and-mouse game went on for ten years.

In the same way, we knew that whenever they would stop the bombing, it meant more American deaths. Didn't our lives mean anything?

I became a physical therapy assistant when I came back to the States. I remember one time on the amputee ward at Fort Gordon. I did the ward rounds for the physical therapy clinic, and since I wore my Combat Infantry Badge on my medic whites, I was the one who would work with the guys first when they arrived from overseas. They were all Southern people—it was the rehab center for the Southeast. And there was this kid from a small town, somewhere in the mountains of Tennessee, who had lost both legs and part of a hand and . . . His father was a big mountain person; he was wearing a plaid shirt. And his mother was a small, thin woman who had a 1940s curly kind of hair. You could tell they didn't have much money. Their wardrobe was on their backs and the look on their faces . . . it wasn't sympathy and it wasn't horror and it wasn't heroism. It was just . . . lost. Like "What are we going to do? What is this? My son I spent years raising and caring and loving, and now he's only half here."

Their communication . . . I remember he had this picture taken in Japan of this general giving him the Purple Heart and shaking his hand—his good hand. And he held that picture, with no expression on his face, as kind of the go-between his parents and himself. And all of them were just blank. Not blank—there was a lot going on—but just speechless. And all he had to show for what happened to him was this goddamn picture of this fucking general shaking his hand.

I remember another time at Fort Gordon when Melvin Laird, who was Secretary of Defense then, came to visit the hospital. The hospital at Fort Gordon was formerly a prisoner-of-war camp for Germans during World War II.

It was built like the old military barracks that are
wooden, one floor and very long, kind of like an intestine.
And during the winter it would get cold in Georgia. It
wouldn't really snow, but it would get cold and the pipes
would freeze and burst, and the hallway would be covered with ice at times, cockroaches, just a miserable place.
They were spending millions of dollars a day on the war at
that time, but they couldn't afford to build a new hospital.

Melvin Laird came to inspect the hospital and we
heard something about it. I was doing the wards. What I
was doing at that time was in the afternoon take the guys
who needed to get whirlpools, that still had open, exposed
wounds, to disinfect them and get the muscles relaxed.
The hallways were maybe wide enough to get a person
and a stretcher through side by side. I'm wheeling this
guy from Florida, this nineteen- or twenty-year-old buck
sergeant. He was a very handsome guy and his wife was
beautiful—beautiful young girl. She was at the hospital
visiting at the time, living at a motel near the hospital.
And you looked at them and they were trying to force a
cheerful relationship, but it's like everything else—all the
electricity and blood was drained out of them. And all of
a sudden comes this entourage of colonels and generals
and Secret Service, and I realized that it was Melvin
Laird. So I'm wheeling this guy on the stretcher who is
quite obviously missing both legs, and he's doped up because he's in a lot of pain. He had a lot of courage—he
wasn't complaining, never complained.

Well, I realized it's Melvin Laird and now's my chance.
My first impulse was to strangle him, to pull a Frankenstein, put a death grip on his neck and not let go until he's
dead. And then I thought, "Well, shit, if this person with
me, this guy on the stretcher, isn't enough . . ." Just that
Laird has to live with knowing that he's sending all these
boys over there to have this happen to them . . .

As they walked by, single file, baldheaded Melvin
Laird in his three-hundred-dollar suit, I looked right for
his eyes. My eyes went for his eyes. And that son of a
bitch walked head on—didn't even look to the right or
left of him. And he's a pretty tall man. I mean, he could
look over my head, he could look over that stretcher. He
didn't bat an eye and he didn't look.

Robert Rawls
Rifleman
1st Cavalry Division
Tay Ninh
Early 1969-Early 1970

A Black GI

I was up at An Khe for a week to go through the little training school up there that the 1st Cav gives you when you first get in country, and then they ship you out to your unit, which was down in Tay Ninh Province. I didn't expect nothing when I got there, but it was just all the way different. It was an LZ beneath the Black Virgin Mountain.

The first night they sent me on OP [forward observation post] and I was as scared as I've ever been in my life. I just said, "How could I do a year over here?" You know, it was too much. The first night was a strain on me. I could feel it inside. It was worse than being a convict locked up in a prison. We just laid out there. So I said, "If the Cong come, we'll be the first ones to go."

On that mountain was where the VC were. There was an American radio outpost at the top, the VC were all up and down the mountain, and we were at the base.

I saw these helicopters land the next morning and I wonders to myself what the hell they is for. They told us to get into the helicopters. I thought, "Oh, we're going to the rear." They put us out there in the middle of the jungle and dropped us off. I was actually bummed out. This

153

was my first time, man, and the helicopter was doing like this and I was so afraid I might fall off because I had two mortar rounds. I finally landed and we started going out on search-and-destroy missions.

Just before our first fire fight, nobody told me our OP was out there. I heard something out there and blew a claymore on my own OP. Lucky nobody wasn't killed. I took my M-16 and opened up. The next morning I got chewed out by the company commander. But I didn't know. They don't tell you anything. They just sent you out there.

We got fire fights after fire fights. My first taste of death. After fire fights you could smell it. They brought the guys back wrapped up in ponchos, those green ponchos. The way they put them on the helicopter really just made me think about it all . . . they just threw them up on the helicopter and put all these empty supplies on top of them. You could see the guys' feet hanging out. I could see those jungle boots. I had nightmares behind them. I can still see those guys . . . I was talking to one guy that morning. His name was Joe Cocaham, he was from New Jersey. They just packed everything up on him and took off. I can remember guys saying, "I wonder how his family is going to feel." I said, "What are we over here fighting for?"

On Ho Chi Minh's birthday, May 19, 1969, I got wounded in an ambush. I got hit under the chin, over the eye and in the leg. Okay. They sent me back to Tay Ninh. That's the farthest I got back to the rear. Just patched me up. Then as the stitches got well, they cut 'em out and sent me back to the unit. By that time my mind had just snapped. I'd write these letters home saying what to do with all of my stuff, like I was making out a will. Because I had a feeling that I wasn't coming back.

But I used to read the Twenty-third Psalm. They say, "Yea, though I walk through the Valley of Death, I will fear no evil, because I'm the baddest son of a bitch in the valley." And on and on.

When I got near the deros, or whatever they call it when you come back to the States, sometimes I wished I had died over there with my buddies. I said, "What's back here?" You know, my wife had left.

I got married a couple of months before I got drafted, and they said they couldn't catch up with the paperwork to keep me out of the draft. I was overdue. I was 1-A about a year and a half. I tried to go to school at that time—they was funny about getting into schools—and I tried joining the National Guard, but they was all booked up. I was working for Cleveland Electric Illuminating Company. When I got back everything was changed. The way I feel about life now . . . it's just a bum trip. I have flashbacks and people can't understand me sometimes. I sit by myself and I just think. You try to talk to somebody about it, they think you're out of your mind or you're freaked out. They want to put you in a strait jacket or something like that. That's why I go to these veterans rap groups that they have now every Wednesday. I just blow off the heat that I have built up inside.

About fifteen guys go to them, all different races. And we just sit there and say the way we feel. We just get everything out of our minds. Like Congress and the United States could spend billions and billions of dollars to bring Vietnamese over here now, but they can't even put up a system that's federally funded by the VA or somewhere to help these Vietnam veterans that've actually been having this ten-year relapse. I mean, you could just look at some of them and just tell that they are . . . just gone.

Most of the guys in the rap group were infantry and Green Berets and Marines. The other day this guy came in. He had lost his arm over there, he had lost his leg over there. And we're talking in the meeting and he told me that he didn't have nothing against the Vietnamese. And I said, I just looked at him, "Man, you've got to be . . . you need help. You done lost your arm and your leg, and you say you got nothing against these people?"

If I see a Vietnamese on the street, I cross and walk on the other side. There are some on the west side, mostly downtown. Sometimes I go downtown to a couple of bookstores or go get fishing equipment, and you can tell them by the way they look, you-know. Just a bummed-out trip.

Where we were it was jungle. Completely jungle. And the company commanders and all of them was like gung-ho-type guys. They were lifers, and I just couldn't cope with the service and what they stood for.

In basic training and in AIT [Advanced Infantry Training], they was beating around the bush. They made a joke out of everything, like "We're going to get old Charlie Cong" and all that old stuff. Instead of being down and serious, they used to beat around the bush. We used to sit up in the bleachers and they'd say, "This is how Charlie really works." They couldn't tell me how Charlie really worked. You had to get over there and experience for yourself how Charlie really worked.

The NVA tried to overrun LZ Grant. That's when our CO got killed. He was a lifer. Our own helicopter killed thirty of our men. We was on a search-and-destroy mission and we could see all this firing way over there. We knew that was LZ Grant. It was being overrun. We had our strobe lights on and this Cobra helicopter thought it was a mortar tube, so the damn thing came down, shot two rockets. *Sshhuuu.* I was in a foxhole and this guy's boot landed next to me with his foot still in it, cut off at the boot top.

Thinking back on the training, all they told us to do was kill. "KILL! KILL!" "What is the spirit of the bayonet?" "TO KILL!" It was just a bummed-out trip. And I just didn't go for it, you know. I can remember this one instance where this guy, he was so depressed, he was walking in the boonies and he said, "I'm going home today." I said, "How you going to do it?" "I'm going home today, man. I can't hardly think no more, all this killing and stuff." So he was walking. The next thing I knew, I heard a gunshot. *Boom. Pow.* He had shot himself through the ankle, through the foot. He said, "I finally made it home." And I thought about doing that to get back home.

Mostly I was by myself. Some guys over there, they were drug addicts, man. Their mind had snapped so bad that they were taking drugs. They'd get them from guys that would come back from R & R. I'd be scared of the NVA soldiers, the VC, and plus I'd have to be scared of my own men. That's too much of a strain. How'd I know this guy might be high or something, sitting up on the bunker, fall asleep, and the VC'd come in and shoot you?

I worked with those ARVNs for about a month at the end of my tour. That was a good sham for me, to go back to the rear and work with them. They weren't worth a cent. In a fire fight those ARVNs would drop everything and run to the rear. That's why I hate them, those Vietnamese. I wish I'd never see one of them as long as I live, 'cause we was over there fighting for them and they was constantly ripping us off. Stealin' stuff. After I came back from R & R, I brought four suits from Hong Kong. When the luggage went through Tan Son Nhut Air Base, I never saw them again. That was the Vietnamese.

After I got back from R & R, I stayed in a place in Saigon they call Soul Kitchen. That's where all the AWOL GIs used to hang out with mama-san and stuff like that. I hung out down there for a while and I felt like stayin' down there, but I got caught by the MPs and they sent me back to the unit. I got an Article 15 [official reprimand] and I said, "So what." Too much stress and strain. That's rough.

The blacks used to make a shoestring that they braided up and tied around their wrist, and everywhere a whole lot of blacks used to go, they'd give a power sign. About six or seven different handshakes. That was about the time that Huey Newton and all them was around. But for the guys in the bush, the grunts, you know, one of my best friends was a white guy. There was no racism between him and me, nothing like that. That was mostly back in the rear. Out in the bush everybody was the same. You can't find no racism in the bush. We slept together, ate together, fought together. What else can you ask for?

I knew this one guy. I could remember how many times a day he pissed, that's how well I knew the guy. We was real close, man, close. He was a Sicilian and I always used to kid him: "Hey, you think I could join the family when we get out of here?" This guy was so close that he should've been my brother, but . . . he died.

I just can't . . . sometimes, man . . . every time I talk about it, it just hurts. But ever since I've been going to these meetings . . . I thought anybody didn't want to listen. But these guys, they listen to me. And if there's any help, you know I need it. The way I was brought up, they'd say, "If you want something, work for it." And that's what I'm trying to do now.

When I was drafted, I said, "I'll go over to Vietnam to help the people out. That's what everybody wants." But after I got there, I said, "These sons of guns ARVNs are laying back in the rear while we're fighting the war."

During the time I was there my marriage fell apart. It fell completely . . . I got back and I could feel it falling. I said, "I know I'm different. I'm not the high-school chap that you knew." She was my high-school sweetheart. It wasn't the same. I was all the way different. I was short-tempered. Actually, I was violent. I used to go to bars sometimes. I'd take a drink and a guy would call me a boy and I'd just try to light into him. After I had fought for a year and come back to the States, he'd call me still a boy. What more do I have to do?

I can't say now if I was one of the lucky ones. Sometimes I wish I could've just went ahead and died with my friends. I used to say, "I'm only dreaming. I'll wake up one day. I will wake up." But I never woke up.

I have nightmares and sweats. I'll be sweating something fierce. My wife will say, "What's wrong with you?" I'll think of something else to say. I've never talked about these dreams with my wife 'cause she can't understand it, you know. She's been a civilian all her life and how would she understand it? The persons I can talk to is the rap group or another Vietnam soldier.

Like they're having this air show down at the lakefront. Yesterday I heard this jet coming over. The way I heard it, it was just like dropping one of those bombs. It brought back another flashback, and that's what I mean about going down there to see one of those planes, because if I feel a flashback coming on, I don't know what I might do. So I tell my old lady, "No. You can go. I ain't going." I didn't tell her why. And I make up an excuse like "I'm going to paint my mother's house."

When I came back to the States, they sent me to Fort Knox. I had several months to kill, so they put me on funeral detail. That was sickening, man. It was sickening for the U.S. Army to put on a damn front like they did. It was a twenty-one-gun salute with blank ammo, a bugler and an honor guard, where you folded the coffin flag and gave it to the mother or the child, with the officer saying, "We really are sorry that your son died while defending his country." You see, I was with these guys who never went to 'Nam. Just before the funeral they used to sit back and drink beer and laugh, almost right before the burial, laugh and shoot the shit, and then they'd say something like this to the guy's family, who were going through all this grief.

One day we went to Pikesville, Kentucky. The family said we was the best thing they could ever do for their son. They invited us in for dinner. They was mostly Appalachian people. They invited us in, we ate, and that was it. But they just didn't know . . . I didn't say anything to them. If I had to talk to them, I'd say, "Let bygones be bygones."

Only thing I can say now is: Have mercy on the younger generation.

Luis Martinez
Team Commander
U.S. Marine Combined
    Action Platoon
Danang
July 1970-July 1971

A Puerto Rican
Marine

I was in what is called a Combined Action Platoon. Eleven or twelve Marines and a Navy corpsman. We were in villages and hamlets along Highway 1.

When I got there we spent a couple of weeks in Danang in the CAP school, where they taught us Vietnamese language and culture and things of that nature so we wouldn't do things to anger the villagers. Certain little things, like pointing your feet when you sit, which they take seriously. To me it was survival because I think as long as you can respect people and treat them the way that you want to be treated, then hopefully if the Viet Cong is going to do something, he remembers you and you have a better chance of surviving.

The VC did win, you know. They had it all the time. We were just visiting. The Americans would go gung ho. The Vietnamese philosophy was "Hey, we're going to sit back. You go in and do your thing, but we're not going to play this hero stuff. We have to live." It was hard trying to teach that to some of the young people that would be coming in, the green troops. "Don't go looking for booby traps, don't go trying to be a hero, because all

160

you're going to do is get killed. And nobody gives a damn once you die. Life still keeps going."

Hispanics in the Marines were no different than anybody else. When you're in a war situation, everyone is green. Sometimes the Armed Forces radio would have a program in Spanish where they would play Puerto Rican music. The other fellows wouldn't want to hear that. They thought it was Vietnamese music or anything they couldn't understand.

I remember when I was wounded in the hospital, I was reading this book where for each state there would be a section where you could write something from whatever city you were from and look up who was there. So I picked up the one for Ohio and I wrote in that. Then I took the one from Puerto Rico and I was going to write in the area from Bayamón. Someone had put, "You fucking spics, why don't you write in English so that we can understand." I was shocked. Here I was in the hospital. And I wrote down, "If I'm good enough to fight and die for this country, I'm good enough to write or speak in any way I please." And a friend of mine who happened to be an Anglo said, "Hey, that's cool. I like that." So I could relate to him because I can't, once again, generalize about all the mentalities.

Someone had told me that 25 to 35 percent of those Puerto Ricans who had served in Vietnam had either been killed or wounded. And it hurt me a lot, you know. My God, that's a lot of people.

When I came back from Vietnam there were people on the base who couldn't speak English. So I tried to help. I think the Marines are always hard up for people. They have a great public relations gimmick or whatever. But when you start seeing kids that really can't read, poor kids that can't take care of themselves and they're in a situation like that, my God . . . you start to wonder about it all. Because I was proud. I read Marine Corps history when I was little. I read all the books on the Marines. I did. And I always wanted to be a Marine. So I joined after I got drafted out of college.

I didn't think that much about college. Well, I wanted to be a teacher, but I thought that the military would be the heroic way of doing things: "Hey, look at me. I've

done something now." Which is completely wrong. I
thought I had to experience things in order to understand.
I've always thought of writing a book. That's why I kept
a diary and things of that nature. But you don't have to
experience things. You can read a book and if you're
perceptive enough, if you're intuitive enough, you can
learn from that. You don't have to experience war. So I
went in kind of an adventurous spirit.

I didn't volunteer for 'Nam. They sent me as a grunt.
They made more of an effort, put more billions of dollars
into killing one or two Viet Cong than they do in dealing
with the problems that we have in our cities, which should
be rebuilt. There's so much to do in education, in all
facets of life. I think that if we would have more emphasis in developing potential that is there, it would be that
much better for our country. We still do love our country.
And if we don't get our shit together, there are a billion
Chinese that are working like ants. And if we can't get
together with the world, if we can't be compatible, obviously we're not going to be dominant very much longer.

That's how come in my work I continue to study—because I figure we are the leaders. There is no one else
out there who we can say to, "Hey, you do it." We have
to do it. In our own little ways, we have to set examples,
we have to do these things that we feel are right, because
we know enough already that there's a bunch of assholes
that have taken the leadership roles and have screwed
things up for so long. You and I have gone through a war
situation. We know each other. We know ourselves. We
have to trust ourselves. We have to trust our decisions and
our philosophies about life so we can keep moving.

Jesus Christ, you know, after a couple of Purple Hearts
and this and that, the Lord says you can live. And you
get to live. I have a home now, a car, a beautiful woman,
who I feel that I'm developing a good relationship with,
a love relationship. We have to look at our positive and
really thank God for what we do have. We made it.

Lynda Van Devanter
Nurse
71st Evacuation Hospital
Pleiku
June 1969-June 1970

Life

VIETNAM was the first place I delivered a baby by myself. It seemed like a Saturday afternoon. It might
have been, I don't know why, but for some reason it
it seemed like a Saturday afternoon. It was very quiet.
There were no other patients around. I was feeling very
depressed and this lady came in. I got pissed off at first,
because we were supposedly there for taking care of military casualties. We were only supposed to take care of
civilian situations if we possibly had the time. But this
particular day, I got her onto a gurney and started leading her back to the OR because I could tell she was very
close to delivery and I had already put in a call to one
of the surgeons to come down and deliver it. He didn't
have time to get there.

She looked over at me and said, "Baby come, baby
come." I looked down and there was the head. I just
grabbed myself a sterile towel and held it under, and that
kid just popped his little head out and turned around
on his side, and popped his little shoulders out, and there
was this little squalling bundle of humanness. And the
life came back again. It was creation of life in the midst

163

of all that destruction. And creation of life restored your sanity.

Those moments when we had a little baby around were very precious. I have a couple of slides of me sitting in the operating room with my foot up on the table, in my fatigues and combat boots, with a scrub shirt over the top of me, holding a little tiny bundle in my arms, feeding it. Those were the things that kept you going. That there was still life coming. There was still hope.

4

Barren
Harvest

Lieutenant Colonel Gary
    Riggs
Adviser
7th Special Forces
Laos
1960-1961
Vietnam
1966-1970

Restraint

WHEN Johnson rolled out and Nixon came in, the emphasis was black and white from where I sit. Well, the emphasis on our operational kind of things. The things we did.

The emphasis became "Let's get the damn thing over. Let's close it out, with as much dignity as we can, but let's just back off and come home." And that permeated all the way down to Snuffy in the field. Not just my guys, but Boonie Rat out there with a commissioned unit. It became a matter of survival then. This was after Tet, February 1968. Because we knew by then that we were going to come out of there.

There were three or four phases of the war. The first one would be up to 1964. In '65 we brought in our first line unit. From the time the 173rd Airborne came off Okie up until Tet, we were pumping everything in there. We had Westmoreland. He waved that flag and said, "Go git 'em." I'm down in the trenches. I have never served above a battalion. I was out in the boonies with the troopies, I had no idea what floated up in the atmosphere,

167

other than that Westmoreland, during the time before General Abrams came in, made his presence felt. He was very aggressive: "We're going to win this mother."

General Abrams come mid-'68. He came with a different message, which was "Contain. Pacify."

Thomas Bailey
Interrogation Officer
525th Military Intelligence
   Group
Saigon
January 1970-August 1971

The Little People

My job was working at the Combined Military Interrogation Center, or CMIC. It was, in theory, a Vietnamese and American combined center. In other words, we also had Vietnamese who did interrogations in the unit. We were located in Saigon.

For Americans to begin to understand Vietnamese, and probably any other people in the world, they first have to understand themselves with some objectivity. For me, that was a lot of my 'Nam experience—seeing America, going through the process of love/hating it, feeling very bad about America, the shame of what they were doing there.

Our trip over there was an exercise in nation-building. We were really trying to define them in our terms without beginning to see what their terms were at all. They've always had a class society—there's a strict sense of upper class and lower class. It's just a question of where the foreigners fit.

The villages seemed to be more equal, but not egalitarian, I don't think. There's not the same sense of rights of man. They don't have their roots in Locke or Rousseau. That's particularly a European idea. And when you

169

take it one step further, export it to the United States and see what we've done with it and how we've incorporated it into our society—I mean, there's a certain sense in our society that there's some things we should be egalitarian about and others that we shouldn't. In fact, that's been one of the big struggles in the last twenty years, of blacks trying to redefine that, perhaps, or other minorities. But within a very narrow framework.

Sometimes I became very frustrated in dealing with Vietnamese, I guess because their civilization was so much older than ours, although we would characterize them as being uncivilized. I would have a difficult time defining the way in which they were more civilized than we were, but they were. It's my gut feeling. Their code of how the society operated was a lot more strongly laid down. Their social codes were real rules—not that they didn't break them—but there was a certain code that was quite strict which the Vietnamese felt very strongly about.

The South Vietnamese thought we were just superhuman. I remember at one point seeing an American female get off a bus in Saigon. I was standing with two or three Vietnamese at the time. They kind of stopped talking and watched her walk by. I said, "What are you thinking?" and they said, "Oh, she's beautiful." She was a pig, but she had blond hair. And I turned to them and said, "Look, each of you is far more beautiful than she is. I mean, look at you. You have clear features and long black hair." And they wouldn't hear of it, of course. It's kind of like you buy the blond-haired, blue-eyed American myth. They saw the posterboards all over Saigon.

Saigon was, at that point, in the grip of what the sociologists call "rising expectations." Without any technological base at all, they had suddenly been given this douche of American shining hardware, stereos and cameras and all the bright shining things that American technology makes. And they wanted it. Intensely. On all levels of society. They just had to have it. I had people come to me who would want something and not even know what it was.

One guy found out I was going to Hong Kong, and he wanted me to buy him a movie viewer. He didn't know that it was a movie viewer. He thought it would be a movie projector. And he didn't have any movies to view on it. But that wasn't the point. He just wanted to have it. He would have to beg, borrow and steal to get it. On the other hand, things like that were also of high value on the black market. So if he didn't want it, he could always turn around and sell it for more.

Bruce Lawlor
Case Officer
Central Intelligence Agency
I Corps
November 1971-December
1973

The Missing
Ingredients

FOR those of us who knew Vietnamese character, they're very much a fiercely independent people. They didn't like us very much, either, the South Vietnamese.

Personal honor came in different ways over there, and one of the things that made me feel the best was a rather senior-ranking South Vietnamese official who had a South Vietnamese friend who was in the literary field. I met this friend and he introduced me to his daughter. I thought no big thing of it. Afterward a South Vietnamese official, a guy I'd worked with, said, "You know, you are the first American that this girl has ever met and talked to. She's seen them all over the streets, but her father would never let her talk to Americans because you are barbarians."

They thought we were animals. A lot of little things that we took for granted offended them fiercely, such as putting your hand on a head. Sitting with your feet crossed, with your foot facing another person, is a high insult.

One of the things that was kind of funny yet kind of sad was America trying to impose its values on an Asian people. When I was there the Agency began a drive toward getting more blacks into case-officer positions. In recent years, I'm told, they're having a drive toward getting more women in the positions. The Agency was becoming a reflection of this society as a whole. And so they sent these blacks and— I've got to preface this by saying I know that every time someone talks about blacks there's an immediate reaction that the guy's racist or whatever, and it's the farthest thing from my mind. But what happened was America said we had to have more blacks in positions of responsibility, and the Agency responded and we had more black case officers. They sent some of these guys to Vietnam and gave them positions in liaison, where they had to speak to Vietnamese colonels and Vietnamese province officials and try to elicit information or even recruit them. The guy walked in the door and already, without saying a word, insulted this Vietnamese beyond belief, since the Vietnamese hate black skin because they associate black skin with the Cambodians, who have been their enemies for centuries and centuries and centuries.

The Vietnamese would come to me and say, "Can't we get somebody else?" and they wouldn't tell you why. "Well, we don't like so-and-so. He doesn't understand us." And you'd try to explain to them he's really a good guy and he's got the ears of the highest man in our organization and it never took. Some of these poor black officers, their careers weren't especially enhanced by the experience because they never got any information. And that's the type of thing we learned over there. All good intentions. Maybe in terms of our society, what we were trying to do was correct. But in terms of trying to get information from the Vietnamese, it was idiocy. But we did it and we had to do it because that's the way it was.

If you went to the base chief and said, "Jesus, you really shouldn't have the black doing this," you got a report in your file that said you were anti-black and discriminating. You went right back to what the Vietnamese said: "Fuck it! If they don't want to know what the information is, it doesn't bother me." And that's what happened. There are so many instances like that where our stupidity was just overwhelming.

One of the greatest ones we had and one of the saddest, I think, was some idiot in the United States came up with the idea that there were a lot of orphans in Vietnam, which there were, so they were going to try to increase the adoption of orphans by the Vietnamese. They had their little ad program and it didn't really take too well. So what they came up with was the idea to provide a stipend very much like foster children have in the United States. A family would take in an orphan through USAID and be given a stipend—a very noble gesture and a very humane gesture. But what they totally ignored was the fundamental character of the Vietnamese family, which is extremely cohesive and extremely anti-outsider, if you will.

Vietnamese in the street—if somebody got run over by a truck, it was a source of fascination. But if it was one of their family, they'd go completely to pieces. And what happened was they adopted . . . sure, there was a rush on the agencies, and everybody back in the United States said, "Oh, what a wonderful thing this is. We're finally accomplishing something in Vietnam." And what they did to these poor kids that they adopted is they made them all slaves. They made the kids do all the dishes and all of the cleaning and all of the . . . I'm serious. And we subsidized it. As Americans we subsidized it and thought we were doing a wonderful thing.

There was a woman over there, and I wish I could remember her name because she was an absolute saint. She was in Danang, and she worked for three or four years trying to convince the American government of what it was doing. She was over there on her own. She wasn't getting paid by any government agency. And we tried to help her. Guys in my organization slipped her a little of this and a little of that, we bent the rules and broke the system for her. If she needed a ride somewhere, we got her a ride. And she ran up against the bureaucratic bunglers, the idiots in Washington. They would say, "Look at the statistics. I mean, we've had x-amount kiddies adopted." And what they've done is created x-amount slaves.

We permitted, we overlooked, instances of flagrant Vietnamese abuse, diversion of funds. I'm not saying "we" as the Agency. I'm saying "we" as a government, because the Agency wasn't involved in these things near the end at all, not the time I was there.

A province chief, for example, would divert the cement intended for Village X to his personal use somewhere, and the province senior adviser [American] would never make a big stink of it because the province senior adviser was probably a full colonel. He was bucking for a star. And that Vietnamese province chief, upon the conclusion of the American's tour of duty, would award him five hundred medals and write a letter about what a wonderful human being he was.

The province chiefs were usually South Vietnamese military types, especially after President Thieu came in. He replaced most of the forty-four province chiefs and put in the military. The people never had any say in voting for who would be the province chief. But I don't think the Vietnamese understood our concept of voting.

They used to like the old province chief because he was "full." What they meant by that was a new province chief just coming in probably hadn't been on the public tit for too long in terms of the type of graft and corruption available to province chiefs, so he'd be running and scrambling to get as much as he could. The extortion would increase under the new province chief because he didn't have his little nest egg salted away. Whereas an old province chief who had been there for years and years had already made his money, and the taxation and the problems that the people could expect were somewhat less because he didn't need as much money as the new guy did. That's the way the villagers looked on their leaders, and they looked on the district chiefs in the same way.

When you interject the concept of voting into that, it doesn't make sense. In the Western mind, voting is very important, but to the Vietnamese mind, the last thing they wanted was an election where they might have to vote in a new guy, because then it meant that they were going to get screwed in the end. So if you're a politician and there's a vote, you're in for the rest of your life because of the way that the system is structured.

The Vietnamese Rural Development Cadre were themselves pretty lazy and pretty corrupt and an inefficient fighting force on top of that. I lay it back on leadership.

I think you've got to differentiate between the average private, corporal, sergeant, the officers and the team commanders that led them. And let's face it, it happened in American units, too.

If you get a second lieutenant who doesn't know what the hell he's doing, his platoon isn't going to have an awful lot of faith in him. The American soldier and the American system eventually disintegrated because of its officer corps over there. I mean, we had so many problems with the troops, and I think it's because they perceived that nobody cared about them. The only thing the officers wanted to do was get their six months in command and then split back to the States and be promoted and go on to bigger and better things. It doesn't take long for the average guy out in the field to say, "Fuck it!" And I think that's what happened to the RD Cadre.

If somebody went out and really broke his ass to try and put up a structure in a village and then was told he couldn't have cement today because the province chief wants to build a new patio, and knows if he complains he's probably going to get shot or put in jail on some trumped-up charge, after a while he says, "Fuck it, why bother?"

The ARVN as a force was undependable. But I think you have to go back to your comparing them to American standards. The American military has fought two major wars in the last century, or three major wars if you include Korea, or four if you include Vietnam. Vietnam was a country that had really been alive only since 1954. Until the U.S. began its massive influx, let's say 1962 or so, there really was no Vietnamese army. There were a few units that were pretty good, but they were always stationed around Saigon to protect the incumbent President. If they were untrustworthy they were stationed way the hell down the other end of the country so they wouldn't be a threat to the presidency. What we tried to do was create an army rapidly. And it never had a chance to shake down.

By the time the country was divided in '54, they had been fighting the French and they had fought the Japanese. But not as a Vietnamese army. They'd fought as guerrillas, the Viet Minh. And the concept of fighting as a guerrilla versus the concept of fighting as part of an American-type army is night and day. And when you put that up against a guerrilla who's carrying a mine down the South China Sea in water up to his neck for hours, you've got a real formula for disaster. Because the essential ingredient is missing, and that's dedication and will and enthusiasm, and that's got to be instilled in the troops by their leaders. I don't think it was instilled in the ARVN, I don't think it was instilled in the Americans, and I don't think it was instilled in the Agency. I think we all gave up. I'm grateful that I went to Vietnam in the position I went in because I knew what was going on. I read the cables. When there was a new offensive or a new strategy, I knew what it was and I could relate it to what was happening in the village. But I knew grunts— the poor bastards jumped out of helicopters in hot LZs and didn't even know where the fuck they were except that guys were shooting at them and mortars were coming in and people were dying and screaming.

Christ, if you're in a situation where you're trying to conduct a guerrilla campaign, how in the hell can you put people like that into a war? How can you inject these type of guys into a situation that requires a tremendous amount of sophistication? You can't. What happens is they start shooting at anything that moves because they don't know. They're scared. I mean, they're out there getting shot at, and Christ, there's somebody with eyes that are different than mine. And *boom* —it's gone.

Expose yourself and draw fire. That was the strategy and that's wrong. That's letting the enemy have the initiative. It's letting them strike when they want to strike, where they want to strike and how they want to strike. And that's guaranteed failure in a guerrilla war. That's the definition of giving your opponent the edge in a war of attrition, because he can raise or lower the levels of casualties that you receive at any given point. So he can do that for his own political purposes. If he needs to make a political point within the country to show American vulnerability, he raises the level of activity: you take more casualties, people see more body bags leaving. If he needed to make a political point in the United States, he could make it. They were conscious of that.

I think the North Vietnamese played us better than we know. They just totally out-psyched us. We lost the war because of will, not military power. For example, I think initially they probably didn't recognize what they were on to. I think they initially looked at Tet in '68 as a disaster, but our reaction in the United States was so overwhelming—I mean, it toppled the President—that all of a sudden it became clear to them that they could make the Americans beat themselves.

Fullback 6

Fᴜʟʟʙᴀᴄᴋ 6, just an example of a colonel who wasn't
worth a shit. He'd been watching too many General
Patton movies. What he wanted to do was promote himself, and he didn't give a damn who it cost or what it
cost. He did not want to win, he just wanted it to look
good. He wanted you to follow the regulations because
that looks good. He wanted a body count because that
looks good.

He liked to send people in without them knowing the
enemy would be there because we wouldn't be as cautious and more likely to get in shit. And his actions were
. . . in fact, I talked to him . . . it was because Ditch
got killed. The colonel knew they were there, but he
didn't tell us about the NVA base camp. I was told afterward by an officer that he knew. And that's when I went
to see him.

I asked him if he knew they were in there. And he
said yeah. Then he tried to give me this bullshit that he'd
told everybody, that we were supposed to know: "You're
supposed to be ready for it all the time," and all that shit.
Well, that's true, and we were ready for it. But if he knew
something positively was in there, we should've been told.
We would've been more cautious. As point man, I'd a run

point a little further out. This is how I remember what happened that day.

I had come to a fork in the trail and I stopped. As point man, I knew what I was doing. One trail continued into the jungle and one came out of the bushes. I came out of the bushes and noticed there was an enemy base camp. I could smell the son of a bitches, and also I had been coming across cut-off logs in the middle of the jungle.

I walked a little ways and there was a break in the goddamn jungle. I found a little hole in a solid wall of brush and as I bent down to go into the hole, I saw something. It looked like laundry or clothing, sticks and a campfire. And when I bent down and went through three or four more bushes into the next clearing, I realized it was a base camp.

I looked up. There's a fucking trench and a goddamn gook standing in it. And lightning fast, I put one right smooth between that motherfucker's eyes. I'll never shoot that good again. He wasn't no more than fifteen foot from me. He was just standing there watching; I guess he was just standing there watching me and thinking, "Look at this goofy motherfucker, just standing there," because he could have killed me fifteen times. He had a big long bolt-action rifle.

Evidently I don't think the son of a bitch saw me. They was concentrating on the men on the trail. What they had was machine guns crossing the trail in ambush so they could catch our guys in a crossfire there.

As I shot I yelled, *"They're in there!"* and I jumped back into the bushes and somehow zipped across and got about four foot from that trail where it T'd.

Well, when it first started it was like sniper fire. And as Ditch and Doc came up the trail to help us, the machine guns opened up and cut them to pieces. I crawled back to where I entered and couldn't get back up because the fucking bushes were over your head. I'd been walking point and crawling through all that thick shit, so I had taken all the grenades out of my pockets. I wanted to crawl up to where the hole was—I figured I'd get back through there and knock a couple of bunkers out. But I didn't have no grenades. Then all of a sudden they opened up from the trees. I was still laying partially on the trail. Missed me? They shot my glasses off. They shot the magazine out from under my rifle. I had three holes in my shirt. Oh, God. If that wasn't the bad part, I went up there two more times. I was the only one lying up the trail and I was trying to fire. That's when they really started shooting. There was little bitty branches and shit on the ground and I was hearing *chink, chink,* and I swear to God, it got so fucking heavy, man, they hit the edge of my glasses and knocked them off. And a little bit later they shot the magazine out of my rifle. It didn't even explode, just *ping*-ed out. Ruined the magazine. I had to lay there 'cause of the sniper. The machine guns were snapping those branches on both sides of my head no more than an inch. And I kept wondering, "Wow, where's the other gun?" But it got so heavy with the snipers, they could see where I was. They were looking right down at me, right over my head.

I laid there and when the snipers quit, I jumped up. RRRRRRRRRAAAAAAAA. They got so goddamn close, hell, three or four times they blinded me. Man, bullets hit right in front of my face and dirt shot up under my glasses.

After about ten minutes of this, it got to where I had to play dead till the snipers stopped. I had to play dead, man, 'cause they would have been all over me. I'd get up and before I'd start shooting, I'd look back to see if I was bleeding, then open up on the motherfuckers. I'd get a magazine off, drop it, put another one in. I did it just for a little while. After they shot my glasses off, I said, "Fuck this shit, man, it's time to cut the retread on this deal." So I crawled back to where the others were, which was about five feet behind me. I decided this forward shit I was doing wasn't going to make it. Then I started to crawl back onto the trail so I could get up, and as I did, somebody said, "Ditch is hit." And I crawled back over to where the trail T'd. He'd fallen to the right. I looked over and said, "Ditch!" I was close enough to touch him. I said, "Are you hit?" and he looked up and just kind of turned over to me and said softly, "Yeah, I'm hit." And as he did he kind of raised up and pulled the medic bag out from under him. Man, it was just soaked in blood.

And he just closed his eyes and died. Right then. I never seen anybody die before that moment. "Yeah, I'm hit. And that was it.

And after that, man, I decided we had to get the fuck out of there, 'cause I wanted to get him out. And I knew Doc had been hit 'cause he wouldn't have let his bag . . . if he'd been alive Doc would have been with his bag and he would have been patching Ditch up.

So I kind of went berserk and stood up and tried to rip a fucking hole for my head. That didn't work 'cause I would have got it shot off. I got down and literally ripped shit out of the goddamned ground and made a tunnel, just like a burrow, and when I got through to where the tracks [armored personnel carriers] had pounded it down, I pulled all the rest of the guys out. We got that lieutenant out and I was going to start back in there to get Ditch. Before we could do it, this other kid got hit —I can't remember what his name was. They got him in the lower back or spine. By then, we were fucking wore out. Man, we had been fighting a long time. Me and Posdle ran up to the kid. I was going to pick him up and carry him out, and hell, we couldn't even lift him. We told him, "Shit, we know you're hit, man, but you're going to have to help us pick you up. We can't lift you." He wasn't that big and we were both pretty big, but we were just fucking wore out. I mean, it was hot and heavy.

The colonel pulled our platoon back. He pulled our company back, in fact. And they wanted to come back in new where they could come in on line, or try to come in on line. They never did get on line. So they pulled back, but I didn't pull back—because you don't leave people in there, man, that just wasn't our way. I didn't pull back. I crawled back up there, trying to get through. I couldn't even find the hole I crawled out of because it was trampled down so fast with tracks moving up in there.

Fullback pulled our company out while I was crawling around in the bushes. I had to find Ditch, I wasn't going to leave him there, because Ditch was the center pillar guy of the platoon. He was older than anybody else, he was 25 . . . he was a very good soldier, the best, and he was everybody's older brother. He was as good a man as I'd ever known. Bravo Company had come in—they were right behind us—but Charlie Company was pulled back and we loggered [camped] out here in the bushes. And when I came out and the second platoon wasn't there, man, it just fucking . . . Oh, man, I went berserk. I walked back and walked in that fucking logger. It was a pretty good ways; the whole battalion had pulled back, in fact, but Bravo Company was still in the bush, like a hundred meters away—far enough not to draw fire. And I crawled back out and couldn't find Ditch and didn't see 2nd Platoon. And I was a mad motherfucker, man. I wanted to get some people to go back up there with me, but of course they had orders not to. And then Angus from third platoon came over and said, "Come on, Mock, we ain't asking anybody, we'll go up there with you."

Angus, he didn't ask nobody, he just took the god-damn squad and we went back up there just as Bravo Company was fixing to go. So I told Bravo's CO, "Man, we've got two men up there and I'm going to get them." He says, "Well, do you know where they're at?" I said, "Yeah, I know where every goddamn thing is. I just got through leading this fucking point through here." He says, "Well, go ahead and take us in there again." They wouldn't let Angus go, so Angus and them stayed in a bomb crater over here, right up close to it. I led Bravo Company in and I got too far to the left. And when the gooks opened up again, they killed the first three men be-hind me. I fell down in the goddamn bushes again and I stayed in there about three hours that time, with Bravo Company coming up on line.

When I come out it was nearly sundown. I got over with Angus and them and we went back in there until about nine o'clock, looking for Ditch. We couldn't find him. Man, I had stayed in there all goddamn day and I couldn't find him. I looked for him that night. The jungle was just . . . Anyway, we found him the next day, but by the time I got back to the company they had put me down as missing in action. This is when I went in and told the colonel he was a sorry motherfucker.

I said, "I just want to tell you what I think about it. You should have told us that base camp was there. You made us walk right into the ambush. That's a sorry god-damn thing to do. You ain't worth shit as an officer."

Wasn't much he could say. Had he said something, it would have drawn attention to what he did. And I really think if a good superior officer had all the facts on what had gone down that day, it would've looked a lot worse on him.

Major Michael Andrews
Platoon Leader
Combined Reconnaissance
    and Intelligence Platoon
3rd Brigade, 25th Infantry
    Division
Dau Tieng
June 1968-June 1969

The CRIP Platoon

THE CRIP Platoon, which was entitled Combined Reconnaissance and Intelligence Platoon, was activated in 1968 for the purpose of bridging the reconnaissance gap between U.S. forces in our area of operations and various Vietnamese reconnaissance forces. It consisted, therefore, of U.S. soldiers who had reconnaissance experience and also a variety of Vietnamese soldiers. There were ARVN, or Republic of Vietnam army, soldiers that were transferred to us, *chieu hois,* or Kit Carson scouts, who were ex-North Vietnamese soldiers. There were some Provisional Reconnaissance Unit soldiers, which were somewhat elite in our province, and other Vietnamese soldiers. The idea was to form one unit and make a united reconnaissance effort.

I had been an infantry platoon leader for four months and then I was reconnaissance platoon leader for the battalion for a short period of time. When CRIP was established, it had a high priority for many reasons. I was pretty much given authority to pick and choose what people I wanted from the battalion, with the stipulation that a company should not be disrupted too much—it should

185

basically be from the battalion reconnaissance platoon. So, as I recall, over half the battalion reconnaissance platoon left with me, and they all were volunteers.

The base of the unit was mechanized infantry reconnaissance. We worked for the U.S. brigade commander and also reported to local MACV headquarters. Also, there were some civilian paid people with the organization, and there were reports that went to the PRUs in the nearest town. So it was, without a question, a coordinated effort, although any final lines of authority had to be with the U.S. brigade commander, who was commander over all. It presented some problems, however, because each component of the unit had its own reporting channel, and sometimes when the unit had success in finding something in an operation, there was some misunderstanding between the ARVNs and the PRU about who had the authority to take what was found. For example, I can recall one time when two VC finance liaison people were captured with a great deal of money on them and there was considerable discussion about whether the prisoners should go to the local MACV headquarters, the PRU headquarters or the U.S. brigade headquarters. The integration of the soldiers was interesting, and there were some problems training and equipping them. One of the biggest problems was simply that of training and explaining to all the various segments of the platoon what the mission was.

There were several instances of Vietnamese soldiers that simply didn't work out. In some cases I elected to send them back to their units. In a couple of cases the Vietnamese soldier simply decided that it wasn't the type of thing that he wanted to do. And the Kit Carsons, after a short period of time, took off in their own directions.

However, I think there was an awful lot of espirit in the unit for many reasons. One was that it was perceived to be a very elite unit. It was different. It was important. I think the soldiers perceived that and did a better job, their enthusiasm was a little higher. Because of the type of operations we had, we were very independent and therefore frequently not tied down with some of the parameters that not only U.S. forces but also Vietnamese forces had to contend with. We were very small and it was easier to keep on the move—to move two or three days and not sleep in the same place or, during an operation, to move very quickly. I think that speed is security. It was very evident in our type of unit. We were never mortared, for example. The only time anybody in the CRIP Platoon was ever mortared was when they went back to the Dau Tieng brigade base camp. We were never mortared when we were on our own.

Second, I think that the people in the platoon—the U.S. forces, anyway—had been through some reconnaissance operations in the battalion before and were cohesive, knew their jobs rather well; and the opportunity of working together day in and day out and being independent and constantly training made the unit tactically proficient and unusually so. There was a lot of teamwork. People knew what to expect from the other person, and without question, it was a good unit to be with for that reason.

Because the unit was small, you could get in and out real fast. For example, with an informer, we'd place a bag over his head, take him into a village, and he would point out what we wanted to find. We were in and out very quickly. It wouldn't take but thirty minutes. I think even had we been hit, we could have been out before we got tied down. This was evidenced by an instance where a whole regiment was headquartered in a village and we went in twice and got out with one casualty. A small unit can do things like that if it's well trained, can go in and come back out without being tied down, even if there are close enemy concentrations. But we were also very lucky.

I felt I'd been well prepared for the type of operations we went on, and I felt rather confident, or competent, in the operations. My initial impression of the average soldier was that he was not—The soldier who had been drafted in Colorado, I had the impression that he did not really know what he was up against, or why he was there in many cases, or what the organization and relationship between the Viet Cong and North Vietnamese regulars were.

In our particular area, unfortunately, the size of the regular American units made them very predictable. The advantage, of course, of a smaller unit with total flexibility is that it can be moving very quickly in and out of operations, can stay one night and then move out and be someplace else the next night. It's very difficult to get any sort of fix on an outfit like that.

The village we lived in was called Khiem Hanh. It was very close to a place called Xombo, about eight miles east of Cambodia. It basically was a military village, ARVNs and their families. It had a MACV compound in the back with a MACV major that worked out of there. Several times I was told to give reports to him, and I went in and gave him whatever we saw or found.

Even though there were heavy U.S. operations in this area for many years, most of the villages were still fairly sympathetic to the other side. It was a notorious area for VC sympathizers. A town called Trang Bang just south was especially notorious. We found out later that there were several major headquarters nearby and a series of very complicated underground tunnels. At the battle of Saigon in '75, the axis of advance out of Cambodia came right through there.

The idea was not to fix on a village for too long a period of time. We lived in that one place and other times we moved around and bivouacked in the countryside by ourselves, and I think that, without question, is the best way to go.

Our mission was twofold. Number one was to respond to anything we were given. Frequently we were given missions. I recall one time I was given an aerial photograph and information that VC tax collectors passed through this area about the first of each month and stayed in one of two huts. We were to wait for them the next time and see if we could pick them up. Which we did and brought them back.

Secondly, the objective was to cover the area as much as possible. We had a rather large area and we just constantly moved, every day, and so became experts in the area of operation and all facets thereof. The villagers were known, the people who ran the local restaurants and laundries were known and were integrated into that particular area of operations because the Vietnamese scouts, simply by staying in a village or eating in a restaurant or talking with people, very frequently found out things that were useful.

There were prolonged discussions with villagers as we began to know and talk to the people in more detail and length. As a battalion reconnaissance platoon leader and rifle platoon leader, I never talked in very much detail to the villagers. But when CRIP came into being I began to talk more and found out that there was considerable anxiety about VC rule and what would happen if the U.S. forces left, but there was a tremendous reluctance to be seen talking with U.S. forces or to be vocal about any kind of criticism against the VC. It was obvious that there was a VC infrastructure and their intelligence net was very effective. But with our Vietnamese platoon members operating independently, once we began talking with them informally and in prolonged discussions, this did surface. There was no doubt about it, there was a real fear. Basically it was being a servant of two masters, not being able to speak out against either without reprisal. A large segment of the population just wanted to be left alone and didn't want either side to have anything to do with them or to further disrupt their lives.

I think one of the things that the CRIP Platoon pointed out very early, long before it became widely known, was that the entire area northwest of Go Dau Ha was a honeycomb of tunnels. That was obvious from a couple of operations we had been on. People would disappear. Or there would be a very strong enemy force that would very simply vanish. They had gone underground.

Jonathan Polansky
Scout
101st Airborne Division
I Corps
November 1968-November
1969

Underground City

ONE time we were on the Laotian border and I wasn't
sure exactly where I was. I called in and asked for a
marker round so I could get my bearing. They shot the
marker round and it landed behind us, so I found myself
lost somewhere in Laos. I realized that we were pushing
more and more in because all our battalion-size movement
was moving further and further in, walking on the Ho Chi
Minh Trail, which was the most incredible thing. Underground hospitals of mammoth size, roads built with all
that red dirt, chains of mountains with two-lane roads
hacked out on the tops just going all the way down, big
complexes of tree houses. Absolutely incredible. You'd
never know that they were there until all of a sudden
you're standing in what appears to be civilization in the
middle of the jungle. Just dug right into the sides of
mountains, dug by hand, by shovel, by who knows what.

We went into one cavern. The tunnel alone was big
enough for trucks to go through underground. Thousands
of rooms full of American equipment—boots, fatigues,
cots, ponchos, helmets. They seemed to have more of our
supplies than we had back at Camp Eagle. We called

B-52s on the whole complex. It was right on the Laotian border. It seemed to be a final waylay station of pulling a unit down to the South. Most of the equipment probably came from the black market and pilfering from the bases. All new equipment. Better stuff than we had.

Thomas Bailey
Interrogation Officer
525th Military Intelligence
   Group
Saigon
January 1970–August 1971

The VC

I think you have to understand something about the general communist structure, or at least Asian communist structure. It's ruled by a committee and it's something that's quite alien to the American mind. I interrogated some prisoners very closely on this, because I couldn't believe that somebody wouldn't come to the head and start running things, that one individual wasn't basically controlling it. But they would have these echelon committee meetings that would make policy and decide how things were going to be done, and they would have the various members of the committee determine how things were going to be done together. I tried to get an idea who the chairman was or how things ran, but I don't like to use the term "consensus" because that's not one that was ever used. They just "struggled" it through. "Struggle groups" are something that comes down from Mao Tsetung.

The committee members would be composed of the people who had to make things run at that echelon, who were the senior persons of the staff—tax collecting, front groups, recruiting, performing the basic functions that make an infrastructure work. What do they need to work? They need money in the form of taxes or however they're going to get it, they need recruits. They used the traditional NLF [National Liberation Front] front groups. That's another misconception, that the NLF was some separate organization apart from the VC. In fact, there was no NLF separate and apart from the VC.

The NLF existed at two levels. At the national level, they had a NLF group that spoke in the sense of having a political voice that was supposed to be more neutralist. And it was eventually replaced by the People's Revolutionary Government in 1969, the PRG.

And then at the local level there were the NLF front groups, that is, the women's group, the farmer's group, whatever. These were organizations run by the communist low-level cadre as a means of getting people to join. And they would share community concerns. One of these concerns might be "Look, the Americans are dropping all this orange stuff out of the skies on us. It screws up the crops, makes our children sick and does terrible things." Or "Jesus Christ, that bomb killed my brother-in-law's family in Hamlet 3," or something like that. In that way, the more politically aware, the more politically active ones, could come out of it and be recruited into the VC infrastructure.

They would be assigned membership in the local committee. They'd be given some task and work their way up. Or they might go into the local forces, the hamlet guerrillas, and then if they showed expertise or if they received training, they might join the local forces—the local area company that usually would have some kind of specialized weapons squad. They were broken down into military regions, which are substantially larger than provinces. Before Tet '68, there was a Saigon military region that encompassed most of the area around Saigon all the way to Cambodia, and what happened was that their cadre was so decimated by Tet '68 that they broke down into subregions.

I was amazed because of the resourcefulness the VC and NVA showed in some areas. For example, at one point the NVA had areas where they had main-force units that would do operations and suddenly they'd drop out of sight. What we finally discovered was that they were evaporating into three- and four-man cells that would just ease into the hamlets and would serve as reinforcement and training, in terms of morale, for the local hamlet guerrillas. Then they'd get the word to re-form their unit. They'd do their operation and evaporate to nowhere again, out to the hamlets. That's pretty resourceful because you get to rely on the hamlets for food and supplies, so you don't have to go on foraging parties. They were resourceful like that.

Bruce Lawlor
Case Officer
Central Intelligence Agency
I Corps
November 1971-December
1973

A Strategy
of Terror

Basically the common villager, which is the bulk of the population, really did not want to have a war. They would not support the Americans, but in that respect they weren't supporting the NVA, either.

I don't think the average villager was politically sophisticated enough to realize the implications of VC rule. I got a lot of bitching from the villagers about having to attend VC indoctrination sessions. They hated the damn things. The poor guys had gone to work all day in the fields behind the water buffaloes and then they'd come in at night and the VC cadre would round them all up and they'd have to sit for three or four hours till ten or eleven o'clock at night listening to some guerrilla harangue them about the glories of communism and all the rest of it. And they used to hate that.

Why did they go along with it? I mean, if someone comes into your hootch at night with a gun, you go. I suppose it wasn't by gunpoint, but the guy who refused was likely to be taken out and eliminated at some point. And you only have to do that once. The VC had a strategy of terror that was excellent. I mean, if you're a purist and think that terror is a legitimate political weapon, it was an excellent strategy.

They used to undermine the credibility of the government and paralyze the population by selective assassination. Selective atrocities. District chiefs, village chiefs, pro GVN village chiefs. They'd only get the effective ones; if you were incompetent and a village chief, they probably would leave you alone because that was an asset to them. If you were corrupt and didn't do anything for your village and bugged the people and overtaxed the people, they probably would leave you alone. But if you were a hard-charging young idealist and really out to make this village motor, you probably were going to get waxed, and in a very unsavory way. Disembowelment, raping your wife and children in front of you, killing your baby. We saw them. We saw people with legs hacked off and guys with . . . Disemboweling seemed to be a big thing. Literally pull a guy's innards out of his stomach, they'd rip his stomach open. But the sad part of it is, he doesn't die right away. Women . . . You know, the sky's the limit. As gruesome as you can think of things to do, they would do. Schoolteachers were a favorite target, and unfortunately a lot of the schoolteachers were idealistic young women.

Robert Santos
Rifle Platoon Leader
101st Airborne Division
Hue
November 1967-November
1968

A Book of Poetry

WE overran an NVA base camp near Hue. We opened the rucksacks we captured for intelligence reasons. And we wanted to use them in place of the metal-framed garbage we wore because the NVA packs were light and comfortable. I opened this one pack, and enclosed were civilian clothes and a tube of Ipana toothpaste. They also had left behind big bags of rice donated by the people of the United States. That really pissed me off. I didn't have any toothpaste. I had to eat C-rations. I hadn't taken a fucking bath. And here the enemy is eating better than I am because the food is donated by the United States.

In the pack I opened up, besides a poncho and all the other crap, there was a box of pastels and a book of poetry, which was written in Japanese and English with Vietnamese handwriting on the inside. I kept it and after I got out of the service I showed the book to a Vietnamese teacher I had in college. I told him where I got it and asked what the inscription was. He said the person who owned it had been a student in Japan and apparently had picked up the book of poetry and written a love message to his girlfriend in Hanoi. He was in the North Vietnam-

ese Army in Hue and was planning to go home and give
her the little book of poetry and the pastels. I still have
them. And the other day I was thinking, you know, maybe I'm waiting to run into that guy and say, "Man, I'm
glad you're alive. Because I kept this for you."

Thomas Bailey
Interrogation Officer
525th Military Intelligence
  Group
Saigon
January -1970-August 1971

Bruce Lawlor
Case Officer
Central Intelligence Agency
I Corps
November 1971-December
  1973

The Phoenix

THOMAS BAILEY: The Phoenix Program was an assassination program designed, as I understand it, to pick out VC cadre at given echleons and nail them. And in this way debilitate the organization. In fact, our Phoenix Program had an old-style computer from Rand Corporation that picked which member of the various local committees you should nail.

BRUCE LAWLOR: If we were going to win the war, what we had to do was get in and eliminate the ability of the VC to control or influence the people. That's what pacification was all about. The buzzword was "root out." We tried to go in and neutralize their political structure.

There were three programs: (1) Census Grievance, (2) RD Cadre and (3) Phoenix. My opinion of the programs is that they were thought of by geniuses and implemented by idiots.

The Census Grievance Program was designed not only to take the census of the population—nobody knew what the hell we were dealing with over there in terms of numbers—but to actually find out what the problems were. It was based on the idea that if the government could see that a group of farmers or a commune or whatever was constantly being harassed by the VC for taxes, rice taxes, levies, if we could identify that problem and if the government could demonstrate its ability to protect those farmers from further levies, then we could've won those people. And that was the purpose of the Census Grievance. Then the RD Cadre, Rural Development Cadre, would come in.

If the problem of a village was lack of sanitation, lack of adequate drinking water, lack of bridges or whatever it was, the RD Cadre could go in, and it would be Vietnamese helping other Vietnamese to build the village back. We'd win the people over that way.

If we found a VC—a tax collector, a civilian-proselytizing cadre, finance cadre, district cadre, whatever—within a given village, then we could use the third phase, the Phoenix Program, to hopefully arrest the guy and talk to him and find out where the other persons in his particular cell were, and in that way root out that structure.

The problem with the thing was it completely fell apart. It never did what it was supposed to do. We permitted the Vietnamese to corrupt the system and we did it because we basically were corrupt ourselves.

It was an extermination program as well. I mean, there's no sense in trying to make a rose out of whatever. The objective of the program was to eliminate VC influence in the village, and each person, I guess, had objectives that they pursued in running or administering their portion of it. My objective was to bring them in and talk to them. It did me no good whatsoever not to talk to these people. Some people felt that the body count was important, and that's what led to the problems. The program, frankly, got used to settle old scores.

I think it was 1968, '69, there was a big stink about it here in the States. The Green Berets were sort of attached to the Agency, and they tried to run this paramilitary-type thing, which created real problems because what the Special Forces were doing was tell their American military commanders, "We can't do this because the Agency doesn't want us to." And then if they didn't want to do something else, they'd tell the Agency, "We can't do this because our military commanders won't let us."

They were playing both sides off against each other to do what they wanted to do. And that created some problems in the system. Eventually they were phased out of the program; that's why they were phased out. I don't know if you'd call it politics. There was a real problem there. The American military wasn't happy, the Agency wasn't happy, and they said, "All right, it's got to be one way or the other." When you say politics, I guess you're talking about press reports here in the United States. That was a factor in shutting down the whole program. But you've got to take it in stages—the Green Berets exit stage left and then the whole program exits stage right because of the political implications of it over here.

Although at the beginning, the outset of the war, the Green Berets were a symbol of counterinsurgency and they were excellent. What happened was that they—Barry Sadler was the worst thing that ever happened to them. He came out with this song and all of a sudden the Green Berets no more were an elite small unit. They got all kinds of cowboys in there, and the cowboys wanted to go out and shoot and kick down doors and beat up people. That's not the way to run a counter-guerrilla outfit. You don't win any friends by going into a village and ripping the place to shreds. The essence of a guerrilla war is to control the population, and I think we found out, we should've found out, that you can't control a population unless you can either subdue them completely militarily —which we could've done, but our political system wouldn't let us, which is good—or win their support.

The Special Forces became overpopulated with cow-

boys. You just had to look at the statistics as to how that
organization grew and how the requirements for entrance
changed. They suddenly dropped the cross-training and
they suddenly dropped the requirement for languages.
And pretty soon they started mass-producing them because everybody wanted to wear a green beanie. And you
get that caliber of person into a very hostile situation that
requires a certain degree of sophistication—they didn't
have it. It caused problems. And I think that's the demise
of the Special Forces, to get some idiots going out and
shooting people in boats. I think it was because they had
some concept of that's the way it was done. They watched
too many John Wayne movies. It just wasn't that way.

The Green-Faced
Frogmen

SEAL was an acronym standing for Sea, Air, Land guerrilla warfare. It was started around 1962 by John Kennedy. Kennedy had sort of a romance with the Ian Fleming 007 character, and that gave birth to a couple of special units. One was the Green Berets, and out of that they decided to come up with a unit called the SEAL teams, the Black Berets. The SEAL teams were the guerrilla-warfare operatives for the Navy, and their responsibilities were something like ten miles of any waterway. So if you look at Vietnam, ten miles of any waterway is a very considerable area, like most of the country. And they were responsible for conducting guerrilla activities within that zone.

My team was originally assigned to a barge floating in the middle of the Mekong. That was for security reasons, as we were about a half mile from either shore. We worked with the Provincial Reconnaissance Units, the PRUs, on the Phoenix Program in the Ben Tre and My Tho areas. The Provincial Recon Units were made up by and large of guys who were doing jail time for murder, rape, theft, assault in Vietnam. The CIA would bail them out of jail under the conditions that they would work in

203

these mercenary units. And we, the SEAL teams, but primarily the CIA, would give them a certain bounty for weapons they would bring in, sometimes ears, depending on what the target was. If they were to assassinate a certain individual, they would have to bring back evidence that the person had been killed. Sometimes that consisted of ears or whatever. Going after weapons became kind of a comedy. One time a South Vietnamese armory was sort of assaulted. The PRUs snuck in and took out a bunch of weapons and sold them back to the CIA. And of course the CIA said, "That was very good to get the weapons, but you got them from the wrong side."

Sometimes we'd go out with a whole pack of mercenaries. They were very good going in, but once we got there and made our target, they would completely pillage the area, which created a lot of ruckus. They would rob everything. It was a complete carnival going back, so we would try to get way ahead of them so they could have their little carnival and if they got ambushed they'd have to deal with it.

At that time the PRU adviser I was working with was a SEAL who subsequently was killed. He was one of the original SEALs, and that's who they had usually working directly with the PRUs. They would bring us in for backup support on specific missions, like one time we were going to knock out a Viet Cong weapons factory.

The other kinds of missions we went on were more with our team. Our team was fifteen SEALs, but we would usually break into groups of seven. Assigned to us were LD&Ns, basically SEAL-trained Vietnamese. I would usually scout with a Vietnamese person. Those kinds of targets consisted sometimes of ambushes. I can remember ambushing a lot of tax collectors. After they made all the collections, you'd hit them in the morning and rob them of all the money and, of course, kill them. And then report that all the money was destroyed in the fire fight. They'd carry a thousand dollars at a time. So we'd have quite a party.

We were really deep in the Delta. The terrain was heavy—heavy vegetation. Some of the places would be well irrigated, so we'd use all the irrigation ditches to move through. We'd never be moving on the land, just the irrigation ditches, in water about up to your chest. We would just wade through the water. That became not a bad place to be because it was quiet for movement, you could relieve yourself very easily as you walked along, if you got shot at you had water surrounding you and that tends to slow a bullet down. I don't think a bullet will travel much more than six feet from the time it hits the surface of the water. You could duck underwater and hide.

The Phoenix Program was a very carefully designed program to disrupt the infrastructure of the Viet Cong village systems. And apparently on some occasions the plan was to come in and assassinate a village chief and make it look like the Viet Cong did it. It was a really difficult program for me because I didn't totally understand it when I was in Vietnam. I was just a scout, and my responsibility was to scout in and get us to a village, get us to a particular spot, go in there and get the person out that we wanted, and then they would be handled. It was my understanding that these people were wanted for questioning, that they were high-level Viet Cong. What I have come to understand since then, and what I really feel was going on at the time, was that we were just going in there to make it look like the Viet Cong came through and killed this person. Now, understand that we are going into areas that have not been touched by Americans. They were Viet Cong strongholds.

There were booby traps all over the place. I was barefoot. We didn't want to make any boot prints. We were walking along barefoot, and Americans don't go into jungles barefoot. I had no identification on me except for a morphine syringe around my neck. If I was hit, I'd shoot morphine. My number was 50, it was on all my clothes. My face was completely painted out black. Often I would wear a black pajama top. I learned how to walk like a Viet Cong, move like a Viet Cong, think like a Viet Cong.

I'm a tall person. I had to learn how to walk small and slump over. There's a certain way you walk through the jungle when you're comfortable with it and I got very comfortable in that style of walking. It's more of an experience . . . it's like a cat who walks and knows where he's going and what he's doing. Most Americans didn't know where they were going or what they were doing in Vietnam. They were kind of tromping around out there. I was moving slowly, hesitating, blending in with my environment, moving up to a structure, getting close to it, trying to blend in all the time. I had, on one occasion, a Viet Cong call to me and talk to me. That's how good I was at moving in this fashion. That was the only way I was going to survive out there, to look and be like a Viet Cong.

We would walk in, and we wouldn't be carrying American-made weapons, either. There were no silhouettes on us that made us look like Americans. At a glimpse we looked like we were a group of men with some guns. Once again, the whole idea was to blend in like the Viet Cong, and at that time I was totally tuned to filling that role. Since I was the scout, I had to look more like a Viet Cong than anybody else.

I was the main point man for that unit. We carried a heavy-equipment person with us, carried an M-60 machine gun fully loaded, ready to knock through trees. We were prepared to hit anything. We hit regimental point units sometimes, just five of us. We were prepared to make contact with anything.

We'd be dropped off in an area that was probably pretty dangerous, in about four or five miles, and we patrolled two or three miles. Sometimes it would take an hour to go one hundred yards, the jungle was that thick. We'd have to crawl underneath it all. We were in there pretty deep. Once again, there were no front lines, but we were in an area that was very, very dangerous. Consequently, we had complete air support. When we were out on certain missions, the pilots had to be in their planes on our frequencies. We would scramble them that quickly. So it was, by military standards, very, very high-level missions we were going on.

On the Phoenix Program, we would go in . . . I had flown over the area the day before in a helicopter, so I knew exactly what it looked like in the daytime, and I'd translate that in my mind at nighttime. Usually I was the only one who knew where we were. Everybody had other specialties. The radioperson's specialty was a whole set of frequencies he had to deal with. The officer's specialty was to execute some of the orders. The medic had another specialty. Each person was an incredibly skilled technician.

I had to be totally tuned up. We were doing Dexedrine. When we'd go out on a mission, we'd take a whole handful of pills, and some of those were Dexedrine. When I hit Dexedrine I'd just turn into a pair of eyeballs and ears. That's probably why I don't remember too many of the details real well, because it was just like I was on a speed trip the whole time I was in the field. When I came in, the crash would be so hard it would totally wipe out anything I'd been through, and I'm sure that works when you need people to go out and do the kinds of things that we were doing, because it would be very hard to debrief us if we were ever wounded or captured. We had the morphine around our neck and we could shoot up immediately, which would make us incoherent for twenty-four hours at least, enough time to shift all the plans around that were predicated on that particular mission.

So when we would go in, I'd be barefoot, I would move up to a hootch. This is maybe during a real stormy night; they're not expecting Americans to be out there in the middle of a storm, they're not expecting them to come walking in at two o'clock in the morning in the middle of a Viet Cong stronghold. A stronghold is a village where they felt really secure. We would go into the hootch. I'd step in and I'd stand there and listen to everybody breathe. If I noticed any change in the breathing patterns of the people sleeping, then I was immediately on alert. I carried with me, more often than not, a duckbill shotgun. A duckbill throws your four-buck [buckshot] at a horizontal; you get a nice wide spray if you have to open fire. God. It was really intense, because you had a whole family sleeping in this one room and you're standing in the middle of them all.

What I would do is, around my head I wore a triangular green bandage. I'd take it off and tie it into a knot in the center and walk over to the bed—I knew exactly what bed this guy was sleeping in. I had a Navy K-bar knife, which is one of the best knives you can get. The blade is about seven or nine inches long, razor-sharp— you could shave with it. I would go over to the person and I would hold their nose shut so they'd take a breath with their mouth and I'd take this rag, which had a couple of knots in the middle of it, and cram it down their throat so it would get down to their larynx, at the same time bringing that knife up under their neck, so that if they moved at all they would be cutting their own throat.

So the person would obviously freeze. With that motion, I would take the gag, grab it from behind their head, the knife under the throat, and literally pick them up just by the head. They were small people, usually sleeping in their black pajamas, and I'd just pick them up and carry them out. Now, if anybody moved in the hootch, the other scout with me, who's Vietnamese, would start talking to them very quietly. He'd have them all lay down on the ground, face down. By then I'd have the person outside. I'd have his elbows secured behind his back. I would pass him to the prisoner-handler. All this time no words are spoken. We were incredibly well rehearsed. This has all taken about a minute, maybe a minute and a half. We would go back inside. The scout would then instruct these people that if they make a move, there's going to be a person at the door that will completely blow them away. Our little group would pull back. We'd only have five or six people and we were dispersed to cover ourselves. We would pull back and start to move for our exit. I would usually sit by the hootch for about five minutes and listen and, while I was doing that, hook a grenade on the door, flatten the pin and run a fishing line across the door so if anybody opened it up, they would drop the grenade and of course they would be killed.

I would sit by the doorway there and be very, very quiet and let them start mustering a bit, then I'd make a little noise outside so that they knew I was there. Once I did that, I'd leave and haul ass back to the unit to scout on the way back. If anybody came out, we could hear the grenade for about a mile if it went off. And these are like families, little kids and stuff. So it was something you just didn't think about. You just did it. It was that second you had to cover.

We did one mission, God, we spent half the night in a pigsty. We got into the area around one o'clock in the morning and climbed into a pigsty, a feeding area, and buried ourselves beneath all the manure and straw. We were looking through the wall. It was like a barn. There were little tiny cracks. We were waiting for our target to come in the marketplace, a tax collector who collected during market time, about eight o'clock in the morning. It was a sizable little village for Vietnam—must have been twenty hootches with a center courtyard—and he came into the area. I'll never forget that. He came walking into the area after we'd been sitting there all that time, and we just jumped up and knocked the entire wall down as we came out shooting. We just blasted everything, bodies were flying around. I just started running for the guy we wanted. It was my job to search him completely. I picked up an arm that had been blown across the courtyard and searched the sleeve. I had to search all parts of the body. The body would be strewn all over the place, kicking and squirming and puking, eyeballs rolling around . . . It was like picking through a broken car . . . It wasn't like a human body any longer.

What blows me away is that my father is a meat-cutter. I couldn't stand the sight of blood as a kid and I still can't. And I can't stand the feeling of pain, either, for myself or somebody else. What's incredible is that I was able to do that so quickly, without hesitation and so calmly. I just did it. I don't think I made a habit of shooting people unnecessarily, but at the same time my fear level was so high that if it meant me being afraid or them being dead, usually the person was dead.

On another mission we went out and we didn't do any face paint—we were getting tired of that; we'd been out for about five months and that was considered to be quite an accomplishment for a SEAL team to be intact that long—and we made contact as soon as we came in. A fellow came walking down the road—I guess this is around midnight—and he has a lantern. If he'd have come over any further he'd have seen our footprints coming from the river. So we opened up on him, since we couldn't afford to have anybody see us. It looked like he had a rifle sling on, and he did. The rifle sling was connected to a little basket. He was out plucking minnows. So we blew him away, and I went over to grab him and drag him into an irrigation ditch and sink the body—we didn't want to leave any bodies around—and I'll never forget, when I went to grab him I searched the front of him, and I flipped him over to search the back and he just opened up like a hamburger. I just took all the pieces and stuff and scooped it into the water—I was in the water by then —and I was scooping this all over me, and he was sinking . . . I couldn't . . . Usually I would stab him in a lung to sink him, which would fill the lungs with water and that weight would keep him underwater.

We patrolled in further and we noticed as we were walking along that behind us about another hundred yards somebody was following us. We could hear the brush moving. So we zig-zagged back through the canals, which ran in all directions. We had another three hours before our pickup boat came at sunrise. So we kind of laid out there by a real wide-open palm grove. Palms are so high they block out all the light along the ground. It's usually real flat, so it's like a playground, and we were just lying there.

The people who had followed us started shooting in the direction that we were lying. It's incredibly frightening to be lying there and to know that somebody knows you're there and they're shooting at you. What they were attempting to do was get us to shoot back so they could identify your position. There were sixteen of them. And they had the perfect advantage over us because we had no cover at all. But we didn't shoot back and they were shooting all around me. Finally we heard them say, "The assholes have left." They thought we had pulled out and gotten our boat and split.

We were digging holes in the ground with the buttons on our shirts, we were so goddamned scared, and we couldn't move. As soon as you move in that position, they can see the shadow of your movement. So our only hope was to make ourselves look like a pile of logs. So we became a pile of logs. It's incredible to explain what you can become, the illusion that you can present to people. You can become a bush, a log, if you just concentrate hard enough on being that. They told us in our training that you could become a master of illusion if you believe enough in the illusion. And it works. I couldn't believe it. Also the power of your eyes, not to look directly at something but to look off to the side of it. You wouldn't concentrate your focus because if you look at something too long, it'll look back at you, and you don't want them to turn around and see you there.

A lot of times we would sit in a bush as close as two or three feet from a trail and watch people walk back and forth for hours until somebody came along with a gun, and then we'd grab them, just reach right out of the bush and grab them by the ankles. This is like you're walking by a bush that you've seen every day in your life, and all of a sudden there's somebody in that bush that reaches out and grabs you. The level of concentration and commitment was just incredible.

Well, on this particular mission they were shooting at us and I had my finger on the trigger and I could feel the bullets rolling out the barrel. I was ready to open up. They figured that we had left. They came around to our right side and lit up a bunch of torches. I could hear women screaming and crying. Apparently they were looking for the guy that we had shot earlier in the night, about four hours before. His wife was out there howling. His family. And they were going to search the area.

So they started coming . . . walking shoulder to shoulder, perpendicular to the way we were lying. We were lying facing one direction and they were walking up on our side. We had no way to turn and shoot at them. They walked up really close, with these lamps . . . We couldn't even look at them. We had to roll our eyes the other way and let them see our hair, as our hair, of course, was darker than our face was. You have to concentrate on whether or not they're seeing you. This kind of intensity, like it's the last second of your life. They came right up on us. I'll never forget how quickly . . . We were all so well tuned to one another, we shifted our positions, opened fire, and I'll never forget seeing all those bodies flying in the air. They were just arching as we hit them with our weapons.

The machine gun opened up and the M-16 and the shotgun, just blowing them away, and the lights were going with them and lit the whole place up. Our instinct was, as soon as we hit we ran forward, we ran right up on them, pursuing them like a dog pursues something—even though you might lose, you still pursue it to throw them off balance. I'll never forget coming up on a guy—his whole face was blown away. He looked like a bowl of spaghetti. His eyeballs were just sitting there, and one of the guys behind me picked an eyeball up and put it in his pocket. I just thought, "Wow, what the hell is going on in this madness?" It was just insane. Just incredible.

Usually when we'd leave we'd get pulled out around sunrise. Our boat would come pick us up and they'd have a lot of beer. I'd climb in, down a couple of beers, and I'd take a rope and jump off the boat and drag behind it in the water back to wherever our base was—sometimes it was a villa and sometimes it was a barge—clean my weapon, drink some more beer, go to bed and sleep all day long and maybe get up around three and get drunk.

And of course, the off times are just as insane as the on-duty times. We'd get in fights, and blow things up, blow Army bases up. We didn't make much distinction about who the enemy was. It was just . . . All you were supposed to do over there was be crazy . . . so we were crazy. It wasn't something that we turned on and off, at least not for me. I was insane the entire time I was in Vietnam. I went out and sold every truck I could get my hands on. My position was "Hey, if you don't like what I'm doing, then put me in jail. It's a lot safer than being out in the field." I'd create quite a bit of havoc, and they would say, 'SEALs are supposed to be crazy. Leave him alone. He's going to die tomorrow." And I think our other attitude was "If you fuck with us, we'll blow you away."

Hell, we're killing people out in the field that I had no bad feeling about at all, so if you're back at an Army area or whatever, and those guys aren't going out in the field as much as you under that kind of exposure, and you can handle whatever comes down, you're not going to put up with shit from anybody. And that was the position we took. They'd really have a problem with us back in the base areas. In fact, even when we got back to the United States they were going to lock us all up in a bunch of big boxes, what they called connex boxes. They said, "We don't know what to do with you guys. You're taking on the Imperial Beach Police Department. You're beating up Hell's Angels. You're doing all this crazy stuff, jumping off piers and insane things."

My particular unit had the least casualties and the heaviest missions, and I take personal credit for getting back a lot of folks 'cause I was scout. As a matter of fact, about a third of the guys that were in my unit are still in. They go out on secret operations. And it's only conjecture, but I know enough about the way that group works and I was in Guatemala this summer and I was noticing how their guerrillas work down there. The SEALs go into areas like Central American and Latin American countries and do the training for right-wing guerrilla-warfare units or terrorist units. I have to conclude that all of that in Vietnam was an advanced boot camp to train operatives for other kinds of terrorist activities that the United States runs all over the world. Usually after guys went on a tour in Vietnam, it was like they proved themselves, and then they would be approached to do more secret kinds of war, individually or in pairs. And that was more common than unusual.

The CIA would orchestrate a lot of the missions. They would identify targets for us. Sometimes they'd go with us. I found them to be a bunch of incompetent drunks, myself. I didn't prefer to go in the field with them because they were too noisy. We would go into a CIA bar. The CIA bar usually had white American women there. That was a big deal. The women worked as staff for AID. The Phoenix Program had three levels: one was AID, Agency for International Development; one was CORDS, Civil Operations and Rural Development Support; and one was USIS, U.S. Information Service, for propaganda.

We sometimes posed as RNK workers. Basically it was a construction company doing work for CORDS, so we were civilians. In fact, when I went into the Binh Thuy hospital—I got hit in the arm—saying I was a member of RNK, and since I didn't have any identification and I had a beard at the time, they assumed that I wasn't a regular Army guy.

God, being in the hospital was so weird, so bizarre. There were guys that were just . . . This is Binh Thuy Naval Hospital. I had been hit in the left arm by one of our own guys. We were doing a daytime mission, apparently because the Navy had gotten interested in our particular unit, since we had gone out on all these missions

and the CIA had written all these flowery reports about
how efficient we were and what good guerrillas, so they
wanted us to go out in the daytime to take pictures of us.
You can't take pictures at night. So we had to go on some
daytime operations, which I protested. I said, "Look,
I'm not trained to scout in the daytime, I'm trained to
scout at night." I was much, much happier to be out at
night than in the daytime. So we went in the daytime, out
on what I call a cowboy operation—it was basically
staged to make us look good. But it was still a hot area,
very hot.

We flew into this place in the U Minh Forest on the
southern tip. Our intelligence said there were twenty-five
POW camps with South Vietnamese and American prisoners in them. The area we flew into was heavily defoliated and they were flying a Viet Cong flag in the middle
of the day. We were broken into three-man teams and we
were just going to search through each of the hootches.
The first hootch I stepped in had a wood carving of Ho
Chi Minh on the wall, so I thought, "Oh, Jesus, these
people are really committed if they have this kind of
paraphernalia around in the middle of the day." They
also had a lot of bunkers, so what we would do is, before
we got to a hootch we would fire a 40-millimeter grenade
from a little tube that fits underneath an M-16 so it could
also be a grenade launcher. Our radio guy had that. I had
a Vietnamese with me; we would fire into a hootch and
then go in and search it. We knew they were in their
bunker, so after firing we'd go in and search the place
and set it on fire and move to the next hootch.

The problem was, I was so tuned to blending in that I
just stood there and blended into one of the hootches and
told the guy to fire and he fired into the one that I was
standing next to. Usually when you fire a grenade into
something that close, you're dead. But because it hit below the dirt embankment around the hootch, what hit me
was the blast and a lot of dirt. It blew me about ten or
fifteen feet. I got shrapnel in my left arm. I just happened
to be holding up my gun; if it had been down, I would
have gotten it right in the lungs. The guy ran back and
said, "Oh"—I mean, we were really close; all the people
I was working with were very, very close—and he said,

"Oh God, Mike. Do you want morphine?" I said, "No. Hey, look at me. You've done enough damage." And the officer came running over and said, "Can you get us out of here?" And I said, "You're goddamn right I can get us out of here," because I knew which way to patrol. I was really pissed off because I didn't want to go in there in the daytime. So finally they said, "We'll medevac you out." They medevacked me to Binh Thuy, and in Binh Thuy I felt kind of embarrassed because I had this small shrapnel wound in my arm and here were all these guys sewn up like Thanksgiving turkeys. This was around Christmas time in '68. I mean, these guys were all wired together.

So here I'm a Navy SEAL passing myself off as a civilian construction worker because I didn't want to hassle with the military bullshit in the hospital. I had on tiger-stripe pants and kind of a weird outfit when I came in, so they didn't know who the hell I was. They patched me up, and I'll never forget, they were showing movies there and giving guys two cans of beer to take to the movies. These guys couldn't even walk or stand up, let alone drink beer, so I went around picking up all the beers from everybody, stuffing them into the sling on my arm and getting incredibly drunk. The doctors and nurses had these little boogie tents; they'd go out there and be dancing and drinking and carrying on. Most of the guys who were in combat couldn't go in there. Screw it. I just had on my pajamas from the hospital. I walked in there drunk, with my beard, and said, "Let's dance."

They wanted to keep me in there for a couple of weeks, but I got tired of it and went over to the warehouse where they were disposing all the old uniforms, found my old one, put it on and left.

I went into Can Tho and stayed with a friend of mine who'd been assigned as an adviser to the CIA. They were living over a whorehouse, the idea being that the Viet Cong wouldn't come in and blow it up because that's their place for recreation as well as ours. So we were living there and we'd go into a bar and drink because it was cheaper there. And it was at that time that we got into a fight with some people from the Army. It wound up that we actually tore down the building ourselves in the course

of this fight, and we also attacked and mauled pretty
badly another SEAL team. I guess they came running
down to help, and in the dark I didn't know what unit
they were—they were just more Army guys coming—so I
hid around the corner, and when they came by I jumped
out and ambushed them just like I would have any Viet
Cong. And all this time my arm was wrapped and it was
bleeding, so people would hesitate when they saw I had a
bad wound there, and at that point of hesitation I would
jump into them. So it was pretty wild. It was like Dodge
City.

We were living for a while at Sadec, which was like the
Viet Cong R & R center. There weren't very many Americans there, so the VC would come into the area to kick
back. We'd just walk around with civilian clothes on,
happy as can be and living in a villa, maybe put a gun in
our pocket, but it was no big deal. Since we looked so
scrungy, they figured we were construction workers and
that's what we told everybody. Sometimes we'd tell them
we were a USO show. We had a boat and sometimes
we'd ride through the middle of town—there was a river
—and we'd ride through naked. Not that we were really
drunk or anything; that's just how we spent our off time,
sunning and stuff.

One of the things that really impressed me over there
in the SEAL team unit was the complete lack of respect I
had, and other people had, for the officers. The officers
were people we just carried along with us. The officers in
my unit were these really gung-ho kind of buffos. These
guys were all tops in their classes out of colleges and uni-
versities, and here I didn't even go to college and I
thought people in college were bright and they were gung
ho, and here I am a scout and I'm thinking, "Wait a minute, man, I've been around a while. I've grown up and
I've been in fights and I'm not going out there and get in
a fight for your lust." So a lot of times in the field a number of agreements were made.

"I'll never forget, on my first mission I went out into an
area that was apparently very secure, but I was scared to
death. I walked into a hootch and there was this poor old
couple there. We had one officer breaking in the new officer in our unit, and he told me to take this person out-

side and finish him off. Here we were questioning them and the old couple was crying and shaking. I said, "What?" And they said, "You know, go take care of him." So I took him outside and I knew what they meant, but instead I bound and gagged him and gave him to the prisoner-handler, another new guy. I felt really good, like I really showed these assholes I'm not going to kill anybody. If I get my hands on them, there's no point in killing them. We're here to collect intelligence. That's what I thought: "We're here to collect people and get some information from them. We're not here to butcher people."

It was like coming into somebody's home at nine o'clock at night and they've got their little Sony TV on and they're totally terrified. Well, they wanted to break me in. They wanted me to "get wet." It's called "getting wet," cutting somebody's throat with your knife so the blood would go all over you so you would then be . . . It was a ritual. And I figured, "Bullshit." But I couldn't tell the officer "Bullshit" out there in the field, so instead I took the guy outside, tied him up and felt really good about it.

They came out, it's dark, and they said, "Did you take care of him?" I said, "Yeah. Everything's cool." So they said, "Get us out of here." Our patrol scattered back out to the river, and when I got back to the water, my job was to wait until everybody was back on and then I'd jump on the last boat. I remember the guy getting on toward the end. He handed me my bandanna, which I had stuffed down the prisoner's throat, but it was all dewy and wet. Of course there would be a lot of saliva, so I put it in my pocket. I jumped on the boat and we're going back up and I noticed we're missing some people. So I said, "Hey, where's the guy that I brought out?" And he says, "Hell, I knifed him, man." And I realized . . . I looked at my bandanna and I realized it was all covered with blood, and I puked and I wanted to cry and . . . I just couldn't do any of that . . . and I went back just totally blown away at what happened to this poor person, and at that point I decided—it was my first mission—that this was a bunch of shit.

We had Rand Corporation people with us. Rand would get this information and do extrapolations on it. It was called perturbation research, perturbation meaning if you go into one village and disrupt the infrastructure of that village and assassinate the village chief and make it look like the Viet Cong did it, then that'll have ramifications throughout the system. And that will break down the entire Viet Cong system in that area—which was bullshit because it doesn't work that way. The Viet Cong did not organize in hierarchies.

If you organize in a big hierarchy and have one king at the top and you wipe out the king, that is going to disrupt the leadership. On the other hand, if you organize in small guerrilla units, you'd have to wipe out every single leader. Plus if you organize in small units, you have communication across units and everybody can assume the leadership. You know all the techniques of the other units and you know that your work penetrated. It is my feeling that later on we were hitting people that the Viet Cong wanted us to hit, because they could feed information through us and other intelligence sources to the CIA and set up a target that maybe wasn't a Viet Cong but some person they wanted wiped out, might have even been a South Vietnamese leader. I didn't understand Vietnamese. The guy could've said he was President for all I knew. He wasn't talking with me. I had a knife on him. So it was just absolute chaos out there. Here we are, their top unit. It was absolutely insane.

A total lack of respect for all officers permeated all relationships. On occasion we'd be called by Marine officers, commandants, whatever, and they'd want to have some big prestigious infiltration thing go on before they'd do their move in a certain area, and we'd just tell them all to go to hell. All the time. Absolutely no respect at all.

Colonels would come into the CIA bar and drink with the CIA people, and we'd be there. One of the things we'd always do is check and see if they had any underwear on. It was a standard thing. Guys on frogmen teams didn't wear underwear. If they had underwear on, we'd rip it off them. With them in it. Lieutenant colonels, colonels, captains—we'd rip it right off them. And there wasn't a goddamn thing they could do, because we were laughing. We'd rip it off and then we'd hang it on the fan. We always had fans in the bars. Their underwear would be blowing. They couldn't do a goddamn thing. And that just reinforced in us the fact that we weren't putting up with shit from anybody. That was our position. So for me, I was more at war with the officers there than I was with the Viet Cong.

The Viet Cong was somebody that I avoided as much as possible, and the officers were somebody that I really kept my eye on because I was certain that they were going to get us killed. It's like being between two hammers that are pounding on one another and you're just there in the middle for no reason.

They finally moved us onto another troop carrier. There were fifteen of us living on a ship that carried three thousand men. We played hide-and-seek on our off time all the time. We'd have these ongoing tag games where you'd lock off the different sectors and compartments, turn off all the lights and climb up the pipes and scream. It was totally insane. Or sit down on our off time and watch *Mary Poppins* seven times in one sitting.

We were totally in tune. We were writing really nice letters home and a lot of us were artists and poets and singers. We could pull off a USO show when we had to. It was that kind of a group of people.

It was a business, and the business was terrorism. Terrorism in my mind is almost a perfect science. And it was approached that way. Each impact that you had in that area had to be interpreted in terms of its terrorist potential, terrifying the people and terrifying the flow of information there and the flow of confidence. We were looking for the maximum impact of that experience.

Absolutely, completely throw them off. Us being in there barefoot, they didn't hear us, they didn't hear any helicopters, they'd come up and the guy is dead. Sometimes we'd paint green on their face, which would mean the green-faced frogmen were in there. We'd go back and read intelligence reports and see that the people were really afraid that the green-faced frogmen were lurking, since they'd never hear us. They didn't hear us come in and they didn't hear us leave.

The green-faced frogmen were the SEAL team guys. In painting somebody green, the body would be dismembered, like an ear would be missing, or sometimes a thing that I don't think our unit ever did but the PRUs would do would be to cut the liver out and take a bite out of it, and that would symbolize that the person would not go into Buddha heaven intact. Not only had you died very violently and horribly, but you wouldn't even be able to enter nirvana intact, and that impact was just incredible. Finding a loved one with a green face and stabbed—in the middle of the road—was incredible terror.

George Lawrence
Helicopter Pilot
717th Air Cavalry
Pleiku
Summer 1971-Summer 1972

Dalat

DALAT was a city built by the French in the highlands between Pleiku and Saigon. We flew to Saigon occasionally for various and sundry reasons and we would always visit Dalat.

When you got to Dalat, you would see ranch-style homes with swimming pools out back that were built by the French before the war. There was a lake in the middle of town with boats that you pedaled with your feet. We'd always land there because of a restaurant that was run by some nuns.

The head nun was French and the rest were Vietnamese, but they all spoke French. You'd go in your combat clothing into this little convent and they would have nice French music playing, real good French food and French wine, and if you could talk them into doing it, all the nuns would come out and sing a song in French with a guitar.

The difference—to go from combat, to fly for an hour or two and be in a setting with culture and good food and nice music—was so dramatic that I'll never forget the feeling. It just felt so good. There were pine trees too.

221

5

Operation
New Wind

Bruce Lawlor
Case Officer
Central Intelligence Agency
I Corps
November 1971-December
1973

The Christmas Bombing

I think the North Vietnamese had exhausted themselves temporarily in the '72 offensive. I think they had shot their bolt for a while. They took quite a few casualties. I don't know what the figures are; I don't suppose anybody will ever know. But the bombing, the American bombing up in I Corps, was certainly extensive. There were these on-again, off-again peace feelers, and then Nixon said, "Okay, guys, we're going to mine the harbors and we're going to blow the shit out of you people." We started pounding them [North Vietnam] in December and it quickly brought them around.

I think the effect of the mining of the harbors, at least perceived from my contacts in Vietnam, was that the North Vietnamese were afraid of Nixon. They didn't know what he was going to do. They believed that the American public was against it and against the war, but they thought he was strong enough so that he'd do it anyway.

Dennis Morgan
Aerial Reconnaissance
U.S. Marines
I Corps
September 1972-February
1973

The Cease-Fire

THE cease-fire went into effect on January 28, 1973, at
0600 hours [6 A.M.] . I took off for my airborne duty
station at 2300 the night before. If you ever look at a
map of where the Cua Viet River runs through Dong Ha–
Quang Tri, you'll see a little spit of land. About eight
hundred meters south of that is where the South Vietnamese marines were up against the North Vietnamese.

The night before the cease-fire went into effect, the Vietnamese marines got together a huge armored force of
fifteen or twenty tanks, armored personnel carriers, vehicles, the whole bit, and went balls to the wall up the Cua
Viet River to cut the NVA off and seize that land and
hold it through the cease-fire. They made the dash up
there, seized the land all the way up to the mouth of the
river, expanded their bridgehead and then just got the hell
shot out of them. The North Vietnamese didn't obey the
cease-fire. They opened up with everything from the other
side of the river. We couldn't do anything because the air
support was turned off at 0600 because of the cease-fire.
And these guys were fighting for their lives.

But what happened is . . . As I say, people join the

military for a number of reasons, and I don't want to get philosophical, that's not the purpose here. Some do it because they have nothing better to do. Some do it because they want to find themselves. Some do it because they want to serve their manhood or find their manhood. And some guys do it because they're overcompensating and want to be macho men. And generally anybody under five foot four inches tall is trying to prove he's a macho man. There's nothing worse than a little guy with a big ego that can't be satisfied. One of the pilots in the Air Force that we were flying with—thank God I never had to fly with him—was one of those guys.

He went out the night before the cease-fire and was screwing around in some damn place he shouldn't have been and got shot down, which really complicated the problem of trying to help the Vietnamese marines who that same night had dashed up the beach and seized that area. We knew he was on the ground. He had gotten out of his bird, the OV-10, and was talking by radio to the air/sea rescue people and other aircraft in the area. He had no business doing what he was doing. He was out trying to win an Air Medal, overcompensating. As it turned out, we couldn't run the air strikes or anything else like that to help the Vietnamese because this yo-yo had been out screwing around and got himself shot down and captured. I think he was eventually murdered or killed or shot dead, executed by the North Vietnamese.

Stephen Klinkhammer
Aviation Ordnance
Aircraft Carrier USS
  America
Tonkin Gulf
October 1972-April 1973

Celebration
Without Victory

I enlisted right out of high school for three years in the
Navy. In 1972 I went to boot camp at Great Lakes.
Right from boot camp I went to aviation school to learn
jet nomenclature, and before I knew it I had orders for
the USS *America*, which is an aircraft carrier, at that time
in the Gulf of Tonkin. It had left Norfolk in August of '72
and I didn't finish my training until September. I heard
that when it left Norfolk, protesters had been in boats out
in the harbor trying to prevent it, and the Coast Guard
had to escort it out. I guess it almost ran over a couple of
the smaller crafts full of people yelling, "Don't go. Don't
go." So after aviation training in Memphis, I had two
weeks' leave and went back home to Michigan and said
goodbye.

By Christmas we had been on line sixty-five straight
days, building bombs aboard the *America*. It got to the
point where I didn't see daylight. I'd wake up and go to
work, the sun would be down—five decks below you
don't see any sunlight—I'd get off work and the sun
would be down. I never saw any goddamn daylight below

ship. I thought I was going nuts. Sometimes we would be working and they'd call a shutdown and we'd just sleep there, on the bombs. You just pick up a piece of cardboard and lay it on a pallet of bombs. It's real cold down there—it's all metal. Around Christmas we had been out so long, everybody was getting edgy and pissed off. We wrote shit on the bombs like "Merry Christmas, gooks" to let off steam.

At that time the craze was to wear bracelets with the names of guys who were missing in action, whose planes were shot down from our ship. You'd buy these bracelets and have the name of the pilot from your squadron who was missing engraved on it. When they came back, if they came back, you could send this bracelet and say, "Welcome back."

We were still flying twenty-four hours a day in January. Then in the end of January, while we were working down there building bombs, the communications system of the ship comes on and says, *"The truce has been signed. The Vietnam War is over."* Everybody is jumping up and down, carrying on.

We had been working all that time over there, bombing the piss out of that country, and all of a sudden it's all over, just like that. No more bombs. Though we did go on and build bombs for a couple more days. Until they fully confirmed it, until we got the order to stop, we were still building and they were still flying. Everybody was in the state of "Well, what the fuck do we do now?" There was a big celebration. The cooks made steaks to order, potatoes, chocolate cake . . . really fuckin' neat.

So we waited around and waited around and some of the troops were pulling out, so we took them on. In April we left the Tonkin Gulf. All we got was one of those traditional "Well done, you did a good job" kind of things by the commander of the ship over the loudspeaker. I couldn't follow that. I said, "Yeah. Does that mean we built as many bombs as we were supposed to or we dropped as many as we were supposed to?" I just couldn't figure it out.

I decided with the time I had left in the Navy, instead of killing people I'd rather be on the other end of it, putting people back together. So I had to go through all these series of interviews with corpsmen and the medical officers aboard the ship. When I got off the *America* I was sent to Great Lakes for training during the summer of '73. I graduated in October. My scores were so good that they recommended me for further training. So I went to operating-room-technician school, and to do that I had to extend my enlistment for thirteen more months. I was assigned to one of the two surgical teams at Great Lakes. I was senior corpsman there.

I worked at Great Lakes when the POWs came back, and some of them were sent there. It was really crazy. There was a lot of people cheering and carrying on. I still hadn't got to thinking much about the war at that time. There was a big party for the POWs. Most of them were pilots and officers. They had malnutrition and had lost a lot of weight. They looked like they had been through trauma, both physical and mental. One of them just did not want to be a part of it and walked away.

The guy who walked away looked like he had a whole lot of bitterness, a whole lot to deal with. I guess the party wasn't the way to go about dealing with the men. That incident made me begin thinking about my involvement. Watching him walk away—the bitterness—I asked myself, "Do I have any of that that I'm really covering up and not looking at?" My involvement was still for God and country at that time, I think. Looking at his eyes and his face and the way he carried himself—he looked like a man who was very tense and very bitter and had a whole lot to say and no one was letting him say it. All these people were cheering him, and it made me think that on one hand I was hearing them cheer, but on the other hand they were trying to cover him up with their cheering and their cake and coffee and booze.

I think whatever experience he did have over there, it was pretty intense for him and nobody was letting him talk about it—like "Okay, you're a hero, you're home," this kind of shit—when I think he needed some time to vent somewhere and that wasn't the appropriate way. His eyes were very intense and he was real skinny. When you have malnutrition your eyes get sunken because the fat is used for energy. He was in his early thirties and he looked much older than that. The intensity of his eyes just freaked me out. I felt like pulling him aside and saying, "Let's talk about it." But I guess at that time I wasn't ready either or didn't know how to do it.

POW

I was shot down on the twenty-eighth of June, 1967, and I was released on the third of March, 1973 . . . My God, then today is the anniversary of my release . . . I didn't even realize that. It's amazing. I didn't think I'd ever not celebrate that day, and now here I forgot today's the day. I was there just a little bit short of six years. I think it came out to be about sixty-eight months.

I was on my second cruise out in the Tonkin Gulf when I was shot down. I was in a Navy squadron that operated from an aircraft carrier. My first cruise I had been executive officer of Fighter Squadron 143 on the carrier *Ranger* in 1966. During that cruise much of our work was done in South Vietnam. We did some things up North, but really a great deal of our effort was in the South at that time. We really hadn't started bombing extensively in the North. We came back to the States in late August of 1966, and then between cruises we trained and went back in April of 1967 on the carrier *Constellation*. I was the commanding officer of the squadron, and about two months after we left the States I was shot down.

All our missions were up in the northern part of North Vietnam—Hanoi, Haiphong and the Red River Delta.

It's what we used to call Package Six. The terminology we used, which divided North Vietnam for planning purposes, was Packages One through Six. Package One was the southernmost. Package Six always had the connotation of "Indian country," because you knew you really were going to have a tough mission if you flew up in there, and all our missions at that time were tough missions in that area.

In 1967, when they saw that we were bombing in the Hanoi-Haiphong complex, they moved all of the antiaircraft missiles, which had been distributed pretty widely throughout the country, concentrating them all in the Hanoi-Haiphong area. And they had progressively built up their MIG force, so it was a very intensive combination of MIGs, SAMs [surface-to-air missiles] and antiaircraft artillery.

On the particular mission on which I got shot down, I was leading a strike into the Haiphong area, the port city area, against what we called "transshipment points," where they would load material off a ship for transshipment to a rail system in the country. It was a flight of airplanes in excess of thirty, and as we came into Haiphong very early in the morning—time on target was supposed to be 7:30 A.M.—there was a thunderstorm right over Haiphong, so we had to divert to our secondary target, which was Nam Dinh. It's the third of fourth largest city in North Vietnam, on the Red River, and was a key transshipment point because the rail system south of Hanoi into the southern part of North Vietnam goes through Nam Dinh and supplies are often barged to that point and loaded onto the rail systems there.

I remember as we were approaching Haiphong, as we looked up ahead, the target was completely covered by clouds. We made the decision to turn left and go down to Nam Dinh, and I remember saying to myself, "Well, I won't have to dodge those missiles today," because the missiles at this time were all ringed around Hanoi and Haiphong. I just kind of said, "Boy, this should not be too tough." So I was shot down by antiaircraft, and it just shows you that you're hit sometimes by what you least expect.

I was in an F-4 Phantom in a squadron and was hit

at twelve thousand feet going in an excess of five hundred knots. That's really quite a shot. It was just a barrage-type flack, we used to call it. I'm sure that the gunner sighted visually because it was a beautiful clear day in that area. I'm sure he saw our flight coming in and he was just throwing barrage flack. We were about thirty-six airplanes. I was in the lead, so he could sight on me.

When I was hit, I knew some damage had been inflicted on me, but although the airplane was starting to get a little bit sluggish, it was still flying, so I made the decision to continue on to the target instead of turning back and going to the sea. As I rolled into my run to drop my bombs, I knew that my control system was going bad. But I got my bombs off and I was able to get the nose of the airplane back up and to turn out toward the sea, and then the airplane went out of control into a spin. I had no control over my flight controls and the airplane was no longer flyable.

Aviators are really kind of eternal optimists. I think you know basically that it could happen to you. At that point in 1967, I'd been in the business for fifteen years. I'd seen a lot of friends of mine that were killed and so forth, just in accidents and back in my days as a test pilot. And it's one of those things that you know can happen, but aviators have, I guess—we have this optimism and confidence that it's not going to happen to me because I'm good enough to prevent it. But we're not naïve. Sure, I had all my personal affairs in order and insurance for my family and had gone through all the survival training and had studied all those sorts of things. You were as well prepared as you could possibly be for any contingency. But I think you have to be fundamentally optimistic or you couldn't do it.

After I was hit I was so busy that I really didn't have a chance to think about much other than trying to make that airplane fly. You're not exactly sure what's wrong. I was doing everything possible to make it fly—it went into a flat spin—I was trying to bring the airplane out of the spin by altering my engines . . . and then I had to think about getting out. I had to send my rear-seat guy out—I told him to go ahead and jump, at about three thousand feet. Then I saw that I was approaching two thousand feet and the airplane just wasn't coming out of it, I was getting very low, so I went ahead and ejected myself. You're so busy you don't have time to think. The same thing after ejection. You're handling all your survival equipment, getting your emergency radio out—we had a little UHF transceiver that we carried with us, so I was transmitting to the planes that were in the vicinity that I was okay. When I reached the ground I was immediately captured by the militia. The kind of local militia that are set up for hamlet defense.

I was shot down right over the Red River Delta. I landed in a rice paddy, up to my waist in water. I looked around and on the bank of this rice paddy was a militia guy waiting right there for me. They had militia throughout the area because there were a lot of raids in there. He had a very old rifle. It was obvious that these local militia were not given modern equipment.

It was really interesting to observe the attitude of the people. It was obvious the militiaman looked upon this as his job. He didn't manifest any particular hatred toward me. The people who manifested the greatest hatred and wanted to strike me were the older people. That kind of surprised me because the kids that gathered around to look at me kind of regarded this as a social experience: "Here's something exciting and new that's happening in our hamlet." I was probably the first Caucasian that some of these young kids had ever seen. Afterward they put me temporarily in a hootch, in the same hootch where they had their pigs, and there was this big sow looking at me like I was transgressing her territory. She eyed me very warily while they were making the decision as to what to do with me.

They moved me from this little hamlet to another point, where their truck picked up me and my rear-seat crewman, and they took us right up to Hanoi. Nam Dinh isn't really that far south of Hanoi, maybe about fifteen miles. We arrived in Hanoi late in the afternoon.

There was no one who could speak English until we got to Hanoi. We stopped at one place en route to Hanoi where some military official put a form in front of me to fill out. I'm sure it was a form they'd made up for the situation of capturing pilots. I refused to do it. I said that under the Geneva Convention regarding the treatment of POWs, all I had to give was name, rank, serial number and date of birth. So I refused to answer and they really didn't push it. It was not until we got to Hanoi that the real brutality occurred.

They kept us blindfolded and would not allow us to speak. If we tried to speak they would hit us with the butt of a gun. We did whisper a little bit, but that's about all we could get away with. We had our hands tied; escape was virtually impossible because we were so well guarded. We were disrobed right down to our skivvies and we were barefoot. But contrary to some POWs who were badly abused in the hamlet, I wasn't. Just a few older people. I think that we were close enough to Hanoi so that the militia had control, and the people in that region were probably indoctrinated more than they would be in more rural parts of the country.

The collection point for the first arrivals was the central Hanoi prison. It was called Hoa Lo. It's a famous prison that goes back to colonial times, probably built by the French before the turn of the century, and it occupies an entire city block in Hanoi. The new arrivals would generally come there and get their first interrogation, and after that some would be taken to other prisons in the Hanoi area. Those of us who were senior remained at Hoa Lo. We always gave names to our camps there, and the camp within the Hoa Lo complex where I stayed for the first almost four years we called Las Vegas. I think people tend to call that Hoa Lo complex the Hanoi Hilton. I was there in Hoa Lo my whole time. I had one month in another camp and then I was brought back to Hoa Lo. But most all the prisoners were brought there for their first interrogation, and the interrogation occurred in an area of Hoa Lo we called Heartbreak Hotel.

They initially interrogated you, I think, with the basic hope that you would give information freely, but they well knew that we wouldn't. We would call upon the name, rank, serial number and date of birth of the Geneva Convention. So they were prepared immediately to start the torture, which they did. They would talk to you, give you a standard spiel and start asking you questions, and then you'd say, "I'm only required to give name, rank, serial number and date of birth." After asking you a couple of times, they left and sent the torturer in.

In those days, one guy tended to do most of it. I think they learned that if they didn't have a guy who was reasonably skilled at doing the torturing, it was really easy to kill somebody. This particular guy developed the nickname of Strap and Bar—we gave a nickname to all the guards in the camp—because he could use metal bars and straps to twist you into all sorts of distorting positions to induce pain, but he was pretty skillful about it. He knew just how far he could bend your arms and legs without breaking any limbs and it was . . . it all had an unreal aspect to it. He would come in there without any emotion. This was his job. He was the professional torturer. And I couldn't believe it. Here's a guy that's inducing all sorts of pain, and hopefully not to kill you or maim you, but just to get you to talk. I think they learned, probably from previous times when they had a few prisoners that were killed by overzealous torturers, that they needed to get a guy like this. They fundamentally wanted to keep us alive because they knew we had hostage value.

Seventy-five prisoners was about the maximum capacity of Las Vegas, and what they would tend to do is, as that camp filled to capacity, move prisoners to other camps. The number of prionsers increased in late '67 as the bombing increased in intensity. As Las Vegas increased in number, they decided in '68 to open the camp at Son Tay, and that was the camp the U.S. commando raid was made on, but it was vacant because they'd moved the POWs several weeks before to another camp.

Basically our camp had seven-foot-square cells because they wanted to keep Americans segregated in individual cells. Many of us were in solitary confinement, and I've seen as many as five prisoners in those seven-foot cells. I spent fourteen months in solitary confinement in one of those cells. And in very few of the cells did you have common walls. You had a space between the walls. They were doing everything they could to minimize communication between prisoners, but we devised communications systems. Very rarely were they able to prevent us from communicating, although they were dedicated to doing so.

In the very early days, it was obvious to us in Las Vegas that we couldn't talk. They had guards constantly patrolling. Some prisoners who were living together developed the tap code, where we took the alphabet, which has twenty-six letters, dropped out the letter K, and made C and K interchangeable. With the twenty-five letters we formed a matrix of five lines of five letters each. The first line was A through E, the second line F through J, the third line L through P, the fourth line R through U, and the last was V through Z. So if you wanted to tap a letter, you would tap down the left side, then to the right. M is the second letter in the third line, so to send M you'd go [*taps three times, short pause, taps twice*]. And you found if you pressed your ear to the stone walls, you could hear light tapping as much as maybe seventy-five feet away. So we could send a lot of messages by tapping on the walls and then relaying that around the camp. One person would start a message and it would go from wall to wall.

But of course it took time because you had to pass the code out and you'd have to take the risk to whisper to get people knowledgeable in the code. If a new prisoner came in, you'd have to carefully track the guards around the camp, and when you were sure that they were not around, you'd whisper the guy the code. We found that it was easier to transmit a message by that code. By carefully looking for the guards and setting up a lookout system, we could talk, whisper sometimes, but it took a tremendous amount of lookout action. There was very brutal punishment for any kind of communication. They would put you in leg irons or they would just beat you to really induce a high level of pain. They used to do a lot of very cruel things. They knew communication gave us unity and helped us to resist their attempts to exploit us, but they also knew we would be formulating escape plans and things like that. But we were always able to communicate. They never shut us down.

In addition to the tap code, we found that you could transmit that code by means of making sound or interrupting a shadow or anything that would signify going down the matrix. For example, we used to have these stiff bamboo brooms. If you had water on those stone floors and swept those bamboo brooms, it greatly amplified the sweeping sound. So we would send the code with the strokes of the broom. The Vietnamese thought we were nuts on the subject of cleanliness because we'd be sweeping every chance we got. In fact, many times I passed up the opportunity to get a bath one day a week just to get that broom and start sweeping messages that everybody in camp could hear.

The messages that you transmitted and relayed around the camp on the wall were messages of lower priority, lower urgency. A lot of times we wouldn't get access to a broom for days on end, so we would have to send things on the wall. Also we developed what I called the voice tap code, where you'd use typical respiratory-ailment sounds for those beats and those lines. Line one would be a cough, line two would be two coughs, line three a throat clear, line four a hack, and line five a spit or a sneeze. So we would send messages that way. In fact, we commonly used to send the message "G B U," which abbreviated "God bless you."

We had a tremendous amount of information to pass out because the Vietnamese were always working on some scheme to induce somebody to write a propaganda letter against the country, and they were not very sophisticated in their methods but they were always trying. So when you went out to be interrogated, if you'd been prepared in advance you could map out a strategy to kind of thwart it. But also we used it for keeping track of people. We really worked hard to keep track of people and how they were doing. Everybody was always trying to pick up intelligence by looking out cracks in the windows and doors. It was amazing how much as a group we knew what was going on. But we always had to compare notes. And we had a military organization. We had a senior officer and a chain of command, everything. We were functioning as a military organization, so communication was really essential.

Our particular camp was all pilots, officers. I was never with enlisted personnel until they moved all of us into Hoa Lo, Christmas 1970. At that time I think there were only three enlisted personnel. They were air crewmen that had been in helicopters. There were some troops that were captured at Hue in the Tet offensive, who were marched all the way up to the North, and it was never clear to us why, but they were. Most of the troops that were captured in the South by the Viet Cong remained in the South. I think the reasons that those troops were brought up North is that they were captured by the North Vietnamese. There really was a separate governmental structure within the VC and the North Vietnamese.

They used to give us radio broadcasts in our prison every day, including Sundays. I don't think they ever missed a day. We used to have these rudimentary speakers in our cells, and often the caliber of the sound was very poor, very distorted, but you could understand. Essentially the hour of radio a day was primarily for propaganda purposes, designed to kind of demoralize us. They had a radio program called *The Voice of Vietnam*. It was an English-language broadcast principally devoted to reading information from the Western press that was derogatory to the U.S. and its involvement in the war.

You learn very early that you had to do certain things. First of all, you learned that you had to have a positive outlook, you just couldn't feel sorry for yourself, and I think that all of us went through that period of "Why me?" where you went over the mission many times and said, "Gee, if I'd done this differently I would have avoided getting shot down." I think that was the common tendency—to refly your mission hundreds of times—and then the full reality of the situation dawned on you, that you were in prison and were likely to be there for a long time with little likelihood of being able to communicate with your family. It was obvious to me after I'd been there for several weeks that they weren't going to allow me to write home or receive mail. So after about a month or so, you realize that you're in there for a long time and you are cut off from the outside world and you are relying purely on your own resources to pull you through. And that's when I started developing some kind of a disciplined type of thought process and exercise program and so forth. I tried to work very actively in the camp communications system. I went for several weeks completely cut off from camp communications, in complete isolation

—I was caught communicating and they did this to punish me.

I was the senior officer in my particular camp for several years. And they were aware of it. My biggest responsibility was keeping communications going. I had to keep it going—not only for military efficiency in terms of keeping people informed of what was going on, but because it was really important for those guys who might be having some psychological problems. You just couldn't let those guys go off the line. It really started worrying me if I'd see a guy that appeared to be reluctant to communicate or he'd drop out of the communications for a while. You really do everything to start getting him back on, so that if he was having some problems . . .

I found that there were a lot of signals you could pick up if a guy was starting to have some psychological problems. His reluctance to communicate was the most obvious one. Usually after a meal they would unlock our cells and we'd go out and put our dishes in one place. Sometimes you could get a feel by looking at the food, seeing who wasn't eating, because some guys tended to put their bowls in the same spot each time. If I saw a guy that we were having trouble communicating with and he wasn't eating all of his food, that gave me a pretty good clue that he was having a problem. I'd really make an extraordinary effort to get him back on the line and see what the problem was. I guess after all the years of pressure and depression, their mental faculties would start to degrade. It was really difficult—I mean, living in these separate cells—to find the problems. But often one of the early indications that the person was having a problem was the appetite: he'd just stop eating. I think a lot of people died more from starving themselves to the point where their resistance had completely declined and then disease . . . a kind of subliminal suicide, in a way. They more or less lost the will to live.

When you were in solitary isolation, you found that you had to develop some very disciplined mental activity. After the initial period, after I got acclimated to the camp, one of the first things I did was to relive my life in very great detail. I'd go back to my earliest recorded memory and come from that point forward. For example, I said,

"Okay, I'm going to try to resurrect the names of as many kids as I can in my first-grade class." I'd dwell on that for hours and hours and hours. Then I'd start on the second-grade class. It was amazing. I think I relived my life in minute detail three times. I think it took about two weeks to go through my whole life, of about eighteen hours a day of very intensive thought. It was amazing how many names out of my first-grade class I could resurrect.

A lot of people were absolutely astonished when I came back to my hometown of Nashville, Tennessee, in 1973—people would come up to me and say, "God, I haven't seen you in thirty years. How did you remember me?" It's amazing how deep in thought you can get in reliving certain family vacations or cruises that I had made in my military career. As I say, I did this three times in the early period. And then after I'd exhausted that, I started to get into more organized mental activity: I'd review history, mathematics, literature, in great detail. For example, I taught myself how to do compound interest. I said to myself, "All right, I'm going to take a hundred dollars at six percent. How much does it accrue over a thirty-year period?" I taught myself how to keep all these things in my head. We had no pencils and paper; we were totally relying on our minds to memorize communications, so you found your mental faculties really got sharp.

There was nothing in your past that you could resurrect that was worse than what you were going through at the time. But you had to develop a positive outlook: "I'm going to keep myself as healthy mentally and physically as I can. I'm going to have to live a day at a time and make the best out of each day." And you got to the point that you no longer spent hours fantasizing or thinking about your family or thinking about the future. You lived that day, that activity that you were in at that time. Your world really got small, but you had to do that. I would get so wrapped up in a particular project that I'd be completely oblivious to anything else.

One time they put me in isolation in a cell we called Calcutta, after the Black Hole of Calcutta. They caught me communicating and they were determined they were really going to break my spirit. They didn't put many POWs in Calcutta—in fact, I know of only one other guy who was there. It was a dark cell, probably about six feet square. It had kind of a tin roof and during the day the sun would beam down on that. I figure the temperature went up to about 120 degrees in the daytime. And the problem that I had was a very bad heat rash. My body was completely covered with heat sores—they advanced from a rash to big sores. I was completely immobile because it was so painful. I said, "I've got to get some mental activity going here."

So that's when I started writing poetry. I could actually see lines of poems in my head. A poem that I wrote was subsequently designated the State poem of Tennessee. I said, "Okay. My project is to write a perfect iambic pentameter poem, like Sir Walter Scott used to write: 'The stag at eve had drunk his fill/Or danced the moon among the trill.'" I said, "Sir Walter Scott had genius, but I've got time. I'm going to stay with this until I can make a perfect iambic pentameter poem." When I was experimenting with various word groupings, I realized that "O Tennessee, my Tennessee" was a perfect iambic pentameter line, so that gave me my first line and my title. Here I was, totally immobilized, just lying completely flat and I don't know how many days it took me—probably two weeks of fifteen or sixteen hours a day of total concentration—and at the end of that time I had completed this perfect iambic pentameter poem. And as I say, I was able to keep all of this in my head. It was a dark room and I could see those lines. It really gave me an appreciation for the mental capacity that you have that very few people ever utilize.

Our whole society is so oriented toward picking up information readily through various media—TV, radio, newspaper—that the average person never gets deep in thought and concentration. The average person works a job that he's familiar with and that doesn't require a great deal of thought. Sometimes I really miss those deep periods of thought . . . I built houses, wrote volumes and volumes of poetry. I was able to resurrect half a dozen poems when I came back.

I also exercised every day, except for that one period in the 120-degree cell. I would force myself to do some calisthenics. And I always forced myself to eat everything they gave me. We were usually given boiled vegetables, sometimes pumpkin, sometimes a bean like black-eyed peas, sometimes rice and sometimes a very coarse bread. Apparently they imported wheat from other communist countries, so it was a bare subsistence diet. I figured that if you ate everything they gave you, you'd probably have around fifty to one hundred calories. Over a period of years we slowly kept progressively losing weight. I lost about forty pounds. And then the last two years, when it was pretty obvious to them that we would be released—I think the negotiations were going on actively the last two years—all of us picked up a little bit of weight. In the last two years I probably gained back twenty of the forty pounds I had lost.

Our relationship with the captors was a very interesting situation. I guess the Vietnamese were very much specialists, and the guards that were in the camp when I got shot down in 1967 remained with us for the whole war. There were some changes, but by and large, when you came into the army to do a job, that remained your job. Over the years we basically accepted each other. And I sensed, as the years went on, a kind of respect that developed on their part for us.

I had no feelings of ill will toward them. I was a military man who was doing his assigned job, and I looked on them as military men doing their assigned jobs. I had no feeling of bitterness. Certainly I—and of course I'm sure now, in retrospect, my emotions have moderated a lot—I probably felt more deeply about it while I was there; the propaganda and so forth bothered me a great deal. But I looked at it from the aspect of their leaders, rather than the individual guards, being the cause of this. I had no bitterness toward those guards.

I had no bad feelings toward the Vietnamese people. I was doing my job as a military man. I would very meticulously try to plan my bombing missions to avoid any impact on civilian population. I briefed and planned my flight to insure that we hit only military targets, because I knew we were at war with a country that was largely rural and that the people were not well-off, and we really worked hard at hitting only military targets and avoiding any unnecessary injuries or death to the civilian populace.

We had some prisoners who collaborated and we were very realistic about this. We realized that prisoners were under great pressure; there was extortion going on by the captors. It was hard on all of us. So we tended to be forgiving to those who were really trying but who, through brutality or for one reason or another, against their will, did something for the enemy. The people who we really have bad feelings about are those who refused to come back into the fold. We identified about five prisoners that had clearly departed the fold and were starting to do things willfully. We finally got into a position where we could communicate with all of them. We exhorted them to come back into the fold: "We realize that for one reason or another they've separated you and they've taken advantage of you, exploited you, but we exhort you to come back in the fold and become like the rest of us and start doing your duty in accordance with the Code of Conduct." We only had two prisoners who refused to do this.

We were all pilots, and so by and large the prisoners there really worked hard to live up to the Code of Conduct. They were fiercely patriotic and had good strong bonds with the other POWs. As I say, there were many who just because of the immense pressure did things that they weren't proud of, but they were always striving to measure up.

In 1970, after the Son Tay raid by U.S. forces to free the POWs that had been held there, all the prisoners in the North at that time were put in one compound. I think it was the day after Christmas when this big consolidation took place. We were moved out of Las Vegas into the other part of Hoa Lo, which we called Camp Unity. Initially they put us in large rooms. I was moved into a room with forty-three other guys. It was predominantly the more senior guys; the tougher resisters were all with me. I think there were about eight other rooms of thirty-five to forty guys. I think we were that way for about a month and a half.

We were holding a religious service one day in our room —three guys were conducting it. A guard looked in and saw that and got very upset. They came in and took those three prisoners out. We were very indignant that they would do this. So by a prearranged signal, that evening

we had a loud protest where we started yelling simultaneously in the camp. We ended it all by singing "The
Star-Spangled Banner." Well, this really upset the Vietnamese. First of all, the administrators of the camp were
very worried because they knew if their superiors were
aware of this . . . and I'm sure that it was heard around
Hanoi that they were losing control, they were having a
prison riot. They really panicked. They had to move
swiftly to do something. All of us who were senior were
pulled out and put back into the small cells again. We
stayed in the small cells for the rest of the war. So out of
the six years, I had a month and a half where I lived in a
group; the rest of the time I lived in a small cell. But as
a result of that, they did allow the guys that stayed in
those rooms to have religious services. We felt that in a
way we had won a victory.

When we were together in those large rooms it was really great because we could have classes and exchange information and really have some very productive mental
programs. There were guys that I hadn't seen for years
and years. It was quite a moving experience when we all
were together and could talk and see each other face-to-
face, people that you knew were in the system but just
had no idea how they were doing. I was really amazed at
the remarkable diversity among the POWs in knowledge
and interests. Any guy that had any degree of knowledge
in a particular field, he was made a professor. I'm quite a
history buff, a Civil War buff, so I taught a course on the
Civil War. I'm very interested in languages, so over a period of several years, just by passing words at every opportunity, I became very proficient in French. We had a
South Vietnamese pilot who was kept with us, although he
lived in solitary confinement. We would get in communication with him and he would whisper words. He was our
French professor. We had people who knew Spanish, people who taught courses in automotive mechanics, photog-
raphy, English, philosophy, you name it. We really kept
ourselves productively occupied. We had to.

I learned an awful lot in that prison experience. I
picked up a lot of knowledge. You'd say, "Gosh, that six-
year void of no access to things that were going on in the
world. Didn't you deteriorate mentally?" In a lot of ways

I advanced by a lot of the qualities that I developed. But I think that the most important thing that you come away from that experience with is a great feeling of inner calm and serenity because you know that there are very few things in life that could happen to you that you couldn't cope with . . . in fact, nothing. And that's a great feeling. It gives you a serenity that you just couldn't buy.

I'm sure that there are POWs that came out of the experience devastated, and that's very unfortunate. But I think the people who were basically pretty solid individuals and were stable and had the wherewithal to cope in there, they came out even better people. I see so much of value that I derived from the experience, and it's a wonderful thing to be at that point in your life where you know that there's nothing that could happen that you couldn't handle. I guess that's the biggest transformation that I've noticed in myself. When you're younger and there are a lot of unknowns ahead, there's a tendency to be concerned or worried about your ability to handle things. I guess it's normal, part of the aging process, anyway, this maturity and confidence you acquire, but I think being in that situation enhanced confidence and maturity by what we gained from it. I was thirty-seven when I was captured and fortunate enough to have that amount of life experience and responsibility at that point. There's no question about it, if you had to be shot down and become a prisoner, if you were over thirty you were far better off.

I forget who I read this from and I'm not repeating it quite as well, but "Bravery is not the absence of fear, it's the ability to keep going in the presence of fear." I think that's one of the really fine things you come out of combat with: you've proven to yourself that you can continue to function, to make yourself function, even though that fear exists.

I guess it was in 1969, when the information started coming back about some of the brutality that was occurring, that the actions taken here in this country and internationally, the kind of overwhelming indignation, made the Vietnamese decide to improve the treatment. They stopped a lot of the bad brutality and they did improve our diet a little bit. And then in 1970, after I'd been there about three years, they finally allowed me to write home and to recieve some mail. The only mail they ever let me receive was from my parents. They never let me receive any from my wife and children for some reason. But we knew from listening to the propaganda broadcasts that although the negotiations had started in 1968, it was going to be a long, hard pull, and I don't think we sensed the end was coming until 1972.

In the fall of 1972, it appeared that the negotiations were progressing to the point that maybe a release was going to occur. I'd say this was about four or five months before we were actually released. But the thing that really made us get our hopes up was when the B-52s came in and bombed Hanoi. Christmas '72. That's when we knew that the attitude among the North Vietnamese had really changed. We could see it in the guards, in the officials that we saw in the camp. That B-52 bombing . . . they changed from cocky confidence to a desire to get the war over. I could see it. They were tired of fighting. After so many years of sacrifice and deprivation, now the war was being brought to the heartland. I think that's when we started to say to ourselves, "It's just a matter of time."

The peace treaty was signed on the twenty-eighth of January, 1973. Under the provisions of the treaty the Vietnamese were required to tell us everything. The U.S. was insistent that the Vietnamese not try to manipulate us right up to the very end. They had to tell us that we were going to be released and the order of release and all of that.

When I got home, it was hardest for my kids. They had to get used to someone that they had not seen for seven years, particularly my youngest—she was seven when I left. She probably had the greatest accommodation, but it was really not very difficult.

It was one of those situations where there was a broken marriage as a result of it. My wife didn't make it through the experience. Those things were inevitable. I don't feel bitter about it. It's just . . . I think it would be unrealistic to think that any marriage could endure a seven-year separation. When I was shot down in 1967 I had been married about fifteen and a half years. So it was just a case of my wife falling out of love with me and in love with another man. When I came back I assessed the situation and

had some very frank discussions with her and just realized
that it happened.

There have been a high number of POW divorces that
have occurred. Now, in my particular case, as opposed to
some other POWs, she had actually completed the divorce
before I came back. So in some respects that was fortunate for me, as opposed to a lot of my friends that had to
go through divorces after coming back.

Clark Air Force Base in the Philippines, our first stop
before returning home, was the first place I found out
about it. So it was difficult to handle that, you know, expecting that you'd come back to a waiting wife and family
and . . . it was quite a shock. I thought my wife would be
the last one in the world that would not be able to get
through something like that. It just happened. She was really a kind of a . . . in some ways, she was a victim of that.
I took custody of my kids when I came back because I
just felt that I could give them what they needed better
than my wife could in her situation. I talked it over with
her and I told her and my kids, "This is what I plan to
do." And I was able to achieve this.

The two older ones, my twenty-year-old son and
eighteen-year-old daughter, were in college, so that was
simple. And the daughter that I essentially have raised and
have kept with me since I got back is now twenty. Everything has gone beautifully. My relationship with my kids
is fine. Their mother is good. There's been no real bitterness or unpleasantness. It's something that we faced up to
intelligently as a family and handled as best we could.

I think, probably, of all the people involved from the
family point of view, the one who had the most difficulty
was my wife. My former wife. She has to live with the fact
of divorcing a man while he was in prison, really being,
essentially now, not with her children for seven years. And
in a lot of respects I feel sorry for her. I think she was a
victim of the war as much as anybody. I hope that she is,
in fact, having a good, happy life now and that this is
something that doesn't prey on her mind. I think she probably is. I hope so. She married a man who has two kids—
he was a widower—so she's raised those kids, and I'm
sure she gets all wrapped up in that family situation.

You would think that "you went through a six-year

void of information. How do you get caught up professionally?" Well, I had to work very hard for several years to fill that void. A lot of reading, a lot of talking with people, just a lot of study. I mapped out a program to do professional study, broad reading and so forth, just to get caught up. It really took me several years to get to the point where I felt I filled in that void.

I think that one of the greatest things that the POW experience gave me was a really positive outlook. I can honestly say that in the seven years I've been back, although I've faced a lot of challenges and increased responsibilities, I've always looked forward to them in a positive way. I've never had any doubts that I couldn't handle the situation. My life since I've been back has been all upbeat, all positive, pleasant, busy, with a lot of challenges. I guess I'm very lucky that I don't bear too many disabling scars from the experience. I've remarried, about eighteen months after I came back, to a super woman. It's been a real great marriage and that's been a good aspect of it all.

Ralph Dennison
Navy Hospital Corpsman
USAID Hospital Compound
Soc Trang
May 1969-May 1970

LBJ

L BJ, Long Binh Jail, was the multiservice jail compound near Saigon. Prisoners would be sent there from all over Vietnam: stockade, watch towers, barbed wire. Prisoners lived in single-story wooden Quonset huts with metal roofs.

One kid was jailed because he married a Vietnamese woman and the military wanted to send him home and he wanted to stay, which any man would: "I want to stay so I can get my papers processed so my wife and baby can come home with me or come shortly after I get home." And the military wouldn't let him. So he went over the hill.

There were several guys who were in there for that type of offense, for staying longer than they were supposed to because they had wives there: "Please let me extend for three months so I can get my family home." The military said, "No. You gotta go. You should have thought of that before. You didn't have our permission to get married." The kid said, "Fuck you. I'm going to stay with my wife."

Some of the guys in the jail hootch went out and got him one night—he was trying to saw his way through a drainage ditch and escape from the prison before the guards caught up to him. The guards would have wasted him,

251

killed him. And this kid was basically a clean-cut Saigon warrior, an in-love young man, which is pretty easy to be because there are lots of beautiful women, and very nice woman, in Saigon. He forgot to ask permission to fall in love.

There were lots of guys AWOL in Saigon then, three thousand in 1969 that the military knew about. And I've really wondered what's happened to them since the troops pulled out. I can't imagine. Some of them were living damn well. Some of them were stoned, were hooked on dope and were living by their wits. But I really don't think the military made a concerned effort to find these guys and say, "Gee, you ought to come home because we're leaving." And I'm sure that they weren't given any priority on the last choppers out. I wonder how many of them were in the MIA files and may be perfectly alive, living in Saigon . . . but the military doesn't want to admit how many guys were gone over the hill.

Dominoes

So they went into Vietnamization, the massive use of air power and Igloo White [seismic sensor operations] and the whole electronic-battlefield concept. But at that point, the United States had practically committed itself to the fact that it wasn't going to win and it was just going to be a question of which President would be unlucky enough to be in power when the thing was lost. It was like a dirty football and it just got passed along. Ford seemed to be the guy they agreed to dump it on. It had fallen apart and he wasn't elected, and for better or worse, the timing all came together at that point.

I once had a fantasy that maybe a couple hundred of us, after everybody else had left, would stay and hold out at the Vietnamese embassy or palace or whatever. And the last forty would be the Trojans who were holding off the Macedonians, and they would say, "To hell with this," and they'd defend it to the last. When Saigon actually fell I just sat and watched the whole thing on TV, which in itself was insane, totally insane. I wanted to feel real happy because, wow, the war was over and I thought the Vietnamese should win and run their own country, and they

were obviously . . . This was it, they were winning and yet
. . . wanting to cry . . . and not knowing whether to laugh
or cry . . . and kind of doing both at the same time and
not being able to let myself feel really bad or really good
. . . it's like . . . too many emotions. It was like an emo-
tional overload, a kind of numbed-out feeling. Feeling like
you needed to go out and party, but you didn't really have
the spirit to do it.

Stephen Klinkhammer
Navy Hospital Corpsman
Aircraft Carrier USS
    <u>Midway</u>
Saigon
April 1975

The Fall of Saigon

ONE weekend I had a pass, so I went up to Wisconsin because my parents were there. I got back at five in the morning to take a shower in the locker room and sit and drink coffee and buy a doughnut out of the machine before scrubbing for the operating room for the day. I was in the shower and the student who was on duty said, "Go home and pack your bags, you're leaving for Saigon." This is April 1, 1975. Being part of a surgical team, you're on call twenty-four hours a day, anywhere in the world.

So I went home to pack my sea bag and call my dad. I said, "Guess where I'm going? I'm going to Saigon." I heard the phone drop. My dad is the president of a bank, and I heard him tell everybody in the bank, "Oh, Stevie is going back to Vietnam," very shocked. This was early in the morning. He picked the phone back up and he said, "When are you leaving?" I said, "We're supposed to be leaving at noon today."

So noon comes by and the Navy couldn't get us a military flight, so they flew us all first-class on a 747 from Chicago to the Philippines. We drank a lot of beer between stops in Alaska and Tokyo. We landed at Manila at two in the morning. It was cold in Chicago, so we were in our dress blues, standing there at the airport in Manila, dripping sweat.

The evacuation of Saigon, the whole thing, was called Operation New Wind or Fresh Wind or Fresh Breeze or something like that. We got to the aircraft carrier *Midway,* and as soon as we got off the helicopter—since I was a surgical tech, my hair was always under a cap and it was rather long, about halfway down my ears—the CO, who was up in the tower, comes down and says, "Get those guys down for haircuts." So right away he gets on us for haircuts. The *Midway* was our base of operations. Our surgical equipment, all the green crates, never did catch up to us. That's known throughout the military, that they never catch up with you, and the *Midway* didn't have an operating room. This is about April 10 or 11.

We were real close to shore at that time, right off Saigon. We heard that we were taking on a whole bunch of civilians. We would be flying in and out with refugees, with American personnel, with reporters. The Tan Son Nhut airport was being bombed with big rockets. You could see the explosions from the sea. We were flying in and taking on refugees, and they were flying out whatever they could. With the refugees there were worms, women going into labor, TB and wounded lying on the choppers because there were a lot of shells coming in. There were a couple dead or dying on the chopper whom we couldn't save. We were landing in Tan Son Nhut. That was our staging point, where everybody was loading.

There were people coming out in boats, half-sinking boats. There were people who had their own airplanes who were flying out. There were all these choppers we had left there; they were using these to fly out, the Vietnamese. The flight deck was so full of choppers that we had to push them overboard because there was no room, we couldn't get our own choppers in. We were flying the big medevac choppers. We had an overload, packing in about twenty-five at a time, both Vietnamese and American. It was total chaos. The Purple Heart Trail, the road that came into Saigon from the paddies west of the city, was so jammed, from the air I could see columns of people that were at least twenty miles long. A lot of children crying. Some had clothes they picked off dead bodies. Most were barefoot. There were oxcarts and they were hauling what they had. There were wounded men on both sides of the road with battle dressings on. The NVA was lobbing these rockets all over the place, they were wiping out civilians . . . There were piles of wounded on the back of ambulances. They were dropping the rockets right into crowds of fleeing people. There were trucks, buses, anything they could get into. Saigon was the last stand, the capital, where the American embassy was.

A lot of American Marines were activated and had put up a perimeter guard around Tan Son Nhut. The NVA was still lobbing these rockets in. In fact, when I took off we were also flying out from the American embassy—a lot of people had been told to go there instead of Tan Son Nhut. It was really a mess. These rockets are lobbing in and a C-130 took off full of people going out to one of the aircraft carriers and it was blown out of the sky . . . that was all over the runway. There were corpses, there were burned-out tanks that people had used to come in, there were pieces of bodies lying in the fields and on the streets. It was just bananas, total chaos. It was one mass of humanity being pushed to where people were being trampled. People screaming, "I want a place on this chopper!" and not being able to communicate because of the language barrier and because they would not listen.

They were raiding the American Exchange. The image I have is this one guy holding up one of those ten-packs of Kellogg's cereal and he's waving it. They were throwing American money up in the air . . . totally berserk . . . total chaos. We were trying to get the wounded first. They were piled in these old ambulances. The refugees were coming up from the Delta as well as from the North. We were trying to get the wounded out first and a lot of them we just couldn't.

Each time we went in, a bunch of Marines would get out and cover the landing zone as we tried to get the wounded on first, but sometimes they were just overwhelmed. They had orders to shoot if they couldn't maintain order. They shot mostly over the heads. I didn't see any of the Marines shoot any civilians. The Marines set up a defensive perimeter and would return fire at the enemy, but like the rest of the war, you never saw the NVA. The ARVN were running, they were coming in, they were bypassing civilians, shooting civilians, trying to get out first all the time. The best way to describe it was every man for himself. There were pregnant women going into labor right there on the goddam landing zone. I delivered a baby right on the chopper. And I also delivered two more on the ships. It was just bananas.

We ended up with three thousand civilians aboard the *Midway*. We had taken all of our squadrons off because they had been there for offensive purposes. The civilians all stayed where the squadrons used to be. There were people sleeping on the floors, all over. Of course, they didn't know what a bathroom was. They were packed in, I'll tell you that. So we'd all take turns walking duty and if someone was puking or if someone had diarrhea or worms, we'd treat that.

On April 30 Saigon fell. South Vietnam had fallen. The Vice-President, Ky, flew out to the *Midway* in his own Cessna. Ky had with him an immense amount of gold bars. A lot of these people, some of the higher-ups in the ARVN and so on, had with them a lot of American money. We confiscated everything from civilians when they came on board. There were pounds and pounds of pure heroin, pounds and pounds of nice marijuana, which I really wanted to sample. People had little cherry-bomb grenades. We picked up guns. A lot of canned fish had to be tossed out. A lot of fever, they had a lot of malaria. So we had these three thousand people packed in there. That was the best we could to. We had a twenty-four watch on a couple of kids down in the sick bay who had 104-degree temperatures. We had an interpreter down there and a bunch of families stayed with him. There were dead bodies we were bagging and bagging. There were still people fleeing Saigon in small boats.

The Vietnamese were scared. I have to put myself in their place—leaving my home, not being sure where I'm going to to, what's going to happen to me. They were very calm, almost in shock. We fed them and had interpreters tell them what to do, and I think the interpreters helped a lot. We had gunnery sergeants, old Marines, who spoke the language. I knew enough to get by, enough to say, "What's wrong with you?" or "I need this" or "I need that." They were basically very calm, sleeping on the hangar deck. They were treated very nice. They were in, I guess you could call it, shock—just a panic, the intensity of the five- or ten-day span there. When I started to come down, I know how I felt: "Holy fuck, what just happened?" The adrenaline runs for so long, then it all stops. The war's ending cut you off just like that. You say okay, but the adrenaline is still running.

I have cried my ass off. I don't have any tears left. I first started letting it out in April of 1977. It took two years. I did that because I just couldn't handle being a soldier anymore. Still a fucking soldier. I got out of the Navy in June of '76, but I still acted like one. I guess I still do in a way. I still sleep with one eye open, you know. And I wake up with bad dreams that I have of taking fire and watching people being murdered and being a part of that process. In fact, around this time of year—Christmas time—it gets really heavy for some reason. My wife knows it. Sometimes she feels inadequate because she doesn't know how to deal with that. I get really upset and I have to cry a lot and talk. Once I start it's like for three or four hours. I'm completely exhausted. I cry myself to sleep wherever I am, or I need to go out by myself. People feel inadequate. My wife feels inadequate. I tell her, "There's nothing you can do that can be any more adequate than just to be here." There is no understanding. My mind isn't mature enough. It wasn't then and it isn't now and it's never going to be able to understand murder.

It's a dull pain, you know. Just a whole lot of knowledge that I think I've gained, and I think I've grown from it. And I have to deal with that maturity, too, in myself. I grew up real fast. Real fast. It seems like a whole block of my life that I can't account for and I want to find that block because I know it's important. I have a certain pride, too, because I was a damn good medic—I have problems with that. I think a lot of times that it's my fault, and it's not my fault—there is no blame. The actual emotions are a fact. I'm a fresh veteran, I'm really not that old—I'm twenty-five, I'm just out. And there's still a lot of things that I'm real close to in there. A lot of that system I didn't mind. But people I know say, "Steve, forget it. It's over." The last thing I need is pity. The last thing I need is someone to feel sorry for me.

My mother told my brother, "Leave Steve alone, he's not the same anymore." This was after my first tour in 'Nam. I guess I was changed and didn't know it. You're the last person to see yourself change. And the fact that you're not going to get any pats on the back, you're not going to get a parade, you're not going to get anything but spit on and misunderstood and blamed—I still feel that sometimes. Maybe I could have done better.

People want me to bury it. I can't bury it. I did learn something and I'm not sure what. But I know it's affected me a whole lot. And I think it's in a good way and I think I've really grown from that, because I don't want to see it happen again and I really care about people. To really try to help people to work through the problems of their own.

Glossary

Agency: Central Intelligence Agency.

Agent Orange: Highly toxic defoliant sprayed on vegetation.

AID: Agency for International Development.

AK-47: The standard rifle used by the North Vietnamese and Viet Cong.

amtrack: Amphibious armored vehicle used to transport troops and supplies, armed with .30-caliber machine gun. Used by Marines.

APC: Armored personnel carrier used by Army to transport troops and supplies, armed with .50-caliber machine gun.

arc light: B-52 bomber strike, shaking earth for ten miles from target area.

ARVN: Army of the Republic of Vietnam. A member of the army.

base camp: Brigade- or division-size headquarters.

bird: Any aircraft, but usually referring to helicopters.

Body bags: Plastic bags used for retrieval of dead bodies on the battlefield.

bush: An infantry term for the field or the "boonies."

bust caps: Marine Corps term for firing rifle rapidly.

C-4: Plastic putty-textured explosive carried by infantry soldiers.

Cav: Air cavalry; helicopter-borne infantry. Helicopter-gunship assault teams.

chieu boi: A voluntary surrendered VC or NVA soldier to be repatriated through a government program.

Chinook: A supply and transport helicopter.

CIB: Combat Infantry Badge awarded to Army infantrymen who have been under fire in a combat zone. Worn on both fatigues and dress uniforms.

CINCPAC: Commander-in-Chief of all American forces in the Pacific region.

claymore: Anti-personnel mine carried by infantry.

clearance: Permission from both military and politicians to engage enemy in a particular area.

clutch belt: Cartridge belt worn by Marines.

261

CO: Command officer.

connex container: Corrugated metal packing crate, approximately six feet in length.

contact. Firing on or being fired upon by the enemy.

CORDS: Civil Operations and Revolutionary Development Support. Created by civilian, MACV and CIA to coordinate American pacification efforts.

COSVN: Communist headquarters for military and political action in South Vietnam.

deros: Date eligible to return from overseas. The sweetest word in military language.

dust-off: Medical evacuation helicopters.

ETS: Date of departure for overseas duty station.

fire base: A temporary artillery encampment used for fire support of forward ground operations.

fire fight: Exchange of small-arms fire with the enemy.

flack jacket: Heavy fiberglass-filled vest worn for protection from shrapnel.

fragging: The assassination of a military leader by his own troops, usually by grenade.

hootch: A simply constructed dwelling, either military or civilian.

I Corps: The northernmost military region in South Vietnam.

II Corps: The central highlands military region in South Vietnam.

III Corps: The densely populated, fertile military region between Saigon and the highlands.

IV Corps: The marshy Mekong Delta, southernmost military region.

in country: Vietnam.

K-bar: Combat knife.

KIA: Killed in action.

lifer: A career military person.

LP: 1. Listening post; forward observation post of two or three men. 2. Amphibious landing platform; used by infantry for storming beaches from the sea.

LST: Troop-landing ship.

LZ: Landing zone for helicopters, usually in a clearing in a rural area.

MACV: Military Assistance Command Vietnam, U.S. Army military advisers to the Vietnamese.

mama-san: Mature Vietnamese woman.

medevac: Medical evacuation helicopters used for fast evacuation of wounded from the battlefield.

M-14: Wood-stock rifle used in early portion of Vietnam conflict.

MIA: Missing in action.

M-1: World War II vintage American rifle.

M-16: The standard American rifle used in Vietnam after 1966.

M-79: Single-barreled grenade launcher used by infantry.

NCO: Noncommissioned officer, usually a squad leader or platoon sergeant.

NVA: North Vietnamese Army.

PF: Popular Force, South Vietnamese National Guard-type local military units.

PFC: Private First Class.

point: The forward man or element on a combat mission.

poncho liner: Nylon insert to the military rain poncho, used as a blanket.

RA: Regular Army, prefix to serial number of enlistees.

R & R: Rest and relaxation, a soldier's three- to seven-day vacation from the war.

react: For one unit to come to the aid of another under enemy fire.

recon: Reconnaissance, small scout patrol to search for enemy activity.

Rome plow: Mammoth bulldozer used to flatten dense jungle.

rotate: To return to the States at the end of a year's tour of duty in Vietnam.

RTO: Radiotelephone operator, a rifleman who backpacks a field radio and is in charge of communications for his unit.

sapper: A VC or NVA commando, usually armed with explosives.

shit burning: The sanitization of latrines by kerosene incineration of excrement.

short-timer: Soldier nearing the end of his tour in Vietnam.

sky crane: Huge double-engine helicopter used for lifting and transporting heavy equipment.

SP pack: Cellophane packet containing toiletries and cigarettes, which was sometimes given along with C-rations to soldiers in the field.

Spec. 4: Specialist 4th Class, Army rank similar to corporal.

US: Prefix to serial number of Army draftees.

USARV: U.S. Army Republic of Vietnam, command of operations unit for all U.S. military forces in Vietnam, based in Long Binh.

VC: Viet Cong.

Vietnamization: President Nixon's program to gradually turn

the war over to the South Vietnamese while phasing out American troops.

wasted: Killed.

web gear: Canvas belt and shoulder straps for packing equipment and ammunition on infantry operations.

WIA: Wounded in action.

the world: The United States.

XO: Executive officer, the second in command of a military unit.

Biographies

DOUGLAS ANDERSON, a native of Tennessee, currently works as a film-treatment writer for United Artists in New York City. A playwright, director and actor, he most recently performed in Shakespeare's *Twelfth Night* at Tennessee Williams' theater in Florida. His play *Short-Timers* was produced in New York in spring 1981.

Major MICHAEL ANDREWS is a graduate of West Point and has also been a faculty member there. Besides being an Army officer who participated in the initial reforaging exercises at Fort Hood, Texas, and Germany, he also has a degree in psychology from Duke University. He currently works for the Army's Recruitment Planning Office in Washington, D.C., where he lives with his wife, Linda, and son.

THOMAS BAILEY is a lawyer in Burlington, Vermont, where he lives with his wife, Tina, and son. He is a captain in the National Guard and a founding member of Vietnam Veterans of America, Vermont chapter.

MIKE BEAMON is a native of northern California. He has been assistant dean of students at the University of California, Irvine. He developed a scuba-diving program for paraplegic veterans, the first of its kind. He and his partner, Jinger Wallace, traveled around the world making a film on women in underdeveloped countries.

JAN BARRY is a newspaper journalist in New Jersey. He was a founding member of Vietnam Veterans Against the War and has edited three poetry anthologies. He lives with his wife, Paula, and two children.

THOMAS BIRD is the artistic director of the Veterans' Ensemble Theatre Company in New York City.

JAMES BOMBARD is a doctoral candidate at Columbia University in public policy and administration. He has worked as a corporate executive for the Aluminum Company of America and is currently employed by the Research Foundation of the City University of New York. He lives with his wife, Patricia, and four children in Port Jefferson, New York.

LEE CHILDRESS is a native of Berkeley, California. He is a truck driver and sculptor, and his plastic sculptures have been considered the vanguard in their field. He lives in Oakland with his wife, Allison, and two children.

BRAIN DELATE is a native of Pennsylvania who currently lives and works in New York City. An actor with a degree in directing from Princeton University, he has been the director and a teacher at the Sun Foundation Creative Theater Program in Illinois for the past three summers. He just completed work in the comic opera *The Dead Shall Walk on the Earth* in Philadelphia.

RALPH DENNISON is a native of Connecticut who currently is a counselor at the Vietnam Veterans Center in Wiliston, Vermont.

JAMES HEBRON is director of the Veterans Advisement Center at the College of Staten Island, New York. He is the New York State director of the National Association of Concerned Veterans and is also president of the Brooklyn Veterans War Memorial Institute.

SCOTT HIGGINS has spent several years in government and politics in New Jersey. A graduate of the Wharton School, he is currently vice-president of Lehman Brothers, Kuhn, Loeb and is active in politics and Vietnam veterans' affairs.

SAMUEL JANNEY has been a restaurateur in San Diego, California. He is now studying computer science.

STEPHEN KLINKHAMMER is the state director of the National Association of Concerned Veterans in Wisconsin. He is a certified alcohol- and drug-abuse counselor and works in a twenty-four-hour crisis center in Racine, Wisconsin. He lives with his wife, Rita, and son.

KIT LAVELL is a native of Chicago. He has been a community activist, working with neighborhood organizations in San Diego and Fresno, California. He has worked for the city of

San Diego and is now developing low-income solar housing. He plans to run for public office in the near future.

BRUCE LAWLOR is a lawyer in Vermont, where he lives with his wife, Carole, and two children. He is a first lieutenant in the National Guard.

GEORGE LAWRENCE is an attorney at the U.S. Environmental Protection Agency in Washington, D.C. He lives in Arlington, Virginia, with his wife, Hazel.

Admiral WILLIAM LAWRENCE is the superintendent of the United States Naval Academy in Annapolis, Maryland. In his thirty-year naval career, he has been a test pilot, fighter pilot and assistant deputy chief of Naval Operations (Air Warfare) at the Pentagon. He is the author of the State poem of Tennessee, composed while in captivity in Hanoi, and is the recipient of the 1979 National Football Foundation and Hall of Fame Gold Medal. He lives with his wife, Diane, and four children.

LUIS MARTINEZ is a native of Bayamón, Puerto Rico. He currently works as project director of the Recruitment and Training Program for minorities and women in Cleveland, Ohio. He has attended the John F. Kennedy School of Government at Harvard University and is the chairman of the Spanish Community Development Task Force in Cleveland.

HERB MOCK is a native Texan. He is currently an electronics technician in the Fort Worth–Dallas area.

DENNIS MORGAN spent ten years as an officer in the Marine Corps. He is currently a real estate agent in Washington, D.C., where he lives with his wife, Connie.

JOHN MUIR is a theatrical casting agent and production coordinator in San Diego, California. He was married recently and is writing a screenplay.

WARREN NELSON is a retired naval officer who now works for the Country Administration Center in San Diego, California, where he lives with his wife, Helen.

KARL PHALER is deputy attorney general for the state of California.

JONATHAN POLANSKY is a bartender, actor and playwright in New York City. In 1979 his play *In Pursuit of Liberty* was performed by the Veterans' Ensemble Theatre Company.

ROBERT RAWLS is a native of Cleveland, Ohio, where he lives with his family.

Lieutenant Colonel GARY RIGGS is deputy director of the Special Forces School at Fort Bragg, North Carolina. He was among the first to wear the Green Beret.

DAVID ROSS works with the Harland Bank Stationery Company. He lives in Vermont with his wife, Wendy, and daughter, Kathryn. He spent seven years as an organizer for Vietnam Veterans Against the War and now does readjustment counseling at the Vietnam Veterans Center in Wiliston, Vermont. He is also a member of the board of directors of the Project to Advance Veterans' Employment.

ROBERT SANTOS is among New York State's most decorated Vietnam veterans. He graduated from University of Michigan Law School in 1978. He currently works as a deputy assistant commissioner of administration at the New York City Department of Parks and Recreation.

DONALD SMITH is a native of Kenosha, Wisconsin. He is a graduate of the Goodman School of Drama in Chicago. He now lives in New York City, acts professionally on stage and radio and can be seen in the forthcoming film *Ragtime*.

GAYLE SMITH is a registered nurse in a rural hospital in Vermont. She is married and has recently become a mother.

LYNDA VAN DEVANTER is a hemodialysis nurse in Washington, D.C., where she lives with her husband, Bill. She is directing a nurses' program for the Veterans Administration and is writing her Vietnam biography.

AL SANTOLI was born in Cleveland, Ohio, and served with the 25th Infantry Division in Vietnam in 1968–1969, where he received the Bronze Star for valor and three Purple Hearts. Currently living in New York City, he is a poet, actor and theatrical director and has had a Rockefeller Fellowship in the arts and education. In 1980 he received the Rukeyser Award for Poetry.